EARLY MUSIC SE

A Treatise on the
Fundamental Principles of
Violin Playing

CONVENIT IGITUR---IN GESTU NEC
VENUSTATEM CONSPICUAM, NEC TURPITU=
=DINEM ESSE NE AUT HISTRIONES
AUT OPERARII VIDEAMUR ESSE.
Cic: Rhet: ad
Lib. 3. XV.

G. Eichler delin.                    Jac. Andr. Fridrich Sc. A.V.

# A Treatise on the Fundamental Principles of
# Violin Playing

by

Leopold Mozart

---

Translated by

Editha Knocker

SECOND EDITION

**OXFORD**
UNIVERSITY PRESS

# OXFORD
UNIVERSITY PRESS

Great Clarendon Street, Oxford OX2 6DP

Oxford University Press is a department of the University of Oxford.
It furthers the University's objective of excellence in research, scholarship,
and education by publishing worldwide in

Oxford   New York

Auckland  Bangkok  Buenos Aires  Cape Town  Chennai
Dar es Salaam  Delhi  Hong Kong  Istanbul  Karachi  Kolkata
Kuala Lumpur  Madrid  Melbourne  Mexico City  Mumbai  Nairobi
São Paulo  Shanghai  Singapore  Taipei  Tokyo  Toronto

and an associated company in Berlin

Oxford is a registered trade mark of Oxford University Press
in the UK and in certain other countries

This translation © 1948 Editha Knocker
Preface and Note to 1985 reprint © Oxford University Press

First published 1948
Second edition 1951
First published in paperback 1985

All rights reserved. No part of this publication may be reproduced,
stored in a retrieval system, or transmitted, in any form or by any means,
without the prior permission in writing of Oxford University Press,
or as expressly permitted by law, or under terms agreed with the appropriate
reprographics rights organization. Enquiries concerning reproduction
outside the scope of the above should be sent to the Rights Department,
Oxford University Press, at the address above

You must not circulate this book in any other binding or cover
and you must impose this same condition on any acquirer

British Library Cataloguing in Publication Data
Mozart, Leopold
A treatise on the fundamental principles of
violin playing.—2nd ed.—(Early music series)
1. Violin
I. Title  II. Versuch einer gründlichen Violinschule. *English*  III. Series
787.1'07'12    MT260

Library of Congress Cataloging in Publication Data
Mozart, Leopold, 1719-1787.
A treatise on the fundamental principles of violin playing.
Translation of: Versuch einer gründlichen Violinschule.
Includes index.
1. Violin—Methods—Early works to 1800.  I. Title.
II. Series : Early music series (London England: 1976); 6.
MT262.M93   1985   787.1'07'14   85-2895

ISBN 0-19-318513-X

9  10

Printed in Great Britain by
Bookcraft (Bath) Ltd
Midsomer Norton, Avon

# Contents

| | |
|---|---|
| NOTE TO 1985 REPRINT. *By* Alec Hyatt King | vii |
| PREFACE. *By* Alfred Einstein. | xi |
| TRANSLATOR'S INTRODUCTION | xxxii |
| TRANSLATOR'S NOTE TO SECOND EDITION | xxxiv |
| AUTHOR'S PREFACE | 7 |

INTRODUCTION TO THE VIOLINSCHULE
    I. Of Stringed Instruments, and in particular the Violin . . 10
    II. Of the Origin of Music, and Musical Instruments . . 17
        A Short History of Music . . . . . 19

CHAPTER I
    I. Of the Old and New Musical Letters and Notes, together with the Lines and Clefs now in use . . . . . 25
    II. Of Time, or Musical Time-measure . . . . 30
    III. Of the Duration or Value of the Notes, Rests, and Dots, together with an Explanation of all Musical Signs and Technical Words . 35
        Musical Technical Terms . . . . . 50

CHAPTER II. How the Violinist must hold the Violin and direct the Bow . . . . . . . . 54

CHAPTER III. What the Pupil must observe before he begins to play; in other words what should be placed before him from the beginning . . . . . . . . 64

CHAPTER IV. Of the Order of the Up and Down Strokes . . 73

# CONTENTS

CHAPTER V. How, by adroit control of the Bow, one should seek to produce a good tone on a Violin and bring it forth in the right manner . . . . . . . . 96

CHAPTER VI. Of the so-called Triplet . . . . 103

CHAPTER VII. Of the many varieties of Bowing
   I. Of the varieties of Bowing in even notes . . . 114
   II. Of variations of Bowing in figures which are composed of varied and unequal notes. . . . . . . . 124

CHAPTER VIII. Of the Positions
   I. Of the so-called Whole Position . . . . . 132
   II. Of the Half Position . . . . . . 140
   III. Of the Compound or Mixed Position . . . . 147

CHAPTER IX. Of the Appoggiature, and some Embellishments belonging thereto . . . . . . . . 166

CHAPTER X. On the Trill . . . . . . 186

CHAPTER XI. Of the Tremolo, Mordent, and some other improvised Embellishments . . . . . . 203

CHAPTER XII. Of Reading Music correctly, and in particular, of Good Execution . . . . . . . 215

INDEX . . . . . . . . . 227

TRANSLATOR'S APPENDIX . . . . . 233

TABLE OF BOWING . . . . . . . 236

# Note to 1985 Reprint

*By* ALEC HYATT KING

IT WAS nearly half a century ago, in 1937, that Alfred Einstein (d. 1951) wrote his preface to Editha Knocker's translation of Leopold Mozart's treatise and she signed her original introduction to it. (The lapse of some eleven years before publication took place, in 1948, was due to post-war shortage of paper, compounded, as she remarked in 1947, by 'enemy air activity'.) Since then, Miss Knocker's scholarly and eminently readable translation has become known as a classic of its kind, but has been out of print for some time. Meanwhile, the study of 'early music' in general has gathered pace, and much attention has been given to the style of performance best suited to the music of the earlier part of the eighteenth century, for the understanding of which Leopold Mozart's treatise is a seminal book.

It owes its great importance partly to the fact that it is the major work of its period on the violin, comparable to Quantz's treatise on the flute and C. P. E. Bach's on the keyboard, and partly to its place in the tradition that it enshrines. For much of what Leopold Mozart wrote was essentially derived from Tartini, and this, combined with its author's historical understanding of musical theory, gives the *Violinschule*, which first appeared in 1755, its enduring quality. Valuable, however, as it is for the understanding of contemporary style in performance, especially in regard to the works of the south German school of composers, it is not a guide to the music of Wolfgang Mozart and other composers of his generation.

The above-mentioned delay in the publication of Miss Knocker's translation allowed Einstein, as he says, to use his preface, partly revised, in his book *Mozart: His character, his work*, which was first published in

1945. While this revision included some changes and excisions, it did not differ materially from the text of 1937. The present reprint allows the opportunity to consider some matters of fact or opinion in Einstein's preface which now need correction or modification, and it is with these that the rest of this note is concerned.

Leopold Mozart himself has been recognized as a musician of greater stature than he was some fifty years ago. While it is partly true that, as Einstein said, he is 'known to posterity because he was the father of a genius', the merits of his best compositions are now better appreciated. This has been established by many studies, mainly by German scholars. The best short account of him in English is Wolfgang Plath's article in *The New Grove*, to which is appended a list of his numerous works in many forms: some are difficult to date with any certainty. To those who read German there may be commended two collections of essays: one comprises a book, *Leopold Mozart. 1719–1787. Bild einer Persönlichkeit* (Augsburg, 1969), edited by Ludwig Wegele, and the other is found in the *Neues Augsburger Mozartbuch*, 1962, which comprises vols. 62 and 63 of the *Zeitschrift des Historischen Vereins für Schwaben*. A good deal more is now known about the background to Leopold Mozart's life in Salzburg, for which the reader should consult the various books cited by Gerhard Croll in the bibliography to his article on that city in *The New Grove*.

Einstein's remarks about Leopold's brothers as 'artisans' are misleading. In the 17th century, an earlier generation of Mozarts had produced 'master-masons' (i.e. designers and architects) and sculptors, thus showing an artistic tendency which found a different outlet in their descendants. Joseph Ignaz and Franz Aloys Mozart were 'master-bookbinders', exponents of an ancient and honourable craft, for whom the term 'artisans' is, to say the least, misleading. They worked in Augsburg in a tradition which produced beautifully designed and finely executed bindings of the type well illustrated by a specimen of the early 18th century reproduced as pl. 21 in Adolf Layer's book *Die Augsburger Künstlerfamilie Mozart* (Augsburg, 1971).

Regarding the state of publication of the letters written by Mozart and his father, the deficiency mentioned by Einstein has been remedied by the completion of *Mozarts Briefe und Aufzeichnungen*, issued by Bärenreiter in seven volumes (including commentary and indexes) from 1962–75. Here, complete, are all the long, fascinating letters which Leopold wrote during his European travels. This collection also includes the first generally available German text of Mozart's letters to his cousin Maria Anna Thekla Mozart, the 'Bäsle'. These, as Miss Knocker remarked, were included in Emily Anderson's translation of 1938, and again in the revised edition of 1966. Such, however, is the changed attitude towards the publication of erotic letters of a scatologic character that Einstein's words—'which by their coarseness still shock prudish souls'—are hardly valid now. Indeed, it may be said that the 'Bäsle' letters are no longer 'shocking', but now make rather tedious reading, because their content has become over-familiar. This is largely due to their use in Schaffer's grotesque play *Amadeus*, and more recently to the exaggerated psychological significance placed upon them by Wolfgang Hildesheimer in his biography of Mozart. The 'Bäsle' herself remains a sad and rather shadowy figure. What little is known about her life and later years (she died in 1841) can be found in Ludwig Wegele's book, *Der Lebenslauf der Marianne Thekla Mozart* (Augsburg, 1967).

Writing of Mozart's last years, Einstein said: 'Leopold Mozart died a comparatively happy man—he was spared the greatest bitterness of all'—by which he meant he did not live to see his son's sad material decline. But this takes no account of the fact that had Leopold lived even another four or five years, his sadness would surely have been relieved by hearing *Don Giovanni*, *Così fan tutte*, *Die Zauberflöte*, and his son's numerous other masterpieces of that period.

One last point of fact. Einstein was not quite right when he said that 'only England and Italy closed their doors to Leopold's *Violinschule*'. About 1812 there appeared in London an edition under the imprint of C. Wheatstone: not, indeed, the whole book, but a selection, sufficient to bring the author's name to a new musical public in England. A copy of this very rare edition is in the British Library; a Russian edition, apparently also unknown to Einstein, was published in 1804: the title-page is illustrated as pl. 51 in Wegele's collection of essays. Einstein's confidence in the vitality of the treatise is further borne out by the publication of excerpts, in Hungarian, in 1965.

It remains to say a few words about Leopold Mozart's translator, Editha Knocker. The outline of her life is recorded only in the fifth edition of *Grove*. Born in 1869, she became a violinist of distinction, having studied with Joachim, and later taught the instrument in association with Leopold Auer in St. Petersburg. In 1924 she established her own school of violin playing in London, and published two textbooks on the subject. She died near Inverness in 1950.

# Preface

### By ALFRED EINSTEIN

LEOPOLD MOZART is and will remain, in the memory of posterity, the father of his son. Without this relationship to Wolfgang Amadeus his name would possess no more significance than those of a hundred other excellent musicians of the eighteenth century who achieved a modest goal at one or other of the many small temporal and spiritual princely courts—and Leopold was not even the highest in his narrow circle, for he never attained the position of first Kapellmeister—musicians who produced many mediocre or even admirable works which were registered in musical bibliographies and recorded casually in musical histories; works which lived, died, and disappeared in the stream of time.

But Leopold was in very deed the father of his son: he had a high ideal, according to his lights, of his task as father of such a genius, and but for his father the son would never have attained the character and eminence he was destined to achieve in the end. Leopold shines in the reflected glory of his son's halo, without which he would have remained in obscurity. But there he stands, plain, plastic, in light and shade; and it is not his talent, but his ambition, his energy, and his will-power that lift him, nevertheless, far above many of his contemporaries. He was no mere dabbler in his art.

And the literary evidence left by him, his *Violinschule*, assures him at all events of a small place in every history of instrumental music. Even without his immortal son Leopold Mozart would always be the author of the *Treatise on the Fundamental Principles of Violin Playing*, which he finished six months after the birth of Wolfgang Amadeus.

Leopold wrote a short autobiography in the first year of his son's life for F. W. Marpurg's *Historisch-kritische Beyträge zur Aufnahme der Musik,* which contains an 'Account of the present conditions of the music of his Grace the Archbishop of Salzburg in the year 1757'. It gives a short outline of his life and achievements up to the age of thirty-eight, and reads as follows:

'Herr Leopold Mozart of the Free City of Augsburg. Is violinist and leader of the orchestra. He composes church and chamber music. He was born on November the 14th, 1719, and shortly after completing his studies in philosophy and jurisprudence, he entered the service of the Prince. He has made himself familiar with all styles of composition, but has published nothing, and not until 1740 did he etch with his own hand, in copper, 6 Sonatas à 3. In July 1756 he published his *Violinschule*.

'Of Herr Mozart's compositions which have become known in manuscript, the most noteworthy are many contrapuntal and ecclesiastical works; further a large number of Symphonies, some for only four, but others for all the usual instruments; likewise over thirty grand Serenades, in which solos for various instruments are interpolated. Besides these he has composed many Concertos, especially for Transverse-Flute, Oboe, Bassoon, Waldhorn, Trumpet, and so forth; countless Trios and Divertimenti for divers instruments; also twelve Oratorios and a multitude of theatrical works, even Pantomimes, and in particular certain Occasional Compositions, such as Military music with trumpets, kettle-drums, drums and pipes, besides the usual instruments; Turkish music; music for a steel piano; and finally a Sledge-Drive with five sledge-bells; not to speak of Marches, so-called Serenades, besides many Minuets, Opera-Dances, and pieces of the same kind.'

We can complete these statements to a certain extent. Johann Leopold Mozart was born on November 14th, 1719, at Augsburg, the eldest of the six sons of the bookbinder, Johann Georg Mozart, whose ancestors on the father's side can be traced back to the seventeenth, and perhaps to the sixteenth, century. His mother too, Anna Maria Sulzer, the second wife of the bookbinder, was a native of Augsburg; she survived her husband, who died at the age of fifty-seven on February 19th, 1736, by more than thirty years and appears to have lived in comfortable circumstances, for Leopold was, just at the time of the production of his *Violinschule*, earnestly considering how to get his fair share as co-inheritor with his many brothers and sisters, of whom each had already received 300 Gulden of their heritage on account.

He must have distinguished himself among these brothers and sisters, for he did not become an artisan like his brothers Joseph Ignaz and Franz Aloys, who both became bookbinders. His guardian, Canon Johann Georg Grabher, placed him as one of the trebles in the choir of the Church of the Holy Cross and St. Ulrich, and out of a church-singer easily evolved a churchman. He learned not only to sing but to play the organ, and his son, in 1777 at Munich, made the acquaintance of a fellow student of Leopold, who still remembered clearly the temperamental organ-playing of the young musician in the monastery of Wessobrunn.

After the death of his father, Leopold was sent to Salzburg obviously under patronage and in the belief that this support would be used for the study of Theology. But Leopold was even at that early age already a diplomatist; he concealed his plans and fooled the clerics with his pretence of becoming a priest.... He studied at Salzburg University, not by any means Theology, but Logic and—as he himself asserts—also Jurisprudence. Presumably in consequence of this, the pecuniary assistance from Augsburg ceased. Leopold saw himself constrained to break off his studies and entered as *valet de chambre*, the service of Count Johann Baptist Thurn, Valsassina and Taxis (the Thurn and Taxis family were known as the Postmasters of the Holy Roman Empire), the President of the Salzburg Chapter.

This is all we know of the first twenty years of his life. What he sang in the Augsburg Cathedral choir can only be surmised; who his teachers were in organ-playing and composition remains dark. What the Free Imperial City of Augsburg, which united Catholics and Protestants within its walls, gave him was perhaps a certain tolerance, or rather let us say an aversion to 'priestdom' which deterred him from pursuing the clerical profession. That Leopold's musical taste was influenced by the robust South German characteristics of his time and that these gave him an impulse towards secular music is shown most clearly in Father Valentin Rathgeber's *Augsburger Tafel-Confect*, a large collection in four volumes of popular songs, choruses, quodlibets, instrumental pieces, all of which were issued between 1733 and 1746 by Leopold's publishing firm Lotter, and which are full of broad, easygoing, *bourgeois*, and at times coarse humour. In the Mozart family these pieces played a great part, and without them Leopold's 'Sledge-ride' or 'Peasant's Wedding' are as little conceivable as Wolfgang's youthful 'Galimathias musicum'.

It is a matter of conjecture what took him to Salzburg, to which place the road from Augsburg apparently went by way of Munich. Ingolstadt, the Bavarian university, lay much nearer for the Augsburgers and offered the same guarantee of a strictly orthodox training. St. Ulrich was one of the Benedictine monasteries which at one time had contributed to the foundation of Salzburg University: perhaps the Canons of the monastery recommended Leopold to Salzburg, which for Leopold as for Salzburg was not without result. His studies of 'Logica' left a deep and lasting impression on his life, both good and disastrous. He became a 'cultivated' musician who occupied his mind not only with the universe and mankind but also with the rules of his art; who interested himself in literature and in the small and great politics of the small and great potentates of his time; who understood Latin moderately well and knew how to handle his mother tongue with extraordinary skill and vitality, with many homely and popular South German turns of speech which lent to his language a special charm. Anybody who has read one of his epistolary descriptions of his journey to Paris or London, or a letter to his son at Mannheim, knows with what vivacity and power of description Leopold Mozart could wield his pen.

This mental superiority, which was augmented still more by the experience and knowledge of the world acquired in his long journeys with his son or the family, was indeed a doubtful asset to Leopold. For it imbued him with a sense of superiority over his colleagues and made him critical of those in authority over him; it made him notably isolated and unpopular; his 'diplomatic perception' often led him to suspect, behind the talk and actions of his fellows, more mystery than existed, and betrayed him into adverse criticism and erroneous judgement, and even into definite error. And who will blame him when, in a letter to Wolfgang of October 20th, 1777, he gives vent to his opinion: 'Hold fast to God who orders all things, for men are scoundrels! The older you grow and the more intercourse you have with them, the more you will find out for yourself that this is the sad truth. . . .'

(Has Leopold read Machiavelli's *The Prince?* 'One can say of mankind generally that they are ungrateful, fickle, false, cowardly in conduct, and greedy of gain. The Prince who trusts entirely to their word comes to grief.') But side by side with this hypochondria stood his tender love for his family, his timely care in all circumstances connected with daily life which showed itself most conspicuously while on their journeys (for round about 1760 it was a really adventurous undertaking to travel through the whole of Europe with a wife and two little children, and to be courier and impresario in one), and his honesty and integrity in all matters of communal and professional life. The tragedy and bitterness of his fate, which he felt deeply, atoned for all his weaknesses. He saw in his son the hope and light of his life; he had to experience that son's estrangement from him, and he died a lonely man to whom nothing remained but the exchange of letters with his daughter and his joy in his little grandson who, by the way, did not inherit a trace of the family genius.

But we anticipate. His service as *valet de chambre* with the Arch-Canon Count Thurn and Taxis was obviously only a roundabout way of guiding Leopold Mozart ultimately to music. In 1740 he dedicated to his master his first work, six Church and Chamber Sonatas for two violins and bass, the notation of which he engraved himself, and in the dedication called the Prelate, with baroque poetics, 'his paternal beacon whose beneficent influence had lifted him out of the harsh gloom of his distress and set him on the road to happiness'. One of the Sonatas from this work, in E flat, has been reprinted (*Denkmäler der Tonkunst in Bayern,* ix. 2, ed. Max Seiffert) and evinces a remarkable mixture of old-fashioned rigidity and a few freer passages of 'gallantry'. Leopold's talent for composition was developing during the unfortunate and difficult time when the austerity and nobility of the old classical style, as represented by Corelli, Handel, and Bach, began to give way to the new 'gallant style' which, inspired by Opera Buffa, gradually forced its way in. Leopold never succeeded in finding a satisfactory compromise between these two schools. This did not prevent him from plunging at once into the vortex of Salzburg musical life, which included not only the magnificent music at the cathedral and at the many other churches of the ecclesiastical residence, but also instrumental music for the Chapter of Prelates and Nobles and theatrical music for the performances of the schools and the university; for the Oratorio and for the Opera. Hence Leopold wrote for Lent, 1741, an oratorio-like Cantata, 'Christ Buried', for three voices, the text of which has been preserved with recitatives, arias, a duet, and concluding chorus. In 1742 he wrote for the smaller hall of the university the music to a school drama *Antiquitas personata*, classical, but ending in a lighter vein. In 1743 again a new Passion Cantata 'Christ Condemned', this time for four voices and chorus.

These works smoothed his path in the Archiepiscopal Court-Orchestra. After 1743 he became a violinist in the orchestra, and in 1744 the instruction of the choir-boys in violin-playing was handed over to him—a proof of his precocious talent for teaching—and shortly after he was appointed Court Composer. He could now think of marriage and domestic life. At an early stage of his life in Salzburg he must have become acquainted with Anna Maria Pertl, the daughter of the Warden of the Foundation of St. Gilgen on the Wolfgangsee, for on November 21st, 1772, he wrote to her from Milan: 'It was twenty-five years ago, I think, that we had the sensible idea of getting married; one which we had cherished, it is true, for many years. All good things take time!'

The remark, in its terse kindliness, characterizes the man and the wife, during whose partnership never a cloud darkened the domestic sky. Anna Maria Mozart, a year younger than her husband (born December 25th, 1720, in Schloss Hüttenstein near St. Gilgen) and orphaned at an early age, had always recognized Leopold's superiority. She was a good, narrow-minded woman, certainly an excellent mother to her family, ready for all Salzburg gossip and all the happenings of the little town; which she judged as kindly as her husband judged them critically and sarcastically. From her Wolfgang inherited all his merry, naïve, and childish traits—all that could be described as 'Salzburgerish' in his character. For, in those days, throughout the whole realm, the Salzburgers enjoyed no great reputation for being a serious people: they were credited, on the contrary, with being much given up to carnal pleasures, and with being averse to intellectual pursuits. They possessed all the attributes ascribed, in the South German Hanswurst—or Lipperl-Comedy (Lipperl = Philip), to the comic hero of this work. Wolfgang was fully aware of these peculiarities of his countrymen. Leopold and Anna Maria Mozart had from their marriage seven children, five of whom died in earliest infancy, leaving two survivors, namely: the fourth, Maria Anna Walburga Ignatia or 'Nannerl', born July 30th, 1751, and the seventh and last, Wolfgang Amadeus, born January 27th, 1756.

The first stirrings of musical genius in his son radically changed Leopold's outlook. He lived from now on solely for Wolfgang Amadeus. Up to 1762 his ambition to rise in Salzburg to the highest position had been thwarted by his superior, the Kapellmeister Johann Ernst Eberlin, who towered far above him as a creative musician, and whom he himself recognized as a pattern 'of a thorough and finished master', as an example of wonderful fertility and ease of production. But some months before Eberlin died (1762), Leopold had departed with his children on his second tour which, as a moral obligation and as a pecuniary speculation, he put far above his official duties at Salzburg. With difficulty, and with scarcely veiled threats that he would turn his back on Salzburg, he obtained on February 28th, 1763, the post of Vice-Kapellmeister, while Giuseppe Francesco Lolli, a very insignificant musician and, until then, Vice-Kapellmeister under Eberlin, was promoted to the vacant post. Leopold never managed to rise above the rank of Vice-Kapellmeister.

On December 16th, 1771, the Archbishop Sigismund von Schrattenbach, who was kindly disposed towards the Mozart family, died and his successor, Hieronymus Colloredo, being less inclined to accept without question the vagaries of his Vice-Kapellmeister Leopold and those of his Konzertmeister, Wolfgang Amadeus, the inevitable conflict arose between authority and genius—in which the guilt lay by no means entirely with the Archbishop. At all events, Leopold received continual set-backs. From 1773 he even had two superiors: Lolli and Domenico Fischietti, and in 1777 Fischietti and Jakob Rust. When Rust left Salzburg Leopold should have become Kapellmeister, and in a letter dated August 1778, he conquered his pride enough to 'recommend himself with the deepest homage' to his master, and to remind him that he 'has already served the Holy Archiepiscopal Church and Chapter for thirty-eight years, and that since the year 1763, as Vice-Kapellmeister, he has during those fifteen years performed nearly all his duties irreproachably and still performs them'. It was of no avail. The Archbishop, it is true, increased his salary but did not give him the desired appointment, and in 1783 another Italian, Lodovico Gatti, succeeded Fischietti. Leopold died a Vice-Kapellmeister. Of the 'irreproachable performance of nearly all his duties' one may be somewhat doubtful. If one reckons the duration of all the journeys which Leopold took with his family, or with Wolfgang only, from January 12th, 1762, till March 13th, 1773, they would probably amount, taken together, to about seven years' absence from Salzburg, and the Archbishop could hardly be blamed when he permitted these journeys only on condition of a reduction of Leopold's salary—it was indeed a considerable favour that he always held his post open against his return. Added to this, Leopold, who extended his horizon vastly during these journeys, returned to the provincial Salzburg a changed man. He became still more critical of his circumstances and his colleagues than before; he now fulfilled his duties only half-heartedly. The development of his son was, as always, his first thought. Wolfgang summed up his father's attitude well when, on September 4th, 1776, he wrote to Padre Martini at Bologna: 'My father has now been thirty-six years in the service of this Court and, knowing that the Archbishop has little liking for people of advanced age, he does not put his heart into his work but devotes himself to literature, which has always been a favourite pursuit of his. . . .' In reality Leopold's only preoccupation was his son. And even during the years of estrangement, after 1782, the son was still a central figure in his thoughts, even when, in his letters to Marianne, he wrote of him merely as 'your brother'. The correspondence gradually became less frequent and was often harsh and resentful on Leopold's side.

The last great pleasure of Leopold's life was the journey to Vienna in February, March, and April 1785; a visit during which he was witness of the full maturity and apparent triumph of the genius of his son, and the climax of his life was, perhaps, that Saturday evening of 1785 (February 12th) when for the first time the three quartets K. 458, 464, and 465 were performed, and

Haydn, to whom they were subsequently dedicated in September 1785, said to Leopold: 'I tell you before God, as an honest man, your son is the greatest composer I know either personally or by name; he has taste and, moreover, the deepest knowledge of composition.' What praise from the mouth of the only great musician who was at that time able to do justice to the greatness of Mozart! Genius and Art united, 'gallant' and 'learned'—the two extremes between which music at that period threatened to fall asunder—were once more welded together! This was the moment which justified all that Leopold had done for his son, and crowned the greatest work of his life.

In order to be quite just to Leopold Mozart one would need to be minutely acquainted with several sides of his activities: as letter-writer, as composer, as musical instructor—in which we must include the instruction of his own children as well as his teaching activities in the Salzburg Chapter House— and his theoretical work. Not all these activities are as fully known as they deserve to be. The greater number of his letters have been published; above all, the whole correspondence with Wolfgang Amadeus and all that concerns Wolfgang Amadeus. But it is only during the last years that we have known, in their entirety, the letters which he wrote to his daughter Marianne at St. Gilgen in the last years of his life (*Leopold Mozart's Briefe an seine Tochter*, im Auftrag der Mozartgemeinde in Salzburg herausgegeben von Otto Erich Deutsch und Bernhard Paumgartner, mit 32 Bildtafeln, 1936, Salzburg)—letters which are full of practical worldly wisdom, full of the sarcastic humour with which the ageing man contemplates all the gossip and small events of the provincial capital; full of a critical love or loving criticism of the daughter married somewhat late in life; full of a secret and resentful admiration for the independent son who has outgrown his fatherly authority; full of sturdy, undisguised tenderness for the little grandson whom he brings up, whose every sign of musical talent he hails with delight—signs which were to prove deceptive. But there has been as yet no complete publication[1] of the letters which Leopold Mozart wrote on his journeys to his landlord,

---

[1] This was written before the appearance, in 1938, of Emily Anderson's complete collection of *Letters of Mozart and his Family*. [Footnote added by Editha Knocker.]

friend, and banker, Johann Lorenz Hagenauer; nor of the extensive letters from Paris (November 1763 to April 1764) and London, where the family remained from April 1764 till the late summer of 1765, covering in all a period of over a year and a half. These letters of the 'Grand Tour', not only from France and England but also from a Germany split up into petty states, from Belgium and Holland, from French and German Switzerland, are a mirror of culture of the first order. Only those who know them are able to appreciate fully Leopold's power of observation, his acuity of understanding, his knowledge of mankind, his interest in all things great and small, and his plastic, homely, virile language. Very few descriptions of travels of the eighteenth century exist which could compare with the letters of Leopold; and had not so-called literary history been too narrow-minded to assess the testimony of a musician like Leopold Mozart at its true value it would long since have placed these letters on an equal footing with the letters from England which Georg Christian Lichtenberg addressed to his friend Boie some twelve years later.

It is not the purpose of this modest preface to pursue in detail the destinies and the inner experiences which were Leopold Mozart's lot during the time when the upbringing and guidance of his son dominated his mind to the exclusion of all else: the journeys to Munich and to Vienna, the great European tour, the second journey to Vienna and Moravia, the three journeys to Italy, and finally those agitating and bitter years when Leopold sent the son with his mother to Mannheim and Paris (1777–8). It proved to be a parting for ever from his wife, for she died while in Paris. This bereavement sent the son home, shattered, changed, wounded to the depths of his being, suspicious of Leopold's every thought and action which he mistook for tyranny or, at best, paternal diplomacy. As a matter of fact, it *was* paternal diplomacy that constrained Leopold in the first instance to send his son to Mannheim, then—when he noticed that dangerous love-meshes were entangling Wolfgang—to Paris; and from Paris back home to the narrow provincial life in a subordinate post at a petty court under an autocratic master—a service which Mozart must have regarded as little better than slavery.

The conflict between father and son was tragic because it was fought between loving authority and genius, and because it was inevitable. Leopold Mozart could never understand his son because he was unable to judge Wolfgang's musical talent beyond a certain point and did not realize that his revolutionary urge towards independence was but the individual, quasi-complementary side of that creative impulse to which Mozart's work bears witness. But in all practical matters how truly was Leopold in the right, and continued to be in the right in his attitude towards his son! What follies the young man committed—after all, he was now twenty-two years old—in Munich and Augsburg! He writes letters to his cousin, the notorious 'Bäsle', which by their coarseness still shock prudish souls and are not yet published in their entirety in Germany[1]—letters which are as different from that moving letter written by Mozart to the Abbé Bullinger on his mother's death as were those of Papageno and Tamino. They were, in the eyes of an anxious father, deserving of censure.

When, at Mannheim, Mozart fell in love with Aloysia Weber, what absurd plans he disclosed to his father, plans which rightly plunged the old man into utter despair! The menace of Aloysia to Mozart's career passed, not owing to any virtue of Mozart, but to the conduct of this 'calculating cold coquette' as Mozart himself called her. Two years later, at the age of twenty-six, he fell like a simpleton into the trap set by Madame Weber and a rascally trustee, and married Aloysia's sister Constanze.

For Leopold it was the final blow: his son had brought to naught the lofty prospects to which his genius entitled him. No one can say whether this marriage was fortunate or unfortunate for Mozart; whether Constanze was a good or a bad woman. No one can say what would have befallen Mozart: whether he might not have lived longer, whether he might not have produced hundreds more masterpieces, had he not married Constanze. Certain it is, however, that in a material sense Leopold was justified in his distrust of this marriage. He died on May 28th, 1787, and thus was spared the knowledge of the deterioration of his son's domestic circumstances: the last dreadful four and a half years, the begging letters to Freemason friends,

[1] Only in England, op. cit. [Footnote added by Editha Knocker.]

the prostitution of his art in order to pay his debts, the desperate and unsuccessful concert tours and—in the end—a pauper's grave. And so Leopold Mozart died a comparatively happy man—he was spared the greatest bitterness of all.

Both space and opportunity are lacking to do exhaustive justice to Leopold Mozart as a composer. Moreover, we have not yet a full record of his creative output, although in the *Denkmäler der Tonkunst in Bayern* (xi. 2, edited by Max Seiffert, 1908) a number of his works have been published: Three Piano Sonatas, two of the pieces which Leopold wrote for the well-known *Horn-Werk* of the Fortress of Hohen-Salzburg, which even to-day still sound over the city; String Trios and a Piano Trio, a Trumpet Concerto, several burlesque orchestral works, and some sacred and ecclesiastical vocal works. Much more could and should be published, and the thematic catalogue, too, which is attached to the volume could be considerably amplified. (For instance, I discovered in Florence orchestral parts of an older form of Leopold's celebrated *Sledge-Ride*, which Seiffert knew only in the Piano arrangement; and in a similar way many of the supposedly lost works have come to light.)

We have already indicated that Leopold was developing during those hard and, for many musicians, dangerous times, when the grand style of the old classics, with their strict forms and polyphonic structure, had become rigid and fossilized and the new 'gallant' style which, in truth, was a permeation of all vocal and instrumental music by the spirit of the *opera buffa*, had not yet arrived at the high-water mark of its distinctive qualities.

Leopold Mozart was not sufficiently great to find a compromise: he 'stuck to his wig', he became old-fashioned in his formality, and remained formal when he embraced the new *buffa* style. Nevertheless, a Litany proved what a sound musician he was, and how justified he was in still producing such works in Munich in 1782, although later he refused to send similar sacred pieces to his son for performance at the Sunday morning musical performances in van Swieten's Palace, and pronounced them to be out of date. But it redounded to his credit that they were able to ascribe many of his works, vocal and instrumental, to the *young* Mozart, which is as pardonable as it is possible, inasmuch as the young Mozart permitted many of his father's works to be ascribed to himself, and Leopold during his long journeys came under the same influences as Wolfgang Amadeus. On the whole, Leopold remained a South German musician even though in the Mozart's house the newest works of a few Saxon and North German masters, such as Telemann or Carl Philipp Emanuel Bach, were as well known as many of the greater and lesser Italian or Italianized masters, such as Hasse or Myslivecek. Leopold made a strong impression on his contemporaries and on posterity with his burlesque orchestral works, the *Sledge-Ride*, the *Peasant's Wedding*, the *Divertimento militaire*, the *Sinfonia di caccia*, the *Pastorals*, the 'Chinese' and 'Turkish' music in which, as we have already intimated, the specific South German Augsburg features are strongly marked. In order to give an idea of these singular symphonies, let us quote Leopold's letter to his publisher of November 6th, 1755.

'Here too comes the Peasant's Wedding. You can, if you think fit, augment the revenue of the Collegium Musicum with the proceeds. There is also a hurdy-gurdy and a bagpipe in it. One could use these at the Carnival festivities. It would be as well to have also a dulcimer or cymbal in it; this would have to be arranged so that they can play from the violin part, and to do it really well they should set the Violin and Bass under each other. In reality it is just as easy to play it by ear. But if you cannot get a hurdy-gurdy or a barrel-organ I will make another proposal. The barrel-organ can quite easily be played by an organist. Herr Stein will be the best for this.

'First comes the March, which must be played very rustically, and in which at the 19th and 21st bars [*a*: musical notation] of the first part, and at the 27th and 29th bars of the second part [*b*: musical notation] *a tempo*, after these notes there must be shouting. But I beg you to see that *piano* and *forte* are carefully observed, and in particular, when the hurdy-gurdy and bagpipe come in, all other instruments must play softly. The violins are in unison, and more copies must be made. The viola part must be taken by two or three players. What is written at the adagio with regard to the lament of the bridal wreath can, so far as I am concerned, be expressed in a better way. I wrote it in haste. The piano part depicts the demure wistfulness of the bride, but at the *forte* her heart is comforted by the whole company: here too the *piano* and *forte* marks must be observed with care. In the March, after the shouting, it may be accompanied each time by a pistol-shot, as is customary at weddings, and those who can whistle bravely on their fingers may also pipe in with the shouting.'

Leopold was occasionally given to such jokes, which have something rustic and boyish about them, and they contrast indeed with his morose character and, often, sarcastic humour. And one cannot help remarking that Wolfgang Amadeus who, as the son of his mother, was in ordinary life often very 'Salzburgerish' and frolicsome to a childish degree, was deeply serious in his art. Tricks such as the so-called 'Musical Joke' (K. 522) are, despite their overwhelmingly funny humour, surely also a perfectly serious satire on charlatanism.

As his greatest original achievement Mozart can point to his *Gründliche Violinschule*. His special gift as a teacher must have shown itself at an early age. Already in 1755 the Master of Arts, Lorenz Mizler, who founded a *Societät der Musikalischen Wissenschaften* in 1738 at Leipzig, had appointed Leopold as Corresponding Member. His *Violinschule* owes its conception and publication to an impulse given by the Berlin musician, or rather musical theorist, Fr. W. Marpurg, in his *Historisch-kritische Beyträge zur Aufnahme der Musik* (1754, and subsequent years), in which he deplores the fact that, despite the great number of musical treatises published, no guide exists as yet to violin playing. Marpurg harps in particular on the *Treatise on Playing the Transverse Flute* by Johann Joachim Quantz, Frederick the Great's flautist, and on Carl Philipp Emanuel Bach's (the second son of the great Johann Sebastian) *Versuch über die wahre Art das Clavier zu spielen*—two epoch-making works, of which the one appeared in 1752, the other in 1753. Both go far beyond the boundaries of mere 'Tutors' of their instruments; they are guides to the whole musical *style* of their time. That Leopold had these in mind goes without saying, when at the end of 1753 or the beginning of 1754 he sat down to the composition of his *Violinschule*, and he owes it to their example that *his* work also is far more than mere instruction in technique.

## PREFACE

As he says, he hesitated long, 'more than a whole year' before making up his mind to publish his book. In the spring of 1755 he entered into negotiations for its publication with Johann Jacob Lotter of his native town, to whom he handed over the first part of his manuscript, as appears from the following letter of July 21st:

'Monsieur, my very dear friend!

'I wish to take this excellent opportunity, when Frau Hagenauer is leaving for Augsburg, of telling you how you can assist me to carry out a scheme. All my brothers and sisters are now married and have all received in advance 300 Gulden of their heritage from my mother. Now it might well happen that in time to come, as I have as yet received nothing, matters might look very black for me. For this reason it has occurred to me that I now have the finest opportunity of likewise acquiring 300 Gulden for myself. I have therefore made a statement to my mother, but especially to my chief guardian, and represented to them that I absolutely must have the 300 Gulden for the publication of my book, hoping, as a result of this, to squeeze out the 300 Gulden, for otherwise, one day or other, the devil may fly away with them. Supposing now that you were asked questions! You must always say that you did not know how costly it would be, but that it might possibly cost as much as 300 Gulden. This is what I wanted to tell you. Moreover, there may well be a fair quantity of manuscript. Indeed I should have forwarded it in view of this excellent chance had you not written recently that I was not to send any more until you requested me to do so. I thought, too, that you would now be in Munich and would possibly not yet have the paper; for I simply could not endure bad paper. Supposing that it did not amount to quite twenty sheets, it would only be so much the easier to sell. However, it will, I think, certainly be that, especially if I include the Preface, Dedication and so forth.

'Fare you well!
'I am,
'the old LEOPOLD MOZART.'

Concerning the range of the manuscript and his Preface we learn from a letter of August 28th:

'... In consequence of your writing that you do not know what length the manuscript will be, owing to the copious music-notation, I have, in the meantime, ended with the eleventh chapter. You must know that all I had thought to put into twelve chapters I have now been compelled to get into only eleven; for if I had divided the eleventh chapter it would have been much too short compared with the rest. You see: The eighth chapter closes with the *Applicatur* (Positions). The ninth deals with *Appogiature*, etc., the tenth with the Trill, and the eleventh with the Tremolo, Mordent and the rest of the arbitrary ornamentations. And my last sheet ends with the 226th page. My manuscript, too, is actually in 226 or 227 pages, and can remain at that. I can close thus if you will not be vexed that it ends abruptly with the eleventh chapter. For to send something of an uneven number is as dangerous as when a hare or a cat runs across your path. You will see that my manuscript does not actually run to 57 sheets. If you permit another to be added, I can subjoin one which people will read with great pleasure. N.B. But there will not be a single music example therein. Do you remember, too, what you told me about a similar kind of instruction book by Wagenseil? If this procrastination does not harm me, it will not affect you; for perchance you still have some copies left of your nice Pandurists, or rather, *Rudimenta Panduristae*? You might sell them in the meantime. . . .'

The twelfth chapter was 'Of Reading Music correctly, and in particular, of Good Execution', which people will indeed read even to-day with great pleasure, and which has become especially necessary as a warning against empty virtuosity and a plea for sound musicianship. The above-mentioned *Rudimenta Panduristae* is a concise instruction-book on violin playing by the Viennese composer, G. Chr. Wagenseil.

In September he was at Augsburg in person, obviously in order to urge the publisher to greater speed in printing:

'Salzburg, 4th October 1755.

'How unwillingly I took leave of you and your dearest wife was easy to read in my eyes. I was very sore at the parting; and happy as I was to enter your household, just as sad was I to leave it. But why cannot people who love each other be always together? Must one seek the best friends one has afar off rather than near at hand? These thoughts and my memory of the kindly and beneficent manner in which your dearest wife received me, occupied my mind all the way to Salzburg. And how happy was I directly I entered my home to find my family in good health; and how my joy was increased twofold when a few minutes later I saw a letter from my friend whom I left with such reluctance! I have a strong suspicion that I am in no way worthy of the good opinion your wife holds of me. An honest fellow am I. That is the truth. That is all. But you betray by that opinion of me your own just disposition: for people commonly judge others according to themselves.

'Now I thank you both again for all courtesies received; and not only is it I who thank you, but my wife also, who presents her best respects, is extremely beholden to you for the same. I have depicted to her the merits of dear Frau Lotter in the liveliest colours, so that her only desire is to meet her herself; and if she were inclined to be jealous she would become so by reason of my constant praises.

'Now I hope to see before long a few printed pages [of the *Violinschule*]. And if you should against all hope pursue me still further with avalanches, then shall I turn to my dear Frau Lotter and implore her that she will interdict a certain nightly diversion until at any rate a few pages are set up.

'Here is the Sledge Ride! The rest will follow soon.'

But Lotter proceeds very slowly with the printing. Two further letters will demonstrate Leopold's impatience:

'Salzburg, the 17th February 1756.

'... Well, to come to my *Violinschule*, I am very much surprised that you wish to say something concerning the engraving and ask for more manuscript, as you are only now beginning to set up the fourth chapter. If you prove to me by your diligence that the delays are my fault, and if you finish what you have in hand within the promised time, I will take the blame on myself. Do you remember what you said to me? That I was to be easy in my mind and believe in your word. I did so. But the 28th of this month is the birthday of His Grace [the Archbishop Sigismund v. Schrattenbach]. Could there have been a better opportunity to present my work? All the Prebendaries are now here and the sales would have speedily turned a few copies into money. And now there occurs another similar opportunity before all the Cathedral Dignitaries disperse: namely Election Day. But dare I say when that is, lest you should at once depend on it too much? You really must not be dilatory, but very diligent, if you do not wish to overwhelm me once more with rage! Election Day is on the 5th April. On this day the Prebendaries are still all here, for they receive the election money. Therefore they all have money on this day. And immediately afterwards most of them go away and do not return until towards the autumn. Now all depends on whether you will not again leave me in the lurch. I implore you, therefore, in the name of all that I can invoke. You surely have enough people who can expedite the work. I beg you once more to do this. You see that I have a good reason.

'To your wife all good wishes from me and mine! Oh, did but Frau Lotter bake as good letters as she bakes doughnuts! In that case, I know, my book would have been ready long ago. Oh, the good woman!

'I remain in daily hope of a few little sheets.

'Your sincerest, most obedient

'LEOPOLD MOZART.'

Between all this, on February 9th, comes the announcement of Wolfgang's birth.

'As for the rest, I must inform you that on the evening of the 27th January my wife was delivered of a boy and, moreover, successfully. She was surprisingly weak and the after-birth had to be removed. But now, thank God, the child and mother are doing well. She presents her compliments to both of you. The boy is called Joannes Chrysostomus Wolfgang Gottlieb.'

At last, presumably in the late summer, the work appeared; at any rate, Leopold's Preface is dated the 26th of July 1756. Marpurg, whose remarks moved Leopold to publish his book, was also the first to announce it (*Historisch-kritische Beyträge*, 1757, iii. 160):

'One has long desired a work of this kind but hardly dared to expect it. The sound and skilled virtuoso, the rational and methodical teacher, the learned musician; qualities, each and all of which make a man of worth, are manifested here.'

Marpurg was not content with this notice but, like Mizler, made Leopold a Corresponding Member of the *Berliner Gesellschaft der Musik Wissenschaft*, founded by him June 23rd, 1759.

'The Society proposes to publish their periodical Essays in the form of letters, and they will take the liberty of addressing their letters to persons of merit, insight, and taste. Having this purpose in view, could they make a happier beginning than with you?'

The success of the book was great, much greater than that of the works of Quantz or Bach. About 1764 the first edition was sold out; Leopold's journeys with his family were the main cause of delay in preparing a second.

In the meantime, however, Leopold experienced the honour and pleasure of a Dutch translation which, typographically and in its general appearance, far surpassed all the German editions. Its title read:

Grondig | onderwys | in het | behandelen | der | viool, | ontworpen | door | Leopold Mozart, | Hoogvorstelyk-Saltzburgschen Kamer-Musicus. | Met 4 Konst-Plaaten een en Tafel van de Regelen | der Strykmanier enz. voorzien. | Te Haarlem, | By Joannes Enschede, | MDCCLXVI. 10 f., 259 p.

In his *Ideen zu einer Aesthetik der Tonkunst* (printed 1806, p. 157) Christian Daniel Schubart, the Swabian poet, music author, and song-composer, speaks of Leopold:

'By his *Violinschule*, written in very good German and with deep insight, he has earned great merit. The examples are excellently chosen and his "fingering" is by no means pedantic.'

Carl Friedrich Zelter, too, extolled the work and wrote concerning it to his friend Goethe (*Correspondence*, ed. Hecker):

'His *Violinschule* is a work which will be worth using as long as the violin remains a violin; moreover it is well written.'

With the second German edition Lotter again took his time. The printing was begun in 1769, but dragged on so long that a number of the copies were not ready till the following year; hence one finds copies dated both with the year 1769 and 1770. The title reads:

Leopold Mozarts | Hochfürstl. Salzburgischen Vice-Capellmeisters | gründliche | Violinschule, | mit | vier Kupfertafeln | und | einer Tabelle. | Zweite vermehrte Auflage. | Auf Kosten des Verfassers. | Augsburg, | Gedruckt bei Johann Jacob Lotter. 1769 (1770) 8 fol. 268 p.

Possibly Leopold lived to see a third edition (an exact reproduction of the second) which appeared in the year of his death, 1787, the only difference being in the title of the firm of the publisher, which read: Johann Jakob Lotter & Son. Yet a fourth, wholly unchanged, edition appeared in 1800, after which Leopold's book was supplanted by other methods more adapted to the advanced technical demands of the new century. In 1801 the first revised edition was published by Täubel of Vienna, in which the name of a Herr Pierlinger appeared side by side with Leopold's, and in 1804 another elaboration was printed by Hoffmeister & Kühnel of Leipzig. A little later an 'abridgement' by Böhme of Hamburg appeared. It was not until 1922 that Bernhard Paumgartner, the Director of the Mozarteum at Salzburg, restored to Leopold his rights and edited a facsimile of the first edition, produced by the Viennese publisher Carl Stephenson.

Between the first and second editions, however, appeared a French translation, of which Leopold for a long time knew nothing—in 1778 he was urging his son to send him a copy from Paris, or to bring one home with him. The title reads:

Méthode | raisonnée | Pour apprendre à Jouer | du Violin | Composée Par Léopold Mozart | Compositeur et Directeur de la Musique de Monseigneur l'Archévêque de Saltzbourg | Traduite de l'Allemand en Français | par | Valentin Roeser | Musicien de S.A.S. Monseigneur le Duc d'Orléans. | On trouvera à la fin de cette Méthode XII Petits Duo et un Caprice faciles à la portée des Commençants, | A Paris | Chez Mr. Le Menu, . . . (ca. 1770) 1 f., 87 p.

Only Italy and England closed their doors to Leopold's *Violinschule*. This is the first English translation of this work and the shades of Wolfgang Amadeus's father are now appeased.

It is superfluous to say much about a work which the reader has before his eyes in its entirety. The book owes its success above all to its *originality*. It may indeed have had forerunners, beginning with the old *Violinschule* of the Nüremburg Lutist Hans Gerle of 1532, or the excellent *Manual of Ornamentation for the Gamba* by the Spaniard Diego Ortiz of 1553, up to the *École d'Orphée* of Michel Corrette of 1738, or Francesco Geminiani's *Technical Instructions*. But Leopold probably knew none of these forerunners and might well have believed himself to be the first in the field. It is evident that his book was the outcome of his personal experience—Leopold was considered to be the best teacher in Salzburg, and his teaching was sought after even in his old age. He did not permit himself to be influenced by Quantz, and still less by Ph. Em. Bach, as is proved by his chapter on Ornamentation, in which he follows the practice of the Italian School of Tartini rather than that of the Saxon or North German musicians. Quite new was his teaching of the 'Applicatur'.[1] In this chapter he bequeathed to posterity a firm basis on which to build. His book is not written for the pupil but for the teacher, whom he instructs from the first how he should teach elementary technique, guiding him finally to the advanced problems of artistic performance. Always must the technician be at the service of the musician. True to his reputation for honesty and integrity, Leopold hated braggarts in art; he preferred a good orchestral violinist to a bad virtuoso. His book is and will remain no mere instruction-book of the *mechanics* of violin-playing, but a guide to 'good performance in general', a treatise on violin playing as an art.

## NOTE

THIS Preface was written in 1937. It has in the meantime been used partly for my book: *Mozart—His Character, His Work* (New York, 1945, Oxford University Press; London, 1946, Cassell & Co.). It has been impossible for me to familiarize myself with the most recent literature regarding Leopold Mozart, e.g. Milton Steinhardt: *Leopold Mozart's Violin School* (thesis for M.M. Degree, Rochester, N.Y., 1937) or: *The Augsburg Mozart Book* (Augsburg, 1943), which contains an article by Ernst Fritz Schmid concerning the connexion of Leopold and Wolfgang Amadeus Mozart with Augsburg.

A. E.

[1] *Applicatur* = positions, fingering.

## Foreword to Translator's Introduction

THIS translation of Leopold Mozart's *Gründliche Violinschule* was advertised to appear in the spring of 1940. Much has happened since then. We have come through a second world war, during the six years of which the publication of books was necessarily restricted by the shortage of paper. The completion of this book was still further delayed by the destruction of type-matter and proofs caused by enemy air activity. These events have necessitated this Foreword to my original Introduction, dated 1937. They have also necessitated the involved labour of reconstructing the 'copy' for the printer. In this connexion I must express my thanks to Ida Oldroyd for her help in deciphering and typing material which was far from being easily legible.

E. K.

1947

## Translator's Introduction

SOME years ago—it was during the war of 1914–18—a friend showed me an old book, still in its original brown leather binding and smelling of the dust of ages. It was to me merely a *Violin Method* by Leopold Mozart—dated 1787, and the third edition.

Our minds were at that time concerned with matters other than literature. So I returned the book to its owner and forgot it. But no—it was not really forgotten. It was tucked away in that wonderful storehouse which we call in these days the subconscious mind, the key of which may be turned by the fingers of association; a sound, a scent, a word, and the door flies open and out tumbles some 'forgotten' thing which has lain on the shelf, covered by the thousand and one activities which, taken together, man calls 'life'.

It was two or three years ago that my storehouse key was turned, and although the door had been ajar several times previously and hastily shut again, this time it opened wide. I wrote to my friend, asking for the loan of the book. It came promptly and I sat down to study it. Before I had read to the end of the 'Foreword' I was enthralled. No thinking person could, I believe, fail to be charmed by Leopold Mozart's dry humour, his wit, his imagery, and his child-like and literal acceptance of history as told in the Old Testament. Nor could he fail to be impressed by his knowledge of the classics and of the general literature of his own day. But more striking still is his ardent desire to help colleagues and students; to improve their standard of musicianship and performance, and to imbue them with his own singleness of purpose—his own intolerance of all that was not 'purity and truth' in his art.

Not only does the Dedication to 'His Grace' prove this beyond all doubt, but in every chapter of his book he emphasizes again and again his desire to 'light a beacon' for the guidance of all who would seek to become worthy of the name of artist and musician.

He even avoids prolixity in order to bring the cost of his book within the means of 'the needy, who are not in a position to put themselves under a teacher for a long period of time'. And yet, despite this absence of 'wordiness', within the covers of his book can be found the whole gamut of good technique, good style, and artistic training.

Truth is unchanging, and his teaching remains in essence as true to-day as it was in 1756.

The great, and I think the most important, difference between Leopold Mozart's teaching and the teaching of our own times is his insistence that each lesson be perfected before the next step is taken. He warns the teacher against letting the pupil *play* before he knows the rules of playing. He stresses the vital importance of correct bowing, and he gives a sound and logical reason for each rule.

No doubt his method of teaching did not get the pupil over the ground as quickly as does the modern system, but I venture to think that those who were trained in his method were not only very able performers who knew their business from A to Z, but also first-rate musicians, possessing that mysterious quality called 'style'.

Let not the reader throw the book down because he thinks it is written in language too 'precious'. Leopold Mozart was a Salzburger of the middle eighteenth century and wrote in a curious mixture of scholastic and bourgeois style. I have endeavoured to catch the flavour of Mozart's language as far as possible whilst adhering closely to the text. This, however, became at times almost impossible owing to his abundant use of homely idioms and popular sayings.

# TRANSLATOR'S INTRODUCTION

Certain German and Italian technical terms, for which no satisfactory English equivalents exist, have been left untranslated.

This translation embodies the first and third editions, dated 1756 and 1787. The differences between the third edition and the second and fourth editions of 1769–70 and 1800 are so slight as to be negligible.

Of Leopold Mozart's life as man and musician I need say no more. In Dr. Alfred Einstein's Preface the reader will find a picture of him, in both capacities, far more vivid than any I can draw. No words can adequately express my gratitude to Dr. Einstein, that great scholar and authority on the Mozart family, without whose untiring help and advice I should never have had the courage to finish my task, and whose encouragement has made that task a labour of love.

I wish to express my gratitude to Miss Emily Anderson and Mr. Brian Fagan for their generous help and advice during the preparation of this work. Acknowledgement is also due to the former and to Messrs. Macmillan & Co. for permission to use extracts from Miss Emily Anderson's translation of the *Letters of Mozart and his Family*.

EDITHA KNOCKER

**NOVEMBER 1937**

# Translator's Note to Second Edition

I HAVE taken the opportunity provided by the call for a Second Edition to revise my translation fairly extensively. The revisions consist for the most part of correction of actual errors; more faithful rendering of Leopold Mozart's meaning (which is not invariably as clear as it might be); more careful tabulation of the differences between the First and Third (1787) editions, re-examination of which showed that in places I had unwittingly telescoped the two; and, finally, clarification of the system adopted in this volume for showing these differences and for distinguishing my editorial additions. For the reader's guidance, this system is as follows:

1. In the text, passages in ordinary (roman) type between square brackets are additions made in the 1787 edition, i.e. they do not appear in the First edition.

2. Leopold Mozart's own footnotes are in ordinary type, unbracketed.

3. My editorial additions in the text are in italics within square brackets, and so are the footnotes which I have added.

For practical reasons certain comments or amendments which I wished to make in this new edition could not be incorporated in the body of the text. These will be found in the Translator's Appendix on p. 232, and a cross-reference thereto is made at each appropriate point in the text.

In all the foregoing revisions I have been greatly assisted by Mr. David D. Boyden, Associate Professor of Music, University of California (Berkeley), who most generously put at my disposal his intimate knowledge both of Leopold Mozart's treatise itself and of the intricacies of translating it. Mr. Boyden volunteered innumerable valuable suggestions, most of which I have gladly adopted.

I also wish to thank my old friend, Mr. Ernest Newman, for his help over the virtually insoluble problem of finding an English word to convey the meaning of the German 'Affect': this is briefly dealt with in the Translator's Appendix.

E. K.

NOVEMBER 1949

# Versuch
## einer gründlichen
# Violinschule,

entworfen

und mit 4. Kupfertafeln sammt einer Tabelle

versehen

von

## Leopold Mozart

Hochfürstl. Salzburgischen Cammermusikus.

---

In Verlag des Verfassers.

Augspurg,
gedruckt bey Johann Jacob Lotter, 1756.

Οτι μὲν ὖν ἡμῖν τὕς τε νέὕς παιδευτέον μὕσικῇ, καὶ αὑτῆς διὰ βίὕ προσεκτέον ὅπη παρείκοι, ὕδένα ἀντειπεῖν οἴομαι.

Esse igitur adolescentes nobis Musica erudiendos, ipsiusque tota Vita, *quantum fieri possit,* rationem habendam, neminem oblocuturum puto.

ARISTIDES QUINTILIANUS, LIBRO II, *de Musica.*

To

the most worthy and noble

Prince of the Holy Roman Empire

# Siegmund Christoph

of the House of the Imperial Counts

von

Schrattenbach;

Archbishop of Salzburg,

Hereditary Legate

of the Holy Roman See

and

Primate of Germany

To my most gracious Prince and Lord:

## Most worthy and noble
# Prince
### of the Holy Roman See
## Most gracious Prince and Lord

MAY I venture to dedicate a humble book of instruction to the eminent name of Your Grace?
And are not rules for the Violin too lowly an offering for the Mightiness of a Prince and Primate of all Germany? An instruction-book can, in the eyes of a great Prince, be no important work; that I know only too well; but I know also that Your Grace is in the highest degree kindly disposed towards all that contributes in the very least to the instruction of youth in the Fine Arts. How many young people, often endowed with the fairest gifts of Nature, would have grown to maturity, untended as the seedlings run wild in the forest, if your right fatherly help had not in good time brought them under the supervision of judicious persons for their upbringing. And how many would have had, in the increase of their years, to famish in want and poverty and to be a burden on the community as useless citizens of the world, if Your Grace had not graciously provided instruction for such, according to their talent and ability, in this or that path of knowledge? Young people of both sexes and of all ranks can boast of this kindness; a kindness which perishes not with the death of the recipient, but lives on in the memory of whole generations and remains unforgettable to the descendants, who can count an array of people who would have remained, if not complete nonentities, at any rate unknown to fame and would have bequeathed to their descendants an inglorious name, had not the kindest of Princes grasped their grandfather by the arm and raised him to a position whereby through his knowledge he, while living, was able to help his fellow citizens and after his death still to be useful to his descendants.

I may, therefore, surely venture to present to Your Grace in deepest loyalty, a book in which I have endeavoured, according to my poor powers, to pave a way for music-loving youth which shall guide them with certainty to good taste in music. Yea, I am confident that Your Grace will not refuse to extend to this, my humble effort, which I have made for the sake of beginners in music, that same gracious protection with which you have to this hour so surpassingly favoured the sciences generally, but in particular the Art of Music.

Therefore I humbly beg to commend to Your Grace's supreme clemency myself and my family; yea, even our whole Company of Musicians; and I pray to that Infinite Trias Harmonica, which transcends all human reason in most perfect divinity, for the preservation of Your Most Precious Person, and subscribe myself
     Your Grace's
          and My most Gracious Prince's and Lord's
               Most humble and obedient servant
                    **Leopold Mozart**

# Preface

MANY years have passed since I wrote down the following rules for those who came to me for instruction in Violin Playing. I often wondered greatly that nothing had been published as a guide to so popular and, for the greater part of music, so indispensable an instrument as the violin, in view of the fact that a sound foundation, and in particular some rules for special bowings, coupled with good taste, have long been needed. I was often sad when I found that pupils had been so badly taught; that not only had I to set them back to the beginning, but that great pains had to be taken to eradicate the faults which had been taught, or at best had been overlooked. I felt a deep sympathy when I heard adult violinists, many of whom often preened themselves not a little on their knowledge, distorting the meaning of the composer by the use of wrong bowing. Yea, I was amazed to see that even with the help of oral explanations and practical demonstration they were often quite unable to grasp truth and purity.

So it came to my mind to publish this *Violinschule*. I even spoke to the publisher. But, great as was my zeal to serve the world of music to the utmost that in me lay, I still hesitated for over a year, because I was too bashful to venture into the daylight with my modest work in such enlightened times.

Finally I received by chance Herr Marpurg's *Historic Critical Contributions to the Advancement of Music*. I read his Preface. He says at the beginning that one need not complain of the number of musical publications. He points out and regrets, moreover, that a guide to the violin is still lacking. This stirred my former resolution once more into life and was the strongest stimulus to send these pages to the publisher in my native city.

Whether these pages, however, be written in accordance with the wishes of Herr Marpurg and other learned musical experts is a question which only time can answer. Besides, what could I say of my work without either blaming or praising myself? The first I refuse to do, because it offends my self-esteem and indeed who would believe that I was sincere? To do the second were to sin against decorum—yea, against reason—and is therefore ridiculous, for everyone knows what an evil odour self-praise leaves in its wake.

# PREFACE

For the publishing of this book I need hardly apologize, seeing that it is, as far as I know, the first guide to violin playing which has appeared. If I owe an apology to the learned world it can only be for the manner in which I have executed my task.

There is still much to be dealt with, and many may reproach me for not having done so. But what are these things? Such matters as belong to the lighting of a beacon to guide the weak judgement of many a concert performer and, by means of rules, to form the good taste of an intelligent soloist.

I have here laid the foundation of good style; no one will deny this. This alone was my intention. Had I wished to deal with all the rest, this book would have been twice the length; and this I particularly desired to avoid. Not much is gained by a book being a little more costly to the buyer, for indeed who has greater necessity to acquire such guidance than the needy who are not in a position to put themselves under a teacher for a long period of time? Are not the best and most gifted people often in the greatest poverty; just those who, if they had a reliable Instruction Book available, could go far in a short space of time?

I could have said a great deal more: I could have followed the example of some authors and enlarged on the material contained in this book, interpolating here and there remarks on other Sciences, and in particular could have dealt much more extensively with the subject of Intervals. But as these are mostly topics which either belong to Composition, or are often intended more to display the author's erudition than to be of service to the pupil, I have omitted everything which would enlarge my book. And just because of this desire for brevity, I have not elaborated the examples for two violins in the fourth chapter and have in general shortened all the other examples.

Finally, I must confess that I have written this *Violinschule* not only for the use of pupils and the benefit of teachers, but because I desire earnestly to convert all those who, by their bad teaching, are making failures of their pupils; because they themselves have faults which they would easily recognize, could they for but a short space of time renounce their self-esteem.

> Decipit Exemplar Vitiis imitabile:
> *Horat. Lib. I., Epist. XIX.*

Perchance they may find their faults clearly depicted in these pages, and perhaps many a reader, even if he refuse to acknowledge it, may be convinced and his conscience roused to better things. One thing only do I expressly forbid: namely, that anyone shall believe that in speaking of a fault here and there in this book with contempt I have aimed my remarks at any particular person. I will here make use of the words with which Herr Kabener, at the conclusion of the Preface to his *Satirical Works*, protects himself against such libel and declares: 'I mean no one excepting those who know whom I have meant.'

> Omni Musarum licuit Cultoribus aevo
> Parcere Personis, dicere de Vitiis,
> Quae si irascere agnita videntur.
>
> *Sen.*

Salzburg, written the 26th of the *Hay-month, 1756.

MOZART

* July

## INTRODUCTION TO THE *VIOLINSCHULE*
## I. Of Stringed Instruments, and in particular the Violin

### § 1

THE word 'fiddle' denotes instruments of different shapes and sizes, furnished with gut strings varying proportionately in thickness, and played with a wooden bow strung with horse-hair. From this it appears that the word 'fiddle' is comprehensive and embraces all the various kinds of stringed instruments, and that it is therefore a misnomer to call the violin baldly a 'fiddle'. I shall enumerate here the commonest kinds.

### § 2

One class of fiddle, already almost obsolete, is the little Pocket-Fiddle or Kit which has four strings, or even only three. It was commonly used by dancing masters while instructing their pupils, on account of its convenient size for pushing into the pocket.

A second, but hardly more practical kind, is the Simple or Board Fiddle, so called because its four strings are merely strung over an arched board or piece of wood, and in this respect it rather resembles an ordinary violin, or Treble-Fiddle.

The third kind is the Quarter-, or Half-Fiddle. It is smaller than the ordinary violin and is used for very small boys. But it is advisable, if the boy's fingers permit, to accustom him to a full-sized violin, so that he may hold his fingers in a consistently even position, harden them, and learn to stretch them. Some years ago one even played concertos on this little violin (called by the Italians *Violino Piccolo*) and, as it was capable of being tuned to a much higher pitch than other violins it was often to be heard in company with a transverse flute, a harp, or other similar instruments. The little fiddle is no longer needed, and everything is played on the ordinary violin in the upper registers.

The fourth kind is the ordinary violin or Treble-Fiddle. It is with this we are dealing in particular in this book.

A fifth sort is the Alto-Fiddle (called by the Italians *Viola di Braccio*, or *Viola*), commonly known as the Bratsche (from *Braccio*, arm). It takes the place of alto as well as tenor, and if necessary the bass to an upper part,[1] for which otherwise a Sixth kind would be needed; namely, the Bassoon-Fiddle, which differs slightly in size and stringing from the Viola. Some call it the Hand-Bass-Viol, which is, however, somewhat larger than the Bassoon-Fiddle. It is customary, as I have already mentioned, to play bass on the latter, but only in company with violins, transverse flutes, and other high-pitched parts, as otherwise the bass would encroach on the upper parts, thus, according to the recognized rules of resolution, often causing unpleasant harmonies. This crossing of the upper with the lower parts is quite a common fault of inferior composers.

The seventh kind is called the Bass-Viol, or, as Italians call it, the Violoncello. Formerly this had five strings, but now only four. It is customary to play the bass part on this instrument, and although some are larger, others smaller, they differ but little from each other excepting in the strength of their tone, according to the fashion of their stringing.

The Great-Bass or the Violon, from the Italian *Violone*,[2] is the eighth kind of stringed instrument. This Violon is also made in various sizes, but the tuning remains the same. It needs to be strung according to its size [albeit the difference must be observed in stringing it]. Because the Violon is much bigger than the Violoncello, it is tuned a whole octave lower. Usually it has four strings [at times only three], but the larger ones may have five. [With these five-stringed Violons, or Double-Basses, bands of rather thick cord are attached to the neck at all the intervals, in order to prevent the strings from slipping, and to improve the tone. One can also perform difficult passages more easily on such a Bass, and I have heard concertos, trios, solos, and so forth performed on one of these with great beauty. But I have observed that in accompanying with any strength for the purpose of expression, two strings are frequently to be heard simultaneously on account of the strings being thinner and lying nearer together than those of a Bass strung with but three or four strings.]

The ninth kind is the Gamba. It is held between the legs, hence its name; for the Italians call it *Viola di Gamba*, i.e. Leg-Fiddle. Nowadays the violoncello, too, is held between the legs, and one can justly call it, also, a leg-fiddle.

---

[1] *The following footnote was added in 1787*: 'I often had occasion to laugh at violoncellists who actually permitted the bass part to their solo to be accompanied by a violin, although another violoncello was present.'

[2] *Ed. 1787 reads*: 'The Great-Bass (il Contra Basso), also commonly called the Violon.'

The viola di gamba is in many other respects different from the violoncello. It has six or seven strings, while the latter has only four. It is, moreover, tuned quite differently, has a more pleasant tone, and serves mostly for playing an upper part.

The tenth kind is the Bordon, commonly spoken of as Barydon from the Italian *Viola di Bordone* [*French:Bourdon*].[1] This instrument has, like the gamba, six to seven strings. It has a very wide neck, the back side of which is hollow and open and into which nine or ten brass and steel strings are inserted, which are touched and plucked by the thumb. Moreover, while the principal part is played with the bow on the gut strings, the thumb simultaneously plays the bass part on the strings under the neck. Consequently, compositions have to be written specially for it. It is, however, one of the most charming of instruments.

As an eleventh kind, we may count the Viola d'Amor after the Italian: *Viola d'Amore*, and the French *Viole d'Amour*. It is a distinctive kind of fiddle which sounds especially charming in the stillness of the evening. Above, it is strung with six gut strings of which the lower ones are covered, while under the finger-board are stretched six steel strings, which are neither touched nor bowed but are merely there to duplicate and prolong the sound of the upper strings. This instrument unfortunately suffers frequently from mis-tuning.

The twelfth kind is the English Violet, chiefly distinguishable from the viola d'amore by having seven strings above and fourteen below, which must therefore be tuned differently. Owing to the number of lower sympathetic strings, the tone is stronger.

An old species of stringed instrument is the Marine-Trumpet, originating from the Trumpet-Fiddle. It has only one thick gut string, a three-cornered body, a long neck, and so on. The string lies on a bridge which on one side scarcely touches the sound-board, thus causing the string, when bowed, to give forth a harsh, rattling tone like that of a trumpet.

These then are all the kinds of stringed instruments known to me, and most of them are still in use; the fourth of which, namely the Violin, furnishes the material for my attempted thesis.

[1] Some speak and write it 'Viola di Bardone'. But 'Bardone' is to my knowledge no Italian word, while on the other hand 'Bordone' is such, for it means a Tenor Voice; means also a large string, a drone, and the soft humming of the bees. He who knows this instrument will agree that the word 'Bordone' rightly describes the tone thereof.

## § 3

The violin is an instrument made of wood and is composed of the following parts. The upper portion consists of an arched roof (belly),[1] and a similar floor (back). The side-walls which join the belly to the back are called by violin-makers the 'ribs', the whole being named by them 'the body'. Attached to this body is the neck, and to the neck the finger-board, so called because the strings drawn over it are grasped by the fingers on this board. A small piece of wood is fastened below to which the strings are attached and these, resting on a wood bridge, are drawn over the neck into pegs, by the help of which the violin is tuned. In order to prevent the strain of the strings from pressing too greatly on the belly and so diminishing the tone, a little piece of wood, called the sound-post, is inserted inside the body under the bridge. At the extremity, violin-makers endeavour to give an air of finish; some by means of a graceful, snail-like curve, some by carving a lion's head. Yea, they often attach greater importance to such decorations than to the main structure. Consequently the violin—who would believe it!—is a victim of the universal deception of external show. He who values a bird for its feathers, and a horse for its blanket, will also inevitably judge a violin by its polish and the colour of its varnish, without examining carefully its principal parts. This course is taken by all those who judge with their eyes and not with their brains. The beautifully 'curled' lion's head can improve the tone of the violin just as little as a fancifully curled wig can improve the intelligence of its living wig-stand. Yet in spite of this, many a violin is valued simply for its appearance, and how often does it happen that clothes, money, pomp, and especially the curled wig, is that which turns a man into a scientist, counsellor, or doctor? But where have I got to? My zeal against this common habit of judging by superficial appearance has wellnigh led me astray.

## § 4

The violin is strung with four strings, each of which must be of the right thickness in relation to the other. I say 'the right thickness', for if one string be a little too thick in proportion to another it is impossible to obtain an even or a good tone. It is true that violinists and violin-makers frequently judge these thicknesses by the eye, but it cannot be denied that the result is often very bad. Indeed, one must go to work with the greatest patience and care if one wishes to string the violin

[1 *For the sake of clearness I shall hereafter use the English names of the parts of a violin.*]

properly and in such fashion that the strings have their intervals in the right proportion to each other, and the right notes lie therefore opposite each other. He who is willing to take the trouble, can test them according to mathematical principles. He can take two well-stretched strings, an A and E, a D and A, or a D and G, each of which is as exactly as possible of the same thickness throughout. That is: the diameter or cross-section must be uniform. To each of the two strings equal weights can be attached. Now if the two strings have been well chosen they should, on being struck, give forth the interval of a perfect fifth, but if one string sounds too sharp and oversteps the fifth, this is a sign that it is too weak and a thicker string is then selected; or the string which sounds flat and is therefore too thick may be exchanged for a thinner string. One must proceed thus until the perfect fifth is attained and the strings are in proportion and truly chosen. But how difficult it is to find evenly made thick strings. Are they not mostly thicker at one end than at the other? How can one make a sure test with an uneven string? I would therefore remind you that the choice of strings must be made with the greatest care and not merely at random.

§ 5

It is most regrettable that our present-day instrument-makers take so little trouble with the finish of their work.[1] Yea, and what is more, each works away according to his own notions and his fancy, without justification for either one or the other. For instance—the violin-maker has perchance, after some experience, made a rule for himself that when the ribs are low the belly must be more highly arched; whilst, on the contrary, when the ribs are high the belly can be less arched and high; and this for the sake of propagating the tone, in order that the tone may not be too much suppressed by the lowness of the ribs or the belly. He knows further that the wood of the back must be stronger than that of the belly; that both the back and the belly must have more wood in the middle than at the sides; that besides this, a certain evenness must be maintained in the increasing or diminishing of the thickness of the wood, and this he knows how to test by means of callipers, &c. How comes it then that the violins are so unlike each other? How comes it that one sounds powerful and another weak? Why has this one, so to speak, a shrill tone; that one a wooden tone; this one a rough, screaming tone; that one a sad and muffled tone? It were vain to inquire very deeply. It is wholly due

[1] Most instrument-makers, it is true, work nowadays merely for their bread, and in one respect cannot be blamed. People demand good work and pay but little for it.

to the difference between the work of one man and that of another. They all decide the height, thickness, and so on by the eye, never attaining any fixed principles; so that while one succeeds the other fails. This is an evil which indeed robs music of much of its beauty.

## § 6

In this direction our mathematical friends might well add to their fame. The learned Herr M. Lorenz Mizler made a proposal some years ago which can never be too much extolled; namely, to establish a Society of Musical Science in Germany. This was actually inaugurated in 1738. It is to be regretted that such a noble endeavour to achieve a reputable improvement in the Science of Music was not given timely and generous support. The whole realm of music would never have been able to repay such a society if it had succeeded in kindling so clear a light for the instrument-makers that by its agency music might have gained vastly in grace. No one will take it amiss if I say frankly that more depends on the accurate research into the making of instruments than on the effort of scientists to prove why two consecutive octaves or fifths do not fall pleasingly on the ear. In any case, sound musicians have banished these long ago and it is sufficient that, because of the effect of their too close relationship on a discriminating ear which expects variety, these octaves and fifths become nauseating owing to unpardonable repetition. Should we not consider rather why it is we meet with so few good instruments, and those of such varied tone-quality, and unequal workmanship, than that we should reckon out whole rows of paper intervals and write them down, especially since they may prove of little or no subsequent use? These learned gentlemen could further the cause of music greatly by means of useful research—for example: what is the best wood for stringed instruments? How can it best be seasoned?[1] Whether in shaping the belly and back the years of the wood should not be in relation to each other?[2] How the pores of the wood can best be closed and whether with this object in view the inside should not be lightly varnished; and what sort of varnish would be the most serviceable? But above all, how high, how thick, and so on, the belly, back, and ribs should be. In a word, how, according to a definite system, the parts of a violin should be proportioned with each other. In this way I say these learned gentlemen could, with the help

---

[1] I have had a violin in my hands the parts of which, before they were assembled, had been smoke-dried with great success.

[2] The varied rings which are shown in the wood are called 'years'.

of mathematics, and the interest of a good violin-maker, be of invaluable assistance to the cause of music.

## § 7

Meanwhile, a diligent violinist does his best to improve his violin as far as possible by changing the strings, the bridge, and the sound-post. If the violin be a large model, thicker strings will undoubtedly have a better effect; whereas if the body be small it will need thin strings.[1] The sound-post must be neither too long nor too short, and must be placed to the right of and slightly behind the foot of the bridge. It is of no small importance to set the sound-post correctly. One has to slip it to and fro many times with great patience, each time carefully testing the quality of various notes on each string, continuing in this fashion until the best tone possible has been obtained. The bridge also affects the tone greatly. For instance, if the tone be too shrill and penetrating or, so to speak, piercing, and therefore unpleasant, it can be softened by using a low, broad, and rather thick bridge which has been but very slightly cut away underneath. Is the tone too weak, soft, and muffled—then one should use a thin bridge, not too broad, and as high as circumstances permit, greatly carved away both underneath and in the centre. Such a bridge must above all be of very fine-grained, well-seasoned wood with well-closed pores. Further, the bridge has its place on the belly midway between the two openings, one on either side, which have the form of a Latin *f*. In order to prevent any suppression of tone, the small piece of wood to which the strings are fastened and which is commonly called the tail-piece, and which is hung on to a small peg inserted for this purpose, must be set in such fashion that the smaller end neither projects into nor over the belly of the violin but lies even with it. Further, one must always keep one's instrument clean, and the belly and strings especially must be cleansed of all rosin-dust before one begins to play.[2]

These few suggestions may suffice an earnest thinker, until in good time my wish be fulfilled, and someone steps forward and widens the scope of my modest inquiry, and reduces everything to proper order.

---

[1] With sharp or flat pitch one has to accommodate in the same manner. Just as the thicker strings give a better result with the flat pitch, so the thinner strings will serve better with the sharp pitch.

[2] Rosin is made of purified resin and is smeared over the hairs of the bow so that they grip more strongly. But one should not smear the bow too much, for otherwise the tone will be rough and dull.

## II. Of the Origin of Music, and Musical Instruments

### § 1

HAVING explained the nature of the violin, I would add a few words about its origin, in order to make known to the beginner something of its pedigree. But the further one probes into ancient history, the more one loses oneself and strays along uncertain paths. Much of that history is based on doubtful foundations and indeed one finds much therein that is more fabulous than probable.

### § 2

Music hardly fares better. Even up to this hour no complete history of music exists. How many squabble even over the name of music? Some believe that the word comes from the 'Muses', who were honoured as Goddesses of Song. Others take it from the Greek μῶλαι, which means 'to search industriously and examine'. Many hold that it has its origin in Moys[1] which means in the Egyptian language 'Water', and Icos which means 'Science';[2] and so it signifies a science invented on or near water; and some even believe that the sound of the river Nile caused the discovery of music. Others deny this and attribute it to the sighing and whistling of the wind or the song of the birds. Finally, it is supposed with good reason to be derived from the Greek Μοῦσα, which really has its origin in the Hebrew word, for it signifies מַעֲשֶׂה; namely, an excellent and perfect work, conceived and invented to the honour of God.[3] The reader may choose which he prefers. I will decide nothing.

### § 3

What can we say of the invention and the inventors of the art of music with any certainty? There is so little unanimity hereon that the matter might be said to turn mainly on conjecture. Jubal has the support of the Holy Scriptures, in which he is called 'the Father of all those who play on the zither and organ'.[4] And some believe that not Pythagoras, as was stated formerly with certainty,[5] but Jubal himself, when listening to the hammer-strokes of Tubal his brother, who is said to

---

[1] Margarita Philosophica, Lib. 5. *Musicae speculativae*, Tract, 1, Cap. 3. Impress. Basileae 1508.
[2] Zacharias Tevo nel suo *Musico Testore*, P. 2, C. 7, p. 10. Stamp. in Venezia 1706.
[3] Mich. Praetor. *Syntagm. Mus.*, T. I, p. 38.
[4] Genesis iv. 21.
[5] Franchini Gafuri, *Theorica Musicae*, Lib. I, Cap. 8. Impress. Mediolani 1492.

have been a smith, discovered the difference between the tones.[1] No musician except Jubal is mentioned in the Holy Scriptures before the Flood. Now whether music was destroyed in the World's Punishment, or whether Noe[2] or one of his sons took music with them into the Ark, we are not told. Only this we know, that the Egyptians first revived it again, from whom it passed on to the Greeks, and from them again on to the Romans.

## § 4

Let us compare the old with the new instruments. Here indeed we shall stray along hazardous paths and wander in darkness. Who can teach us what sort of instruments were the ancient harps, zithers, organs, lyres, pipes, and so forth? Let us listen to what an entirely new and costly book[3] tells us in detail of an instrument of which Jubal is supposed to be the inventor. 'This instrument, the *Tinyra*, was used by the Phoenicians and Syrians. The Hebrews called it Kinnor; the Chaldeans, Kinnora; and the Arabians, Kinnara. This instrument is said to have been invented by Jubal and was therefore known long before the Flood.[4] It is supposed to be the instrument on which David played before King Saul[5] and which is commonly thought to be a harp. It was made of wood,[6] strung with ten strings and was plucked on one side with a Plectrum, but grasped by the fingers on the other side', and so on.[7] With which of our modern instruments could one compare this Kinnor? They are all entirely different. This statement itself rests on conjecture, and the musical dictionaries are in disagreement with one another. The learned editors of these important works have taken the greatest care to give their information a reasonable foundation, but in respect of musical instruments this uncertainty is betrayed by the following words:[8] 'In worshipping the image erected by Nebuchadnezzar, the Prophet Daniel mentions Trombones, Trumpets, Harps, Psalters, Lutes and all kinds of stringed instruments.[9] We will, however, not guarantee that these instruments had the same appearance as those which we call

---

[1] (Petrus Commestor in *Historia Scholastica*.) Marg. Phil., L. 1, Tract. 1, C. 4. Tevo, P. 1, C. 11.

[2] Also called Noah.

[3] *New Collection of the most Remarkable Stories of Travel*, Book II, p. 60, par. 20.

[4] I Moses iv. 21.

[5] I Samuel xvi. 16, 23.

[6] I Kings x. 12. II Chronicles ix. 11.

[7] Joseph, *Antiq.*, Lib. 7, Chap. 10.

[8] In Book I, p. 68, par. 67.

[9] Chap. iii. 5.

to-day by the same names.'[1] We have, then, little or no certain information of the true constitution of the ancient instruments.

## § 5

We are no more certain when we search back for the inventors of musical instruments. The parentage of the renowned lyre of old is still disputed. Diodorus says, 'Mercury, after the Flood, rediscovered the course of the Stars, the harmonizing of song, and the Ratio of Numbers'. He is also supposed to be the inventor of the three- and four-stringed lyre. Homer and Lucian agree with this but Lactantius ascribes the invention of the lyre to Apollo, while Pliny has it that Amphion was the father of music-making.[2] And even if Mercury be hailed by the majority as the rightful inventor of the lyre[3] (which, after him, came into the hands of Apollo and Orpheus),[4] in what way can such instruments be compared with our own of to-day? Is indeed the shape of this lyre known to us? And can we in truth assume Mercury to be the creator of the violin family? Before I go further, I will venture to try to sketch out a very short history of music for the sake of beginners.

## A Short History of Music

God gave the first human beings, soon after the Creation, every opportunity to invent the excellent science of music. Adam was able to distinguish the difference between human voices; he heard the song of the various birds; he perceived the changes of the whistling of the wind through the trees, varying from a high to a low pitch; and the tool for singing had been given to him from the beginning by the good Creator, planted in him by Nature. Then what shall prevent us from believing that Adam, moved by the urge of Nature, essayed an imitation of, for instance, the cheerful songs of the birds and so on, and discovered in them a variety of notes? We cannot deny Jubal's merit, for the Holy Scriptures themselves honour him with the title of Father of Music, and it is not improbable that music, either through Noah or one of his sons in the Ark, and after the Flood by means of instruction, came down to the Egyptians from whom later the Greeks, who were

[1] Read what Calmet has remarked in his *Commentaire sur les Psaumes* on the music of the ancients.
[2] Giuseppe Zarlino, *Instit. & Dimost. di Musica*, P. 1, C. 1.
[3] Tevo, P. 1, C. 12, p. 11. (Roberti Stephani, *Thesaurus Linguae Lat.*, sub Voce Chelys.)
[4] *Dizionario univers. di Efraimo Chambers*, sub Voce Lyra. And Polidorus Vergilius, *de rerum Invent.*, pp. 51 and 52.

at great pains to improve it, learnt, and finally handed it on to the Romans and other peoples. As to whether these were Ham and his son, Mizraim, nothing definite is told in the Holy Scriptures.[1] That in Laban's and Jacob's time music had already advanced, even to being used as a mark of honour when escorting those who were setting forth on a journey, is quite certain; for Laban said to Jacob:[2] 'Wherefore didst thou flee away secretly, and steal from me and didst not tell me, that I might have sent thee away with mirth and with song; with tabret and with harp?' The Song of Miriam is familiar to us[3] and how she, with other women, played on timbrels during the journey through the Red Sea.[4] No less do we know from the Scriptures that Moses had ordered two trumpets to be blown on stated occasions.[5] We know of the trumpets blown by the Levites, by means of which the walls of the city of Jericho were caused to fall in ruins.[6] We know of the musical regulations made by David;[7] and that they had several kinds of instruments in his time we learn from the titles of his Psalms. Asaph, the son of Berachiah, was his bandmaster and the instruments were under the care of Jehiel, who might therefore also be called a leader of the band.[8] The Prophets made use of music when they wished to prophesy; Saul being a proof of this.[9] And in the Holy Scriptures we read it also of the children of Asaph, Heman, and Idithun.[10] That after the Hebrews the Greeks were the oldest musicians there is no doubt. Mercury, Apollo, Orpheus, Amphion, and others are known to us. And if there be some who assert that no such man as Orpheus ever existed in this world—yea, even that the word 'Orpheus' meant in the Phoenician language 'a wise and learned man'—yet most of the testimonies of the ancients point to this Orpheus having lived.[11] That much of a fabulous character is mixed with this is quite certain; but in these fables be many truths.[12]

[1] Kircherus was of this opinion, and Tevo writes thus in his *Musico Testore*, Cap. 12, p. 11.
[2] Genesis xxxi. 27.                  [3] Miriam was the sister of Moses and Aaron.
[4] Exodus xv. 20 and 21.              [5] Numbers x. 2.
[6] Joshua vi. 4 et seq.
[7] I Chronicles xv, xvi, et seq., also Cap. 23, 5, 30.
[8] Ibid., xvi. 5.                     [9] I Samuel x. 5, 10.
[10] I Chronicles xxv. 1, 2, 3, 4, 5, 6 (also written 'Jeduthun').
[11] His writings are supposed to be: the *Argonautica*, *Hymni*, and *Praecepta de Lapidibus*. The latest edition is said to have been published by Andr. Christ. Eschenbach at Utrecht 1689, with scientific, literary annotations.
[12] At the time these men lived, learned people were idolized. And this is the very reason why everything seems so fabulous. Who knows? Perchance the poets of future centuries may have cause enough to celebrate as gods our present-day virtuosi of song, for it really seems as if old

Up to the time of Pythagoras no change occurred in music, he being the first who tried to measure the differences between sounds. A mere chance led him to this, for once, when he was in a smithy and heard hammers of varied sizes beating on the anvil, he noticed that the difference of tones varied according to the weight of the hammer. He experimented with two equal strings, on one of which he hung a weight of 6 lb., on the other a weight of 12 lb., and found that when striking these two strings, the second was in ratio to the first string of 2 to 1, for it sounded the higher octave. In the same way he found the fourth and fifth, but not the third, as some erroneously believe. This sufficed, of course, to give a different form to music and to create an instrument with several strings, or at any rate to add one more to it. But soon a musical war broke out; for after Pythagoras came Aristoxenus of Tarentum, a pupil of Aristotle. And because the one tested everything by ratio and proportion, but the other everything by ear only, a protracted quarrel ensued, which was finally settled by the proposal that reason and ear should judge equally. The honour of this arbitration is ascribed by some to Ptolemy, by others to Didymus, although some hold Didymus himself to be a follower of Aristoxenus. In the meantime, the Pythagorean method of teaching is supposed to have endured for a period of five to six hundred years in Greece. Those of the Pythagorean persuasion were called Canonici, while the followers of Aristoxenus were called Harmonici.[1] From their time to that of the birth of Our Blessed Saviour, and after that till about the year A.D. 500, and even towards the year 1000, an effort was made here and there to improve some details in music. Several notes were devised, as for instance the major third by Ptolemy; and some intervening notes by a certain Olympus.[2] But the essentials were not changed. Besides this, indeed, about A.D. 502, or A.D. 515, Boëthius, a noble Roman, taught the Grecian music to the Romans as far as in him lay. He translated many Greek writings into Latin and as many believe, introduced singing above the Roman letters instead of over the

times might return. It was usual in those days, as has been said, to deify scientists and artists in many places with loud bravos, without honouring them with any other becoming or distinguished reward. But surely such meagre eulogies should imbue the virtuosi also with the nature of gods, and clarify their bodies, so that they might be enabled to subsist on heavenly visions, and ne'er be in want of temporal necessity.

[1] Pythagoras probably lived in about the 3,430th year of the world, and Aristoxenus in the 3,620th year.

[2] Ptolemy discovered, it is true, the real relationship of the major third, but this was only serviceable in harmonic relations. Joseph Zarlin, an Italian, first discovered the relation between the major and minor third.

Grecian. No less did the sainted Pope Gregory the Great take great pains to improve music about the year A.D. 594. In order to bring more method into music he did away with unnecessary letters and so made music considerably easier. We have to thank him for the Gregorian Church music.

In spite of all this, however, music remained essentially Grecian until at last Guido d'Arezzo invented a so-called Newer Music in the year 1024 (or perhaps, as others have it, in 1224); which, however, became still newer and livelier owing to the invention of a certain learned Frenchman, Jean de Murs, who put music in an entirely new light.[1] This remarkable change is supposed to have taken place, according to some, in A.D. 1220, or as others insist, in 1330 or even 1353. One after the other ventured to add something more and by degrees music took on the lovely form which we admire to-day. The oldest authors are those who, transcribed first by Boëthius and later by Meibom, were translated from Greek into Latin.[2] These were followed by Wallace of Oxford, England, who in 1689 published the remaining Greek authors in both Greek and Latin.[3] Glarean, Zarlin, Bontemps, Zacconi, Galilei, Gaffur, Berard, Donius, Bonnet, Tevo, Kircher, Froschius, Artusi, Kepler, Vogt, Neidhardt, Euler, Scheibe, Prinz, Werkmeister, Fux, Mattheson, Mizler, Spies, Marpurg, Quantz, Riepel, and others whom either I do not know or whose names do not occur to me at the moment; all these are men who by their writings on music have earned great credit in the scientific world. But these are only theoretical writings. He who seeks practical authors can find hundreds of them if he searches the dictionaries of Brossard and Walther. The former wrote in French, the latter in German; both having achieved honour by these works.

## § 6

Now I will proceed with my thesis, and meanwhile name Mercury as the inventor of stringed instruments, until someone else establishes a better right to the title.

---

[1] Guido was a Benedictine in the monastery of Pomposa in the district of Ferrari. He was called Aretinus because he was born in Arezzo in Italy. What he and Jean de Murs did for music will be told, in short, in Chapter I.

[2] Marcus Meibomius published Aristoxenus, Euclid, Nicomachus, Alypius, Gaudentius, Bachius, Aristides, Quintilianus, and the ninth book of Martianus Capella in Greek and Latin, in Quarto, at Amsterdam A.D. 1652.

[3] He who would make himself more familiar with the history and precepts of old and new music, let him read Marpurg's *Introduction to the History and Precepts of Old and New Music*; and in Mizler's *Musical Library*, too, he will find much information. [*This footnote does not occur in the 1st edition, 1756.*]

# INTRODUCTION—SECOND SECTION

Both the old and the new writers are agreed that when the Nile, which had flooded the whole of Egypt, returned at last to its banks, Mercury found among the drowned animals left in the meadows and pastures the shell of a turtle in which nothing remained but the dried nerves and sinews. These, when touched, gave different tones according to their length and thickness, and are supposed to have inspired Mercury to the invention of a similar instrument.[1] And this was the so-called lyre of the ancients; the first stringed instrument[2] from which by degrees, by multiplying the strings, of which at first there were only three or four, and by changing the form, many others have sprung. As further proof of this we have the word 'Chelys', which in Latin means a violin, and 'Chelysta' often denotes a violin player. But as its origin is Greek, and χέλυς denotes a turtle[3] no less than Mercury's lyre,[4] how can we doubt that our present-day violin has indeed descended from Mercury and the turtle that he discovered, and finally from the oft-mentioned lyre?

## § 7

That they, however, strung the instrument with gut strings, as we do to-day, is amply proved.[5] The Latin *Chorda*, the Italian *Corda*, and the French *la Chorde*, are all borrowed from the Greek χορδή, which is the correct word used by medical men for the intestines.[6] In all the languages quoted here they are called gut, because they are mostly made from the entrails of animals.

## § 8

Now we still have to examine whether the ancients also bowed their instruments. If we believe Glarean, even the popular lyre was bowed; for he writes—speaking of an instrument called Tympani Schizan—the following words: '... arcu, quo Lyrae Chordas hodie equinis setis, pice illitis, radunt verius quam verberant, pulsatur aut verritur potius'.[7]

---

[1] Polidorus Vergilius, p. 51. Roberti Stephani *Thes. Ling. Lat.*, sub Voce Chelys.

[2] *Dizionario univers. di Efraimo Chambers*, sub Voce Lyra, pp. 187, 188.

[3] Joannis Scapulae *Lexicon Graeco-Latinum*.

[4] Rob. Steph. *Thes. Ling. Lat.*, loco jam cit.

[5] Homer, from *The Hymn of Praise to Mercury*, ἑπτὰ δὲ συμφώνους ὀίων ἐτανύσσατο χορδάς: 'but seven strings tuned in right relation to each other, and made from stretched sheep-guts'. And Horace says of Mercury: 'Tuque testudo resonare septem Callida nervis.'

[6] *Dizion. univers. di Efr. Chambers*, sub Voce Corde, p. 212.

[7] Glareanus in *Dodecachordi*, Libro, I, C. 17, p. 49. He wrote this, his ΔΩΔΕΚΑΧΟΡΔΟΝ in the year A.D. 1547.

What does this indicate but a violin bow, strung with horse-hair and smeared with resin? And does it tell us other than that the lyre was bowed, or rather, according to their style of playing, scraped? There exist also more modern writings which are of this opinion,[1] and if we agree with Tevo we can no longer have any doubt. Yea, we even know the inventors of the violin and violin bow, for he (Tevo) says: 'The violin was invented by Orpheus, the son of Apollo; and the poetess Sappho conceived the bow strung with horse-hair, and was the first who fiddled in the present fashion.'[2] So that, according to this statement, we really have to thank Apollo for the invention of the violin; Sappho for the method of bowing it; but as regards the whole history of the matter, Mercury was responsible for the origin of all fiddle instruments.

[1] *Dizion. univers. di Efr. Chambers*, p. 188.
[2] Tevo, P. 1, C. 12, p. 11.

## CHAPTER I
## I. Of the Old and New Musical Letters and Notes, together with the Lines and Clefs now in use

§ 1

IT is necessary that the beginner, before the teacher puts the violin into his hands, should impress not only the present chapter, but also the following two on his memory, as otherwise, if the eager pupil stretches both hands out for the violin at the beginning, learns this or that piece quickly by ear, surveys the foundations superficially, and rashly shuts his eyes to the first rules, he will certainly never make up for his neglect, and will therefore stand in his own path to the achievement of a perfect stage of musical knowledge.

§ 2

All our perceptions originate in the external senses. There must therefore be certain signs which, through the eyesight, affect the will instantly, and cause the production of various tones either with the natural voice, or on different musical instruments, according to these various signs.

§ 3

The Greeks sang by means of letters, which were written either lying down, standing up, on the margin, or even upside down. There were about forty-eight of them and no lines were used, but each note had its own letter, by the side of which they wrote dots in order to indicate thereby a time-measure.[1] These dots gave the ancients much trouble and had mainly three or four meanings, namely: Punctum Perfectionis, Divisionis, Incrementi, and Alterationis.[2]

§ 4

The sainted Pope Gregory abbreviated the letters. He chose the following seven—A, B, C, D, E, F, G—and set them on seven lines, according to the height

---

[1] Gaffurius in his *Practica Musicae*, Lib. 2, C. 2. Read also Marcus Meibomus.
[2] Zarlin, P. 3, C. 70. Glarean, L. 3, C. 4. Artusi, *l'Arte del Contrapunto*, p. 71.

and depth of which one could recognize the distance between the tones. Each line therefore had its letter, and one sang also by means of these letters.

### § 5

About five hundred years later came Guido, who was responsible for a considerable change. He noticed that it was very difficult to pronounce the letters, and therefore changed them to six syllables which he took from the first verse of the Song of Praise, composed for the Festival of St. John the Baptist, namely: ut, re, mi, fa, sol, la:

|  |  |
|---|---|
| *ut* queant Laxis, | *re*sonare fibris |
| *mi*ra gestorum, | *fa*muli tuorum |
| *sol*ve polluti, | *la*bii reatum |
|  | Sancte Joannes![1] |

### § 6

It did not remain at that. By degrees he changed the syllables too into big dots which he set on the lines, and wrote the syllables or words underneath. He even went further, and it occurred to him to put dots also in the spaces between the lines.[2] In this way he saved two lines, as in fact he reduced the former seven lines to five. That was a great achievement, but in consequence of the similarity of the dots, music remained slow and sleepy.

### § 7

This difficulty was overcome by Jean de Murs.[3] He changed the dots into notes, and this resulted at last in a better system of time-division such as had not previously existed. Firstly, he devised the following five figures:[4]

**Maxima, Longa, Brevis, Semibrevis, Minima**

After this a new venture was made by adding two more, the Semiminima

---

[1] Angelo Berardi condensed the syllables into one line: *ut re*levet *mi*serum *fa*tum *sol*itosque *la*bores.

[2] From these dots arose the word counterpoint, which style of composition everyone must understand who would be called a sound musician.

[3] What kind of people Guido and Jean de Murs were, has already been told in the introduction.

[4] Glareanus, L. 2, C. 1.

(crotchet) and the Fusa (quaver). For example, they made out of a minim a semi-minima by blacking it in: ♩ or they left it white but added a little crook at the top ♩. In the same way the fusa, or quaver, was blacked in, but was differentiated from a semiminima by a crook: ♪ or it was left white but was given two crooks ♪. The instrumentalists finally took the liberty of dividing even the quaver and invented a semiquaver. This discovery indeed evolved rapidly. One gave two strokes to the black note ♪, or if it remained white gave it three strokes ♪.[1] Finally, in the course of years music grew and climbed with slow steps and through much suffering to its present-day state of perfection.[2]

## § 8

We set our notes now on five lines which, like a ladder, enable us to recognize at once the rise and fall of the notes. These are written also above and below the lines, namely when the height or depth of the instrument and the melody demands this.

## § 9

Each instrument is recognized by a sign which is called the Clef.[3] This clef is always placed on a line. It governs a certain letter from which we recognize the melody and the sequence of the music-ladder. This will be made clearer by means of illustration. Here are the clefs:

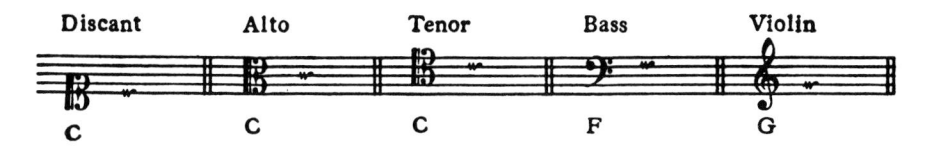

| Discant | Alto | Tenor | Bass | Violin |
|---------|------|-------|------|--------|
| C | C | C | F | G |

[1] Glareanus, *eodem loco*.
[2] Let no one be startled by the word 'perfection'. When we look into the matter carefully and rigorously there are, in truth, still heights above us. Yet I believe that if it be true that the Greek music healed diseases, then should our modern music certainly call even the dead from their coffins.
[3] The word clef is here used figuratively. For as a key made of iron opens the lock for which it has been made, so in the same way the musical clef opens to us the way to the song to which it applies.

The Discant, Alto, and Tenor have their clef on the C, so that the ascending notes will be D, E, F, and so on. The Bass Clef is on the F, so descending notes will be E, D, and so on; but if ascending, they will be G, A, and so on. The Violin clef has its place on the G, as we shall see in the explanation of the letters.

§ 10

But the violin is not the only instrument which can boast of this clef, for various other instruments make use of it: for instance, the trumpet, bugle, the transverse flute, and all such wind instruments. And although the violin is distinguishable, partly by its height and depth of pitch, partly by passages which are peculiar to the violin only,[1] it would be a very good thing if the clef were changed at least for the trumpet and bugle. Such a change would enable one to know immediately whether one needed a C or D trumpet, or a C, D, F, G, or A horn, and so on. One could then write thus:

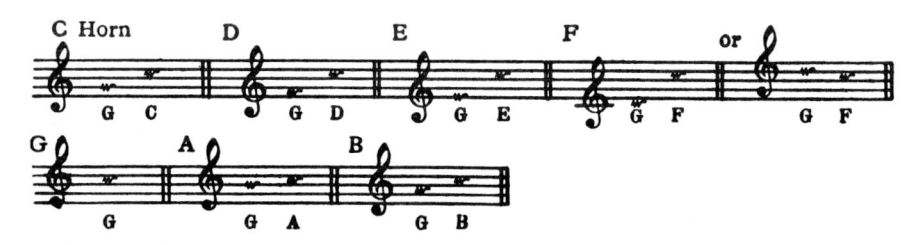

The clef remains throughout in G and if one counts up to the space where the usual C of the violin stands, one knows at once what sort of horn the clef indicates. In this manner, in former times, they often wrote the G clef three tones lower, in order to be able to set down the very high notes conveniently on paper. It was then called the French clef; for instance:

---

[1] This is the critical point at which many a so-called composer shows himself in his true nakedness. One sees at once from the composition whether the composer understands the

## § 11

Notes are musical signs which indicate by their position the height or depth of pitch; and by their shape the length or duration of those notes which we try to produce with the human voice or on a suitable instrument. Here are the present-day notes and their names:

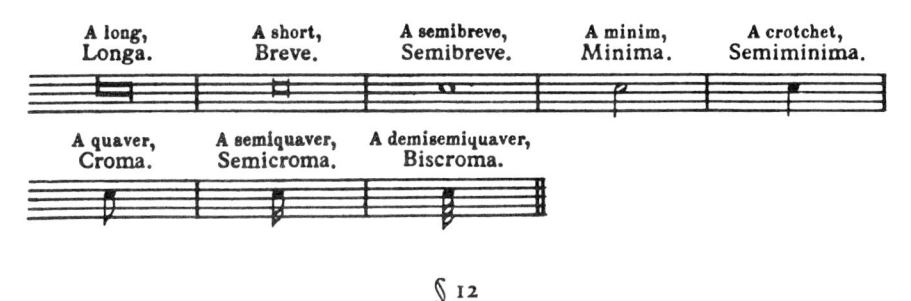

| A long, Longa. | A short, Breve. | A semibreve, Semibreve. | A minim, Minima. | A crotchet, Semiminima. |

| A quaver, Croma. | A semiquaver, Semicroma. | A demisemiquaver, Biscroma. |

## § 12

We have to this hour retained in music the seven Gregorian letters by which the notes, according to their position and therefore also their pitch, are differentiated. They are as follows: A, B, C, D, E, F, G, which are perpetually repeated.

## § 13

The violin has four strings, each of which is named after one of these seven letters, namely:

G  D  A  E

The smallest, or thinnest, string is named E; next to it a somewhat larger or thicker A; the next D, and the thickest G.

---

nature of the instrument. And who indeed would not laugh when, for instance, he is required to play on the violin such passages, leaps, and duplications that four extra fingers would be needed? [*The first sentence in this note is in the first edition (1756), but is omitted from the third edition (1787).*]

## § 14

Now in order to vary the pitch, one has to place the fingers on the strings. This is done in the following manner:

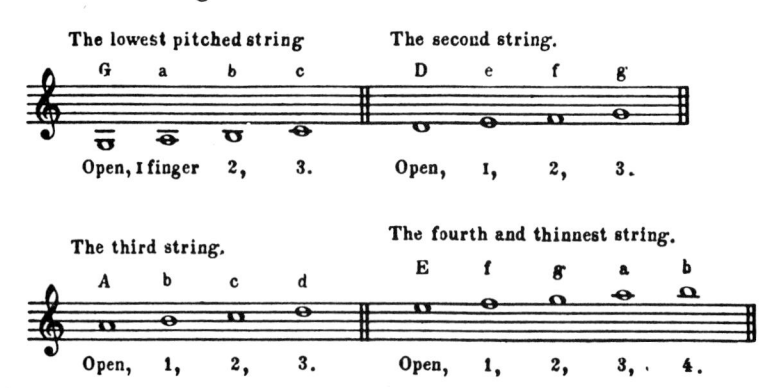

```
The lowest pitched string          The second string.
   G    a    b    c                   D    e    f    g
Open, I finger  2,   3.           Open,   1,   2,   3.

The third string.                  The fourth and thinnest string.
   A    b    c    d                   E    f    g    a    b
Open,   1,   2,   3.              Open,   1,   2,   3, .  4.
```

We see quite clearly the four open strings marked in capital letters, and after each the intermediate notes which are to be taken by the fingers. The pupil must impress this well on his memory, so that he can play without looking at the letters over the notes and may know at once without much reflection what letter-name each note bears, no matter where it is placed. No less is it to be noticed here that the B occurring among the seven letters and marked with the sign ♮, or b♮ must at all times be called H. The reason for this will be explained in its proper place.

## II. Of Time, or Musical Time-measure

### § 1

Time makes melody, therefore time is the soul of music. It does not only animate the same, but retains all the component parts thereof in their proper order. Time decides the moment when the various notes must be played, and is often that which is lacking in many who otherwise have advanced fairly far in music and have a good opinion of themselves. This defect is owing to their having neglected time in the first instance. Everything depends on musical time-measure, and the teacher must use the greatest patience in seeing that the pupil grasps it thoroughly, with diligence and attention.

## § 2

Time is indicated by the lift and fall of the hand, according to which all those who sing or play together must accommodate themselves. And just as the doctors call the movement of the pulse 'Systole' or 'Diastole',[1] so one calls the down beat 'Thesin' and the lift of the hand 'Arsin'.[2]

## § 3

In ancient music there were conflicting methods of notation, so that everything was in great confusion. They signified time by whole circles and half circles which were sometimes cut through, sometimes turned round, and sometimes distinguished by a dot inside or outside.

As, however, it no longer serves any purpose to scribble down their poor, obsolete stuff, amateurs are referred to the ancient writings themselves.[3]

## § 4

Time, nowadays, is divided into even [*simple or common*] and uneven [*triple*] measure, and is indicated at the beginning of every piece. Even time has two parts;[4] uneven has three parts. In order, however, to make the even time-measure more comprehensible to the pupil, even or simple time is divided into four parts, and therefore called four-crotchet time. Its sign is the Latin letter C. Here now are all the customary kinds of time-measure.

**The Even Time-measure.**

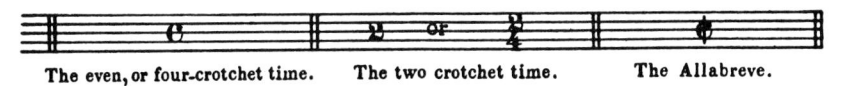

The even, or four-crotchet time.     The two crotchet time.     The Allabreve.

**The Uneven Time-measure.**

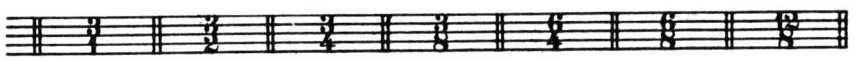

The semibreve triple time.   The minim triple time.   The three crotchet time.   The three quaver time.   The six crotchet time.   The six quaver time.   The twelve quaver time.

---

[1] Συστολή, Διαστολή.

[2] Θέσις, Ἄρσις, Giuseppe Zarlino, Cap. 49. This is derived indisputably from τίθημι, *pono*, and αἴρω, *tollo*.

[3] Entertainment of this kind can be found, among others, in Glarean, L. 3, C. 5, 6, and 7. Read also Artusi, pp. 59, 67, et seq., and Froschium, C. 16.

[4] That even time be mostly only duple, a good composer must know best himself; for how

These species of time are sufficient to show in some degree the natural difference between a slow and a quick melody, and also to make it convenient for him who beats time.[1] For in $\frac{12}{8}$ time-measure, a quicker melody is more suitable than one in $\frac{3}{8}$ time, as, in a rapid tempo, the latter cannot be beaten without moving the spectators to laughter; especially if the conductor desires to distinguish the first two crotchets [*L.M. obviously means 'quavers'*] by means of a high lift of the hand and a separate down beat for each, which results in a most laughable sight.

## § 5

Among the time-measures, common time is the principal measure, with which all the others are brought into relationship: For the upper number is the numerator while the lower one is the denominator. We may say then that of the notes of which four make a bar of common time, two go to a bar of $\frac{2}{4}$ time. From this we see that $\frac{2}{4}$ time has only two parts, the up beat and the down beat, and because four black notes or crotchets, go to common time, two of the same value must therefore go to $\frac{2}{4}$ time. In this manner are all time-measures scanned. For in the same way we see in a triple bar of three semibreves, namely $\frac{3}{1}$, that of the notes, one of which constitutes a bar of $\frac{4}{4}$ time, three must necessarily make the $\frac{3}{1}$ triple bar. This we shall understand more clearly in the next section.

## § 6

Allabreve is an abbreviation of common time. It has only two parts, and is nothing more than the $\frac{4}{4}$ time divided into two parts. The sign of Allabreve is the letter C with a stroke drawn through it: ₵. In this time-measure but few ornaments are used.[2]

---

poorly does the work praise the master, when many such close a cadence on the second or fourth beat. In only few, and especially in peasant dances or other unusual melodies, can this be excused.

[1] Let not our friends the critics be startled if I omit the times in $\frac{4}{8}, \frac{2}{8}, \frac{9}{8}, \frac{9}{16}, \frac{12}{16}, \frac{12}{24}, \frac{12}{4}$. In my eyes they are worthless stuff. One finds them seldom or not at all in the newer pieces; and there really are enough variations of times for expressing everything, to be able to do without these last. He who likes them, let him grasp them with might and main. Yea, I would even generously present him with the $\frac{3}{2}$ time, were it not that it still gazes defiantly at me out of a few old Church pieces.

[2] The Italians call simple time 'tempo minore'; but Allabreve they call 'tempo maggiore'.

## § 7

This is only the common mathematical division of the bars, which we call the time-measure and the beat.[1] But now we come to an important point, namely, the question of speed. Not only must one beat time correctly and evenly, but one must also be able to divine from the piece itself whether it requires a slow or a somewhat quicker speed. It is true that at the beginning of every piece special words are written which are designed to characterize it, such as 'Allegro' (merry), 'Adagio' (slow), and so on. But both slow and quick have their degrees, and even if the composer endeavours to explain more clearly the speed required by using yet more adjectives and other words, it still remains impossible for him to describe in an exact manner the speed he desires in the performing of the piece. So one has to deduce it from the piece itself, and this it is by which the true worth of a musician can be recognized without fail. Every melodious piece has at least one phrase from which one can recognize quite surely what sort of speed the piece demands. Often, if other points be carefully observed, the phrase is forced into its natural speed. Remember this, but know also that for such perception long experience and good judgement are required. Who will contradict me if I count this among the chiefest perfections in the art of music?

## § 8

Therefore no pains must be spared when teaching a beginner to make him understand time thoroughly. For this purpose it will be advisable for the teacher constantly to guide the pupil's hand according to the beat, and also to play to him several pieces of different time-measures and varied speeds, allowing him to beat time himself, in order to prove whether he understands the division, the equality, and finally the changes of speed. If not, the beginner will play many a piece by ear without being able to beat good time. And to whom will it not seem laughable when I tell him that I myself have seen a player who, although he could play the violin fairly well, was quite unable to beat time, especially to slow melodies? Yea, not only so, but instead of indicating the four beats correctly, he imitated, with his hand, all the music played to him; lengthening his beat at the long notes and quickening it with the quick notes; in fact, in a word, expressing all the movements that he heard in the music by a similar movement of his hand. How can this happen except by giving the violin into a pupil's hand at once and before he has had proper

---

[1] *Tempus, Mensura, Tactus,* Latin. *Battuta,* Italian. *La Mesure,* French.

instruction? Therefore he must be taught from the first to beat each crotchet of the bar carefully, rhythmically, with spirit and zeal, and to express and to discern. After which he may take the violin in his hand with some profit.

## § 9

Beginners will suffer no little harm if they accustom themselves perpetually to count the quavers. How is it possible for a pupil, whom the teacher perplexes with such fallacious teaching, to get on in even a moderately fast tempo if he counts every quaver? And, what is worse, if he divides all the crotchets and even minims mentally into quavers, by making perceptible accents with the bow, and also (as I have heard myself) counts in a loud voice, or even taps so many beats with the foot? People excuse themselves on the grounds that this way of teaching has arisen out of the necessity to accustom the beginner to grasp quickly the proportional division of time. But that kind of habit remains, and the pupil depends on it and becomes finally unable to play one bar correctly without this counting.[1] One must therefore try to instil the crotchets thoroughly into his mind and then so arrange the instruction that the beginner may be able to divide such crotchets into quavers with exactitude, the quavers into semiquavers, and so on. In the following chapter this will be made clearer to the eye by means of examples.

## § 10

It is true that the pupil sometimes understands the division, but is not exact in the equality of the beat. In such case one must watch the temperament of the pupil that he be not spoilt for ever. A cheerful, merry, ardent person will always hurry more; a melancholy, idle, cold-blooded one will dawdle. If one allows a person who has fire or spirit to play quick pieces at once, before he knows how to perform the slow ones exactly in time, the habit of hurrying will cleave to him all his life.

[1] Certainly special means have to be devised at times when teaching some people who have no natural ability. In this way I was once obliged to invent quite a special explanation of the notes. I represented the semibreves as so-called Batzen, or four Kreutzer-pieces; the minim as a half Batze, the crotchet as a Kreutzer, the simple quaver as a half-Kreutzer or two pfennigs, the semiquaver as a pfennig, and finally the demi-semiquaver as a Heller. Is this not laughable? But laughable and silly as it sounds, it succeeded, for this seed had the right relation to the soil into which it was thrown. [*A Batze is approximately equivalent to twopence; a Kreutzer to a halfpenny, and a Heller to half a farthing.*]

On the other hand, if one gives nothing but slow pieces to a frosty, melancholy 'moper', he will remain for all time a player without spirit; a bad and sleepy performer. One can therefore combat such faults as originate from the temperament by means of reasonable instruction. The hot-head can be held back with slow pieces, and his spirit by degrees be tempered; while the slow, sleepy player can be enlivened by cheerful pieces, and at last in due time be turned from a half-dead into a living person.

§ 11

Above all, one should not give a beginner anything difficult before he can play easy things well in time. Further, one should not give him minuets or other melodious pieces which remain easily in his memory, but should let him at first take the middle parts of concertos wherein are rests, or fugal movements; in a word, pieces in which he has to observe all that is necessary for him to know and to read at sight, and he is obliged therefore to show whether or not he has understood the rules which have been taught him. He will, otherwise, accustom himself to play by ear and at random.

§ 12

Especially must the pupil be at great pains to end a piece in the same tempo in which he began it. He avoids in this way the common fault which one observes in many musicians, who conclude a piece much faster than they began it. He must therefore, right from the beginning, start with a certain reasonable moderation and in particular, if he undertakes more difficult pieces, he must not begin them faster than he can rely on being able to play correctly the rapid passages which occur in the piece. He must practise these difficult passages again and again with great attention, until he achieves the executive ability to play the whole piece at the correct tempo throughout.

## III. Of the Duration or Value of the Notes, Rests, and Dots, together with an Explanation of all Musical Signs and Technical Words

§ 1

The form of the notes in common use to-day has already been put before you. Now the duration or value of the notes, their differences, the shapes of the rests, and so on still remain to be explained. I shall speak first of the rest; then notes in conjunction with rests, and shall put under each note the rest of the same relative value.

## § 2

The rest is a sign of silence. There are three reasons why the rest was discovered to be a necessity in music. Firstly, for the convenience of singers and wind-instrumentalists, in order to give them a little respite during which to take breath. Secondly, from necessity, because the words in songs require punctuation and because in many compositions one or other of the parts often has to remain silent if the melody is not to be spoilt and made unintelligible. Thirdly, for the sake of elegance. For just as a perpetual continuance of all the parts causes nothing but annoyance to the singers, players, and listeners, so does a charming alternation of many parts and their final union and harmonization give great satisfaction.[1]

## § 3

One sort of rest is the 'Sospiro'. It is so called because it is of short duration.[2] I will here set each rest under the note which is of the same duration or value.

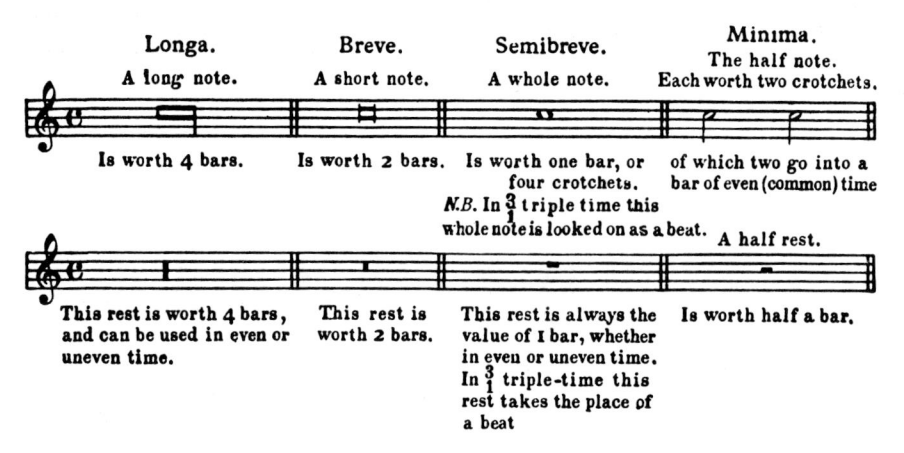

| Longa. | Breve. | Semibreve. | Minima. |
|---|---|---|---|
| A long note. | A short note. | A whole note. | The half note. Each worth two crotchets. |
| Is worth 4 bars. | Is worth 2 bars. | Is worth one bar, or four crotchets. N.B. In 3/1 triple time this whole note is looked on as a beat. | of which two go into a bar of even (common) time. A half rest. |
| This rest is worth 4 bars, and can be used in even or uneven time. | This rest is worth 2 bars. | This rest is always the value of 1 bar, whether in even or uneven time. In 3/1 triple-time this rest takes the place of a beat | Is worth half a bar. |

[1] Much depends on whether the composer knows where to place a rest. Yea, even a small rest or silence used at the right time can achieve much.

[2] From the Italian *sospirare*, to sigh.

# FIRST CHAPTER—THIRD SECTION

### Semiminima.
The quarter note.
Each is worth a quarter bar.

4 go to the bar of even (common) time.

A quarter rest.

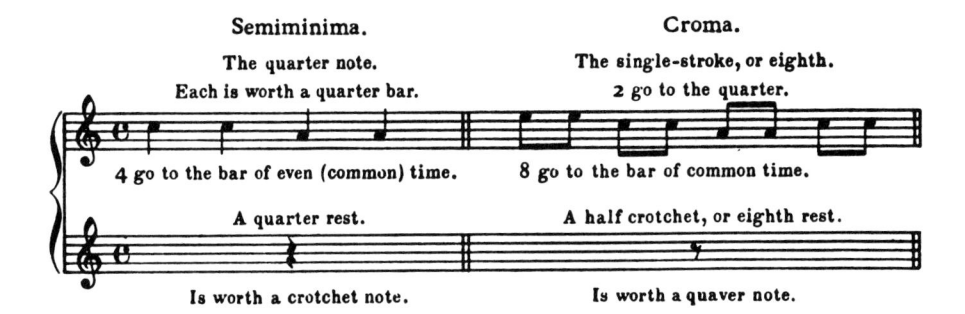

Is worth a crotchet note.

### Croma.
The single-stroke, or eighth.
2 go to the quarter.

8 go to the bar of common time.

A half crotchet, or eighth rest.

Is worth a quaver note.

### Semicroma.
The two-stroke note or sixteenth.
4 go to a crotchet.

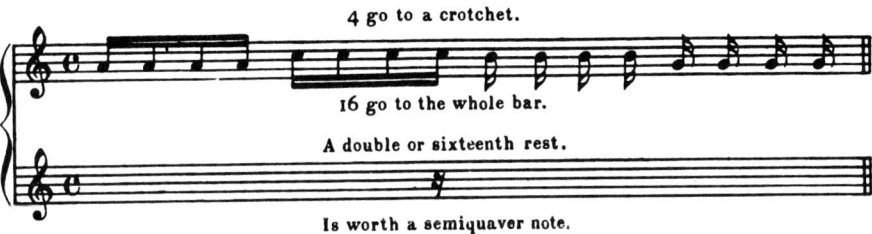

16 go to the whole bar.

A double or sixteenth rest.

Is worth a semiquaver note.

### Biscroma.
The three-stroke or 32nd note.
8 go to a quarter.

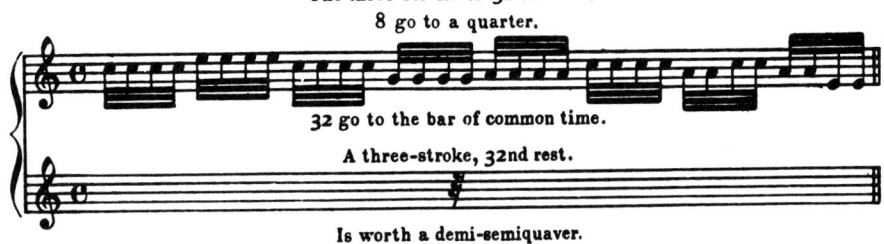

32 go to the bar of common time.

A three-stroke, 32nd rest.

Is worth a demi-semiquaver.

[*The German division of note-values is as follows: whole note = semibreve; half note = minim; a quarter = crotchet; an eighth = quaver, and so on.*]

## § 4

The values of the notes are here as clear as daylight. We see that a semibreve-note, two minims, four crotchets, eight quavers, sixteen semiquavers, and thirty-two demi-semiquavers are of the same value, and that the semibreve, as well as the two minims, and four crotchets, and the eight quavers and so on, amount to a whole bar of common time.

## § 5

But because these various kinds of notes and rests and 'Sospiro' are, in modern music, mixed up together, a line is drawn between the bars for the sake of greater clarity, so that the notes and rests lying between the bar-lines must always amount in value to as much as the time-signature at the beginning of the piece demands. For example:

The C is a crotchet-note, and is therefore the first quarter of the bar; the D and E notes are two one-stroke notes or two quavers, and therefore make the second quarter; the double sospiro (semiquaver rest) and the following three notes F, G, and A, amount together to four semiquavers and make, in consequence, the third quarter; while the G as a quaver and the two semiquavers E and D, make the fourth quarter. A line is drawn here, for here ends the first bar. The four semiquavers C, G, E, and again G, are the first quarter of the second bar, the crotchet C the second quarter, and the following rest amounts to two quarters, for it is a minim rest, and therefore makes the third and fourth quarters. After that comes another line and here ends the second bar.

## § 6

Even so is it in uneven time-measure. For example:

The first rest is worth a quaver, and therefore worth half a crotchet; one then adds the following quaver note C, and has then the first crotchet of the bar. The two-stroke 'Sospiro' with the three semiquaver notes G, E, and D, are the second crotchet. The single-stroke quaver C and the two double-stroke semiquavers D

## FIRST CHAPTER—THIRD SECTION

and E make the third and last crotchet of the first bar, which is divided from the second by the bar-line. The quaver-notes D and G are the first crotchet and the two crotchet rests are the second and third crotchets of the second bar. And so on through all varieties of time-measure.

### § 7

The notes also are often so mixed that one, or even several, have to be divided up. For example:

The quaver-note C is here worth only half a crotchet. The following crotchet-note C must, first only mentally, but afterwards actually be divided up by the bow; and while the first half of the crotchet is reckoned as belonging to the first quaver C, the second half is reckoned as belonging to the second quaver-note E. He who does not perceive this clearly enough must imagine the above example as written simply in the following manner:

and must play them too, just as he sees them here. But later he must take the second and third C with the same value of time in one bow-stroke, and in such manner that the division of the notes is made clear by an accent of the bow on each note. For example:

This can also be done where several such notes, which must be divided as above, follow each other consecutively. For example:

For, because the two notes D and E must be divided, one can, in order to achieve the exact value of them, play them first straightforwardly:

but later on play thus: [music] Where the two notes D are taken together in the up stroke, and the two notes E in a down stroke, they must be distinguished from each other by an after-pressure of the bow.[1] In particular one must be at pains not to shorten the second part of the divided note but give it the same value as the first part, for this inequality in division of notes is a common fault which soon causes the tempo to quicken.

## § 8

The dot which stands next to a note prolongs the preceding note by the half of its value, so that the note after which the dot stands must be held half as long again as its natural length. For instance, if the dot stands after a semibreve, the former is worth a minim.

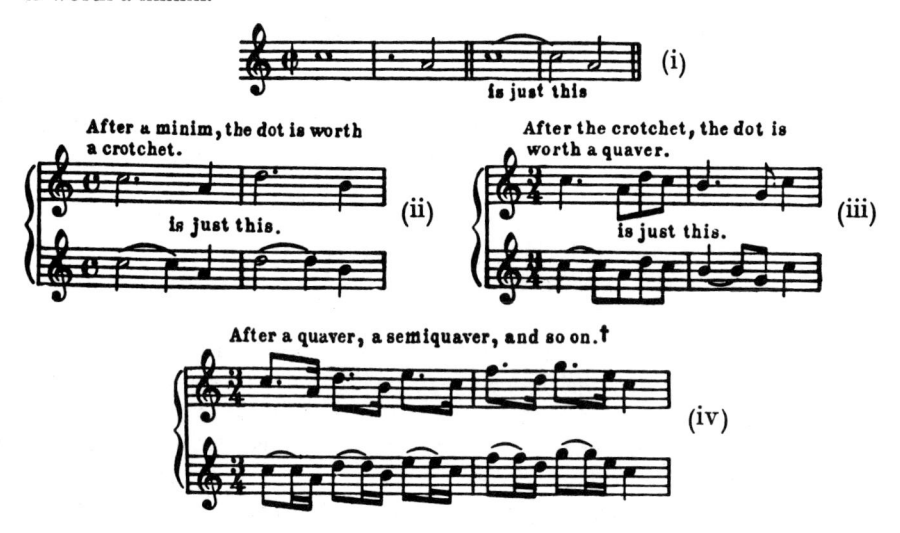

(i) *is just this*

(ii) After a minim, the dot is worth a crotchet. *is just this.*

(iii) After the crotchet, the dot is worth a quaver. *is just this.*

(iv) After a quaver, a semiquaver, and so on.†

---

[1] When we come to discuss musical embellishments in due course, then shall we deal with these notes in quite different fashion.

[NOTE.—*The above footnote is as follows in the edition of 1787*: 'The division of these notes by the bow occurs only at the beginning until the pupil understands exactly the right division of time. Then, however, the division must no longer be heard. Read the following § 8.]

† I am quite unable to understand how people explain their composition, who teach that the

## FIRST CHAPTER—THIRD SECTION

### § 9

In slow pieces the dot is at first to be made noticeable by an after-pressure of the bow, in order to play strictly in time. When, however, one has established oneself firmly in the time, the dot must be joined on to the note with a gradual fading away, and must never be distinguished by means of an accent. For example:

### § 10

In quick pieces the bow is lifted at each dot: therefore each note is separated from the other and performed in a springing style. For example:

### § 11

There are certain passages in slow pieces where the dot must be held rather longer than the afore-mentioned rule demands if the performance is not to sound too sleepy. For example, if here

the dot were held its usual length it would sound very languid and sleepy. In such cases dotted notes must be held somewhat longer, but the time taken up by the extended value must be, so to speak, stolen from the note standing after the dot.

In the above example, therefore, the note E with its dot is sustained longer, but the note F is taken with a short stroke of the bow and so late that the first of the four 'G' notes comes punctually at the right time. The dot should in fact be held at all times somewhat longer than its value. Not only is the performance thereby

dot is worth exactly the same as the note following it. If, for example, here: the dot, according to such rule be worth a semiquaver, and here is worth only a demi-semi-quaver, such a teacher will come off badly with his reckoning of the bar.

enlivened, but hurrying—that almost universal fault—is thereby checked; for otherwise, owing to the shortening of the dot, the music easily tends to increase in speed. It would be a good thing if this long retention of the dot were insisted on, and set down as a rule. I, at least, have often done so, and I have made clear my opinion of the right manner of performance by setting down two dots followed by a shortened note:

It is true that at first it looks strange to the eye. But what matters this? The point has its reason and musical taste is promoted thereby. We will see it in dissected form. The note E is a quaver; the first dot is half of its value and therefore a semi-quaver. The second dot is worth half of the first dot and therefore a demi-semi-quaver; and the last note has three strokes. We see then, as a result of the two dots, a single-stroke note, a double-stroke note, and two triple-stroke notes, which together make the value of a crotchet.

§ 12

The pupil must be tested constantly as to whether he knows how to divide the dots and rests, mixed with notes of various values, correctly into crotchets. One must lay before him various kinds of time, and not allow him to undertake anything else until he understands thoroughly all that has been explained. Indeed the teacher would act very sensibly if he wrote down for the beginner the varieties of notes in all kinds of time, and in order to make it more comprehensible, wrote each crotchet exactly below the other.

Here is a pattern of simple time which the pupil must first study and then play, if he has learnt the chapter on the art of bowing.

*N.B.*—Here belongs the table at the end of this book.

§ 13

Now we come to the remaining musical signs. These are the sharp (♯), the flat (♭), and the natural (♮), which the Italians call the B quadro or the square B. The first, namely the sharp (♯), signifies that the note before which it stands must be raised a half-tone. So the finger is moved a half-tone forward.[1] For example:

The notes marked with ♯ are called: A sharp, B sharp, C sharp, D sharp, E sharp, F sharp, and G sharp.

The second sign, namely the flat (♭), is a sign of lowering the note, so that when a flat stands before the note the finger is drawn back and the note is taken a half-tone lower.[2] For example:

The notes lowered by means of ♭ are called: A flat, B flat, C flat, D flat, E flat, F flat, and G flat.

The third sign, namely, the natural (♮), banishes both ♯ and ♭ and calls the note back to its own pitch. For it always occurs when one of the other signs stood recently before the same note, or after the clef at the beginning.[3] For example:

Here the first note is played lower because a ♭ stands before it. But because the next note is the same, and a ♮ is put before it, the finger must be pushed forward for this note, which restores it to its natural pitch. In the second bar of the same example, the second note C, which had been raised in the previous bar by the ♯, is again lowered by the sign ♮, and so on.

[1] It is called Diesis from the Greek (Δίεσις). Also Signum intensionis.
[2] That is the Signum remissionis.
[3] Signum restitutionis. Those who will not use the sign ♮ in their composition are in error. If they do not believe this, let them ask me concerning it.

## § 14

When it comes to playing such raisings and lowerings of the notes, it appears that they often occur on the open strings. Where the notes fall on an open string note, they must at all times be taken by the fourth finger on the next lower string; particularly when they are to be flattened. For example:

\* On the A string with the fourth finger    \* On the D string with the fourth finger.

If a ♯ stands before an open string note ⟨music⟩ it can, it is true, be taken on the same string with the first finger, but it is always better to take it by an extension of the fourth finger on the next lower string.

## § 15

Here we must speak of what was mentioned in the first section of Chapter I, § 14. The Interval, or Space, from H to C, makes the natural large half-tone.[1] Hence one must say B ⟨music⟩ when a ♭ is written before it, in order to make a difference; whereas when it stands without ♭, one must use the letter H. For example: ⟨music⟩ a, h, c. One would otherwise, if it were always called

---

[1] Hemitonium maius naturale.
[*This custom of calling B natural by the letter H still obtains in Germany.*]
§ *15 in the 1787 edition reads thus:*
'Here we must speak of what was mentioned in the first Section of Chapter I, § 14. The interval, or space, between B♮ and C makes the natural large half-tone. (Hemitonium maius naturale.) It was customary until now, if a ♭ was prescribed, to call it ⟨music⟩ b, c; but the natural B was named H. For example: ⟨music⟩ a, h, c; and this was done in order to distinguish Mi from Fa. One called it, therefore, when a sharp ♯ stood before it ⟨music⟩ His, Cis. But I do not see at all why one should not call the Natural B, by its own name, and why one should not call B lowered by a Flat (♭) Bes, and the B raised by a B Sharp (♯) Bis.
[N.B.—*Instead of using the words sharp or flat after each letter, the Germans add 'is' to denote a sharp, and 'es' to denote a flat. For instance, D sharp is Dis, and D flat is Des.*]

B with the flat before it, have to call the H the B. In reality, therefore, this naming of the H arises in order to distinguish the MI from the FA.

### § 16

Among the musical signs the slur is of no little importance, although many pay but little attention to it. It has the shape of a half-circle, which is drawn either over or under the notes. The notes which are over or under such a circle, be they 2, 3, 4, or even more, must all be taken together in one bow-stroke; not detached but bound together in one stroke, without lifting the bow or making any accent with it. For example:

### § 17

It happens also that under the circle or, if the circle be under the notes, over the same, dots are written under or over the notes. This signifies that the notes lying within the slur are not only to be played in one bow-stroke, but must be separated from each other by a slight pressure of the bow. For example:

If, however, instead of dots small strokes be written, the bow is lifted at each note, so that all these notes within the slur must be taken in one bow but must be entirely separated from each other. For example:

The first note of this example is taken in the down stroke but the remaining three in the up stroke, with a lift of the bow to each note, and detached from each other by a strong attack of the bow in the up stroke, and so on.[1]

---

[1] Many composers put such signs commonly against the first bar only, when many similar notes follow. One must then continue with them until a change is indicated.

## § 18

This slur is also frequently carried on from the last note of one bar to the first note of the next. If they be different notes, they are played according to the first rule given in § 16. But if they be both the same note, they are held on as if they were but one note. For example: is exactly the same as if it were written . The first crotchet of the second bar must be at first differentiated and made apparent by an after-pressure of the bow but without lifting the latter, which procedure merely ensures that strict time be kept. Once, however, the time is secure, the second note which is tied to the first must no longer be accented but only held on as a minim.[1] It may be played this way or that, but always one must be at pains not to shorten the second note, for this is a common fault, which changes the tempo and hurries it.

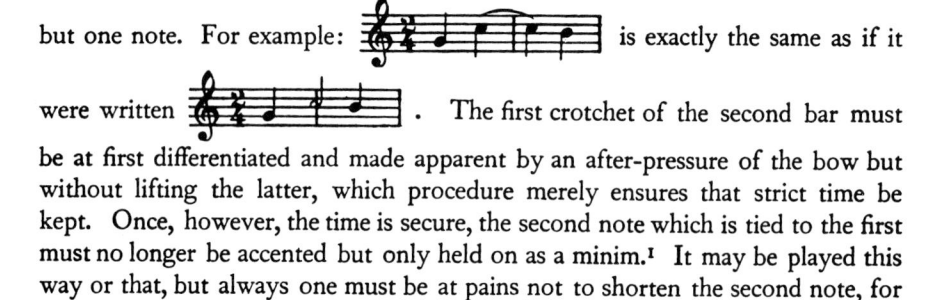

## § 19

When a half-circle stands alone over a note which has a dot over it, it is a sign that the note must be sustained. For example:

It is true that such sustaining is to be made according to fancy, but it must be neither too short nor too long, and made with sound judgement. All concerted players must observe each other, not only in order to end the pause together, but also to recommence together. Here it must be noticed in particular that the tone of the instrument must be allowed to diminish and die entirely away before beginning to play again; also that care be taken to see whether all the parts should begin together, or whether they should enter one after the other; the which can be dis-

---

[1] It is bad enough that people exist who flatter themselves greatly on their art and who yet cannot play a minim, yea, hardly a crotchet without dividing it into two parts. If one wished to have two notes, one would certainly write them down. Such notes must be attacked strongly and, with a gradual dying away, be sustained without after-pressure; just as the sound of a bell, when struck sharply, by degrees dies away.

cerned from the rests and from the movement of the leader, on whom one must at all times keep an eye.[1]

The Italians call this sign 'La Corona'.

### § 20

A composer often writes notes which he wishes to be played each with a strongly accented stroke and separated one from another. In such cases he signifies the kind of bowing by means of little strokes which he writes over or under the notes. For example:

### § 21

One sees often in musical pieces, above one or other note, a small letter ($t$) or ($tr$). This signifies a trill. For example:

But what a trill is will be dealt with in detail in its proper place.

### § 22

To bring order and division into each bar and into the composition itself, various kinds of lines are used. As already mentioned in § 4, all bars are divided by lines, which are called the bar-lines. Pieces themselves, however, are generally divided into two parts, and where the division occurs it is marked by two lines which have dots or little side strokes. For example: :‖: or ⫶‖⫶. In this manner is it indicated

---

[1] *Following the word 'eye', the 1787 edition, § 19, continues*: But, when this sign (which the Italians call 'La Corona') stands over or under a rest or pause, the rest is silent for a longer space of time than the value of the bar demands. On the other hand, a pause over which this sign is seen is not held long, but is often observed as little as if it were not present.

The conductor who beats time, or the leader, must be watched carefully, for such matters depend on good taste and right judgement.

that each part,[1] which is thus marked, is to be repeated. But if only one or two bars are to be repeated, the indication is marked thus:

Whatever is enclosed within such strokes is to be repeated.

### § 23

The little notes which are always seen (particularly in modern music) in front of ordinary notes, are the so-called Appoggiature or Grace-notes, which are not reckoned in the value of the bar. They are, if played at the right moment, indisputably one of the most charming of ornamentations, and therefore never to be neglected. We will deal with them separately. They are in appearance as follows:

### § 24

In the example just given there are, to begin with, only two semiquavers, therefore only half a crotchet; then follows the bar-line. This is called the up beat, which, so to speak, makes the introduction to the ensuing melody. This up beat has often three, four, or even more notes. For example:

### § 25

If the music be very chromatic[2] it often happens that a note which is already

[1] *Edition of 1787 reads 'bar' for 'part' here.*
[2] After the various modes of the ancients were altered, only two species were retained: The

# FIRST CHAPTER—THIRD SECTION

sharpened according to the key, has another sharp added, which is written (𝄪) or (×). Therefore the previously sharpened note must be raised another half-tone. For example:

Here is the F double-sharp which is now G natural, since the numerous subsemitones and consequently the many divided keys[1] were, for the convenience of cembalists, done away with and the Tempered Tuning was discovered. One does not play the F double-sharp with the third finger, but usually moves the second up.[2] Even so does it happen in the double-flattening of a note which is not shown by any special sign, but merely by two flats (♭♭) [or one large flat (♭)]. One uses then no other finger than that which falls in any case on the same note.

## § 26

At the end of almost every musical line one sees the sign (𝄁), which is called the Custos Musicus, and is merely put there to indicate the first note of the following line, and thereby, especially in quick pieces, to aid the eye in some degree.

## § 27

Besides the musical signs already mentioned there exist many technical terms which are indispensable for the purpose of indicating the pace at which the piece should be performed, and how to express the emotions conformably with the composer's intention.

---

natural, namely Genus Diatonicum, which suffers neither ♯ nor ♭ in its course; and that which is mixed with sharps and flats is called Genus Cromaticum.

[1 *i.e. each black key was divided on the manual into two parts, anterior and posterior, in order to distinguish between, for example, F sharp and G flat.*]

2 If, now that the divided keys on the organ are abolished, one tuned everything in pure fifths; then, with the progression of the remaining notes, there would arise an intolerable dissonance. They must therefore be *tempered*. That is, one has to take something from one consonance and add something to the other. They must be so distributed and the notes so balanced with each other that they are all tolerable to the ear. And this is called Tempered Tuning. It would be too wide a subject to cite here all the mathematical researches of many learned men. Read Sauver, Bümler, Henfling, Werkmeister, and Neidhardt.

## Musical Technical Terms[1]

*Prestissimo* indicates the quickest tempo, and *Presto Assai* is almost the same. For this rapid time a light and somewhat shorter stroke is required.

*Presto*, means quick, and *Allegro Assai* is but little different.

*Molto Allegro* is slightly less than *Allegro Assai*, but is quicker than

*Allegro*, which, however, indicates a cheerful, though not too hurried a tempo, especially when moderated by adjectives and adverbs, such as:

*Allegro, ma non tanto,* or *non troppo,* or *moderato,* which is to say that one is not to exaggerate the speed. For this a lighter and livelier, but at the same time somewhat more serious and rather broader bowing is demanded than in a quicker tempo.

*Allegretto* is rather slower than *Allegro*, usually having something pleasant, charming, neat, and playful, and much in common with the *Andante*. It must therefore be performed in a pleasing, amusing, and playful manner, which pleasantness and playfulness can be as clearly described, in this tempo as in others, by the word *Gustoso*.

*Vivace* means lively, and *Spiritoso* is to say that one has to play with understanding and spirit, and *Animoso* has nearly the same meaning. All three kinds are the mean between quick and slow, and a musical composition before which these words are placed must show us the same in various aspects.

*Moderato,* moderately, temperately; neither too fast nor too slow. This too is indicated by the piece itself, during the course of which we cannot but perceive its leisurely character.

*Tempo Commodo,* and *Tempo Giusto,* again throw us back upon the piece itself. They tell us that we must play it neither too fast nor too slowly, but in a proper, convenient, and natural tempo. We must therefore seek the true pace of such a piece within itself, as has already been said in the second section of this chapter.

*Sostenuto* means drawn out, or rather held back, and the melody not exaggerated. We must therefore in such cases use a serious, long, and sustained bowing, and keep the melody flowing smoothly.

[1] Termini Technici. One should indeed use one's mother tongue throughout, and might just as well write 'slowly' as 'Adagio', to a musical piece; but am I then to be the first to do this?

*Maestoso*, with majesty; deliberately, not hurried.

*Stoccato* or *Staccato*: struck; signifying that the notes are to be well separated from each other, with short strokes, and without dragging the bow.

*Andante*: walking. The very word tells us that the piece must be allowed to take its own natural course; especially if *Un poco allegretto* be added.

*Lente* or *Lentemente*, quite leisurely.

*Adagio*: slow.

*Adagio Pesante*: a mournful *Adagio*, must be played somewhat more slowly, and with great tranquillity.

*Largo*: a still slower tempo, to be performed with long strokes and much tranquillity.

*Grave*: sadly and seriously, and therefore very slowly. One must, indeed, indicate the meaning of the word *Grave* by means of long, rather heavy and solemn bowing and by means of consistent prolonging and maintaining of the various notes.

To slow pieces are attached yet other words, besides those already explained, in order to make the intentions of the composer still clearer, such as

*Cantabile*: singingly. That is: we must endeavour to produce a singing style. This must of course not be too artificial but played so that the instrument, as far as possible, imitates the art of singing. And this is the greatest beauty in music.[1]

*Arioso*: like an aria. It means the same thing as *Cantabile*.

*Amabile, Dolce, Soave*, all require a pleasant, sweet, charming, and smooth style, for which the part must be moderated and not torn at with the bow, but rather a suitable charm given to the piece by varying between soft and medium tone.

*Mesto*: sad. This word serves to remind us that we must imagine ourselves in a mood of sadness, in order to arouse in the listeners the melancholy which the composer has sought to express in the piece.

---

[1] Many imagine themselves to have brought something wonderfully beautiful into the world if they befrill the notes of an *Adagio Cantabile* thoroughly, and make out of one note at least a dozen. Such note-murderers expose thereby their bad judgement to the light, and tremble when they have to sustain a long note or play only a few notes singingly, without inserting their usual preposterous and laughable frippery.

*Affetuoso*: affectingly, ordains that we seek the emotion which lies in the piece and play it therefore impressively and touchingly.

*Piano*: means quiet, and *Forte*, loud or strong.

*Mezzo*: means half, and is used for modifying *Forte* and *Piano*: namely *Mezzo Forte*, half strong or loud; *Mezzo Piano*, half soft or quiet.

*Più*: means more. So that *Più Forte* is stronger; while *Più Piano* is weaker in tone.

*Crescendo*: means increasing, and tells us that the successive notes, where this word is written, are to increase in tone throughout.

*Decrescendo*: on the other hand, signifies that the volume of tone is to fade away more and more.

*Pizzicato*: be it written before a piece, or only against several notes, means that the whole piece or the same notes are to be played without using the bow. Instead the strings are plucked with the index-finger or with the thumb of the right hand, or as some are wont to say: pinched. The strings must never be plucked from underneath, but always pulled sideways; as otherwise they will strike the finger-board in the rebound and rattle, and so at once lose their tone. The tip of the thumb must be placed against the saddle at the end of the finger-board, the strings being plucked with the tip of the index-finger, and the thumb only used when whole *chords* are to be taken in one. Many pluck always with the thumb, but the index-finger is better for the purpose, because the thumb, by reason of its fleshiness, damps the tone. Just make the experiment for yourself.

*Col Arco*: means with the bow. This is to remind you that the bow is to be used again.

*Da Capo*: from the beginning; signifying that the piece is to be repeated from the beginning. But if

*Dal Segno* be written, that is: from the sign, you will find such sign marked to guide you to the place from which you are to repeat. The two letters V.S. (*Vertatur subito*), or also only the word *Volti*, stand usually at the end of a page, and signify 'turn the page quickly'.

*Con Sordini*: with mutes. That is: when these words are written in a piece of music, certain little attachments which are made of wood, lead, tin, steel, or brass, are to be put on the bridge of the violin in order to express better something quieter and sadder. These attachments muffle or damp the tone. They are therefore also called 'Dampers', but more commonly 'Sordini', from the Latin *surdus*, or Italian *sordo* = muted. It is best, when using the Sordini, to avoid playing on the open strings, for they are too shrill compared with the stopped notes and cause, in consequence, a marked inequality of tone.

From all these above-explained technical terms is to be seen, as clear as sunlight, that every effort must be made to put the player in the mood which reigns in the piece itself; in order thereby to penetrate the souls of the listeners and to excite their emotions. So, before beginning to play, we must consider all things which can possibly be necessary to the reasonable and correct performance of a well-written musical piece.

## CHAPTER II

# How the Violinist must hold the Violin and direct the Bow

### § 1

WHEN the teacher, after careful examination, finds that the pupil has understood clearly all that has been discussed up to now, and that it has impressed itself thoroughly on his memory, then comes the time when the violin (which should be strung with rather thick strings) must be held correctly in his left hand. Now there are mainly two ways of holding the violin which, because they cannot be clearly enough explained in words, are here represented by drawings, thus depicting the several ideas.

### § 2

The first way of holding the violin has a rather pleasant and relaxed appearance. (Fig. I.) Here the violin is quite unconstrained; held chest-high, slanting, and in such fashion that the strokes of the bow are directed more upwards than horizontal. This position is undoubtedly natural and pleasant to the eyes of the onlookers but somewhat difficult and inconvenient for the player as, during quick movements of the hand in the high position, the violin has no support and must therefore necessarily fall unless by long practice the advantage of being able to hold it between the thumb and index-finger has been acquired.

### § 3

The second is a comfortable method. (Fig. II.) The violin is placed against the neck so that it lies somewhat in front of the shoulder and the side on which the E (thinnest) string lies comes under the chin, whereby the violin remains unmoved in its place even during the strongest movements of the ascending and descending

Fig. 1 is the frontispiece, opposite the Title-page

Fig. II.^da

The Faulty Position

Fig. III.ta

hand. One must, however, watch the right arm of the pupil unremittingly; that the elbow, while drawing the bow, be not raised too high,[1] but remains always somewhat near to the body. Observe the faulty position in the picture.. It is easy enough to acquire the wrong habit, but not so easy to wean oneself from it. (Fig. III.)

## § 4

The 'handle', or rather the neck of the violin, must not be taken into the whole hand like a lump of wood, but held in such a manner between thumb and index-finger that it rests on one side on the ball at the base of the index-finger, and on the other side against the upper part of the thumb-joint, but in no way touching the skin which joins the thumb and index-finger together. The thumb must not project too far over the finger-board, for otherwise it would hinder the player and rob the G string of its tone.[2] The lower part of the hand (namely, where it joins the arm) must remain free, and the violin must not lie on it, for in so doing the nerves which connect the arm and fingers would be pressed together and so contracted, and the third and fourth fingers prevented from stretching. We see daily examples of such clumsy players, who find everything difficult because they restrict themselves by an awkward position of the violin and the bow.[3]

---

[1] *After the word 'high' in § 3 above, the 1787 edition reads as follows*: 'but is always held rather near the body, albeit unconstrainedly. Observe the fault in the picture Fig. III. This fault can be avoided if the part of the violin where the E string lies be turned somewhat nearer to the chest, in order to prevent the right arm from requiring to be raised too high when playing on the G string.'

[2] *The following passage is inserted in the editions of 1787 and 1806 after the word 'tone'*: 'It must be held more forward towards the second and third fingers than backward towards the first, because in this way the hand achieves greater freedom in stretching—try it for yourself. The thumb will ordinarily come to rest opposite the second finger when F or F♯ is played on the D string.'

[3] *The editions of 1787 and 1806 continue*: 'In order to avoid this evil, one must take advantage of the following exercise. Place the first finger on the F of the E string, the second on the C of the A string, the third on the G of the D string, and the fourth or little finger on the D of the G string, but in such a fashion that none are lifted, but all four fingers lie simultaneously on the right spot. Then try to lift first the index-finger, then the third; soon the second, and then the fourth, and to let them fall again at once, but without moving the other three from their places. The finger must be lifted at least so high as not to touch the string and you will see that this

## SECOND CHAPTER

### § 5

The bow is taken in the right hand, at its lowest extremity, between the thumb and the middle joint of the index-finger, or even a little behind it. Observe the illustration, Fig. IV. The little finger must lie at all times on the bow, and never be held freely away from the stick, for it contributes greatly to the control of the bow and therefore to the necessary strength and weakness, by means of pressing or relaxing.[1] Both those who hold the bow with the first joint of the index-finger and those who lift up their little finger, will find that the above-described method is far more apt to produce an honest and virile tone from the violin if they be not too stubbornly attached to another method to try this one. The first, namely, the index-finger, must however not be stretched too far over the bow or too far from the others. One may, at times, hold the bow with the first or second joint of the index-finger, but the stretching out of the index-finger is at all times a serious error. For in that way the hand stiffens because the nerves are taut, and the bowing becomes laboured and clumsy; yea, right awkward, as it must then be performed by the whole arm. This error is to be seen in the illustration. (Fig. V.)

### § 6

Now when the pupil understands all this well and thoroughly, he may make a beginning and play the scale of A B C (given in the first section of the first chapter, § 14), with careful and constant observance of the following rules.

Firstly, the violin must be held neither too high nor too low. The medium height is best. The scroll of the violin is then held on the level of the mouth or, at the highest, level with the eyes; but it must not be allowed to sink lower than the level of the chest. It is of great advantage if the music which is to be read at sight be placed not too low, but brought level with the face, in order that there be no need to stoop but rather that the body remain upright.

---

exercise is the shortest way to acquire the true position of the hand and that thereby one achieves an extraordinary facility in playing double-stopping in tune when the moment arrives.'

[1] § 5, *in the 1787 edition, begins thus*: 'The bow is grasped in the right hand at the lower part (not too far from the nut attached below at its extremity) by the thumb and the middle joint of the index-finger, or even a little behind it; not stiffly but lightly and freely. This can be seen in the illustration, Fig. IV, and although the first finger must contribute most towards increasing and diminishing the tone, yet the little finger must always be on the bow, for it adds much to the control of the bowing by means of pressing and releasing. Both those . . .'

*Fig:* **V.** The Error

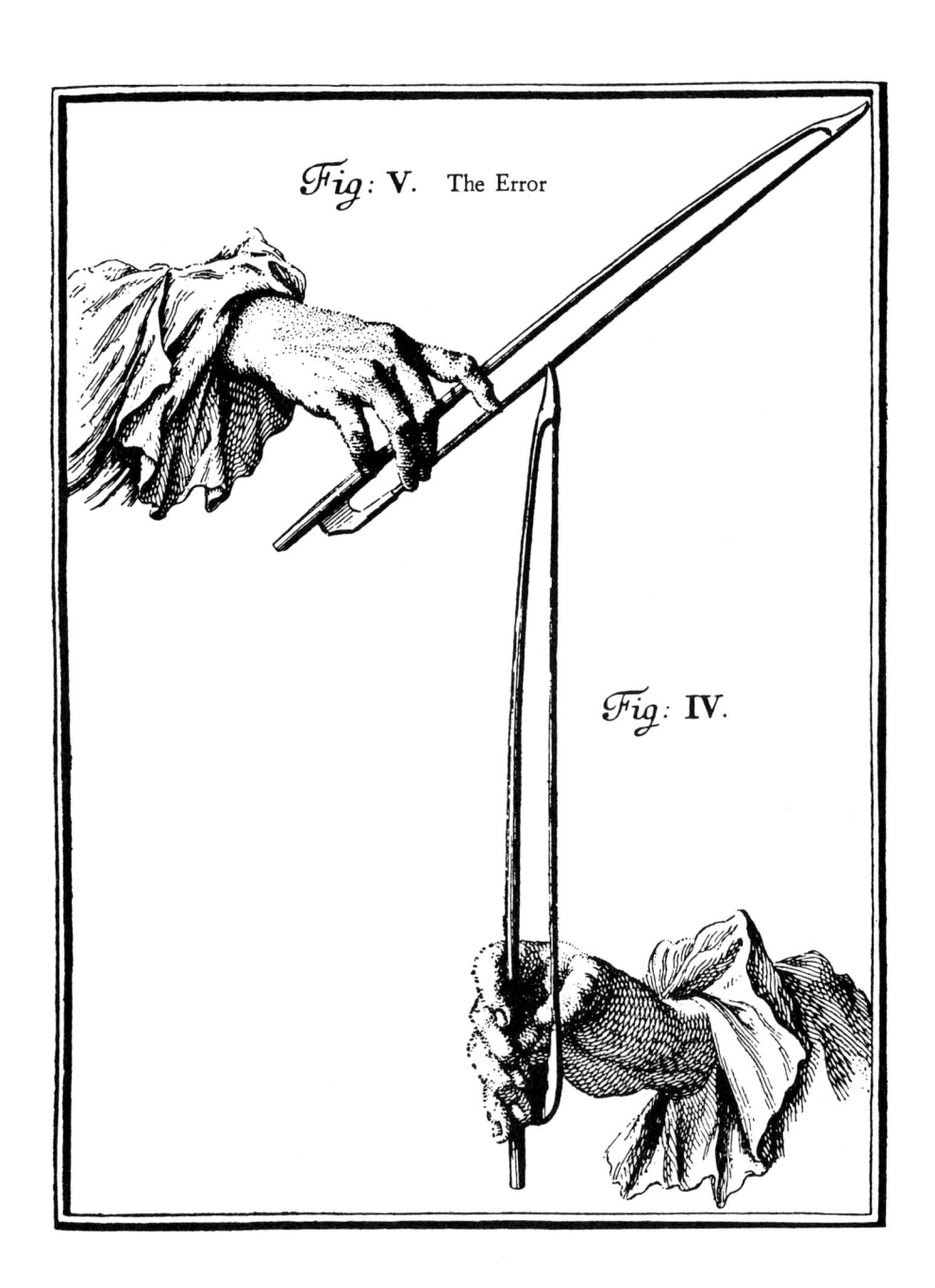

*Fig:* **IV.**

## SECOND CHAPTER

Secondly, the bow must be placed more straight than sideways on the violin, for in this way more strength is gained and the error avoided of which some are guilty, who play with the bow so much on the side of the hair that they, when pressing even slightly, play more with the wood than with the horse-hair.

Thirdly, the stroke must not be guided by the whole arm; the shoulder should be moved but little, the elbow more, but the wrist quite freely and naturally.[1] I say that the wrist must be moved naturally. I mean by this: without making ridiculous and unnatural twistings; without bending it too much outwards, or holding it perchance quite stiffly; but on the contrary, the hand must be allowed to sink when making the down stroke, and in the up stroke the hand must be bent naturally and freely and neither more nor less than the course of the bow demands.[2] For the rest it must be observed that the hand especially the index-finger, has the most to do with the control of the tone.

Fourthly, one must accustom oneself from the beginning to draw a long, uninterrupted, soft, and flowing stroke. One must not play away at the point of the bow with a certain kind of quick stroke which scarce touches the string, but must always play solidly.

Fifthly, the pupil must not play first on the finger-board and then near the bridge, or with a crooked bow,[3] but must at all times remain on a part of the string not too far from the bridge, and there seek to draw a good tone from the violin.

Sixthly, the fingers must not be laid lengthwise on the strings but with the joints raised, and the top part of the fingers pressed down very strongly. If the strings are not pressed well down, they will not sound pure.[4]

Seventhly, it must be observed, as an important rule, that the fingers, once placed, must be left unmoved until the constant change of the notes necessitates their being lifted, when they must be left hanging exactly over the note just played.

---

[1] *The 1787 edition has the following footnote*: '(a) If the pupil will not bend his elbow, and consequently plays with a stiff arm and with violent movements of the shoulder: then place him with his right arm near a wall. He will, if he knocks his elbow against the wall when making a down stroke, quite certainly learn to bend it.'

[2] *In these days we should use the word 'wrist' in place of 'hand'.*]

[3] *The 1787 edition continues from here as follows*: '. . . but must guide the bow consistently on a part of the string not too far from the bridge and, by means of moderate pressure and release, be at pains to seek and retain a good and pure tone.'

[4] *The 1787 edition continues as follows*: 'The remedy given at the end of § 4 must always be kept in mind. A pupil must not be too fainthearted and allow himself to be discouraged by the little discomforts caused at first by this exercise owing to the stretching of the nerves.'

One must guard against stretching out one or several fingers into the air; contracting the hand when the fingers are lifted; or sticking the little finger or even others under the neck of the violin. The hand must always be held in the same position and each finger over its note, in order to achieve both certainty in placing the fingers, and purity and velocity in playing.

Eighthly, the violin must remain immovable. By this I mean that you must not allow it to turn backward and forward with every stroke, making yourself laughable to the spectators. A sensible teacher will watch all such faults from the beginning, and perpetually observe the whole position of the beginner so that he may not overlook the smallest fault; for by degrees this will become an iron habit which can never be overcome. There are a great many such bad habits. The most common of these are the moving of the violin; the turning to and fro of the body or head; the twisting of the mouth or wrinkling of the nose, especially when something a little difficult is to be played; the hissing, whistling, or any too audible blowing with the breath from the mouth, throat, or nose when playing a difficult note; the forced and unnatural distortion of the right and left hand, especially of the elbow, and finally the violent movement of the whole body whereby the floor or the whole room in which he plays is shaken and the spectators are moved either to laughter or pity at the sight of so laborious a wood-chopper.

## § 7

If now the pupil has, with careful observance of the afore-given rules, begun to play the musical scale or the so-called musical A B C, he must continue with this until he is able to play it in tune and without fault. Here lies really the greatest error committed by masters as well as pupils. The first often have not the patience to wait, or they allow themselves to be led astray by the disciple, who deems himself to have done all if he can but scratch out a few minuets. Yea, many a time the parents or other guardians wish to hear that sort of untimely little dance at an early stage and then think miracles have happened, and how well the money for the lessons has been spent. But alas! how greatly they deceive themselves. He who does not, right from the beginning, become thoroughly familiar with the position of the notes through frequent playing of the A B C, and who does not by diligent practice of the musical scale arrive at that point where the stretching and contracting of the finger, as each note demands, becomes so to speak second nature, will always be in danger of playing out of tune and with uncertainty.

## SECOND CHAPTER

### § 8

If at first the beginner does not succeed in holding the violin freely in the prescribed manner (for all have not equal ability), let him hold the scroll of the violin against a wall, particularly if he fear to let it fall and if he cannot hold it otherwise than with the whole hand with pressed-down fingers. Then arrange his hand according to the instruction of § 4 and § 6, and in this position let him, while observing all the above-given rules, play the scale. Let him repeat this exercise alternately 'free', and against the wall. Remind him frequently to impress thoroughly on his mind the position of the hand, and so to continue until he is finally able to play freely without the support of the wall.

### § 9

Experience teaches that, because the index-finger has a natural tendency to fall forward, the beginner, instead of playing the F (fa) or natural F with the first finger on the E string, will always take the F♯. If the pupil has by now accustomed himself to playing the F on the E string in tune by drawing the first finger back, he will also, from force of habit, wish to draw his first finger back below the B♮ on the A string, and the E on the D string; since these two notes, being natural large half-tones, must be played higher. The master must carefully watch such matters during the lesson. Yea, it will be necessary to make the pupil play from the note C until he can play in tune the natural half-tone in this scale and the pure F; otherwise he will find it hard, or impossible, to rescue himself from a habit once rooted of playing insecurely and out of tune.

### § 10

At this point I cannot but touch on the foolish system of teaching which is pursued by some when instructing their pupils; namely, that of affixing little labels with the letters written thereon, on the finger-board of the pupil's violin, and even of marking the place of each note on the side of the finger-board with a deep incision or, at least, with a notch. If the pupil has a good musical ear, one must not avail oneself of such an extravagance. If, however, he lacks this, he is useless for music and it were better he took a wood-axe than a violin in his hand.

## § 11

Finally, I must remind you that a beginner should at all times play earnestly, with all his powers, strongly and loudly; never weakly and quietly, and still less should he dally with the violin under his arm.

It is true that at first, the rough character of a strong but as yet unpurified stroke greatly offends the ears. But with time and patience the roughness of sound will lessen, and with the strength of tone the purity thereof will be retained.

## CHAPTER III

# What the Pupil must observe before he begins to play; in other words what should be placed before him from the beginning

### § 1

BEFORE playing a musical piece, three things must be observed; namely, the key of the piece, the time and the kind of movement demanded by the piece, and therefore the technical terms at the beginning of the piece. What time is, and how from the word written over a piece the necessary speed thereof can be known; both these have already been explained in the first chapter. Now we must speak also of the keys.

### § 2

In the music of to-day there are only two keys, the major and the minor.[1] They are recognized by the third; that is, the third note above the key-note from which the piece springs, or in which the piece is composed. The last note of a piece generally shows what key it is in, but the sharps (♯) or flats (♭) written before the piece indicate the third of the key. If the third be large the key is major; but if the third be small, it is minor. For example:

---

[1] To a violinist my explanation of the keys will of a surety be more useful than if I prattle to him of the Dorian, Phrygian, Lydian, Mixolydian, Aeolian, Ionian, and by adding the Hypo, yet six more keys of the Ancients. In the Church they enjoy the right of liberty; but at Court this is not suffered. And even if all the modern keys seem to be made only from the scale of C major and A minor; yea, in reality are only built up by adding ♭ and ♯: how comes it then that a piece which, for instance, is transposed from F to G, never sounds so pleasant, and has quite a different effect on the emotions of the listeners? And whence comes it also that practised musicians, on hearing a composition, can instantly specify the key note if it be not indeed different in character?

# THIRD CHAPTER

Here we see that the example closes with D. F is the third note from D, and is therefore the third of the key. It is, however, the pure or natural F, for we see no sharp at the beginning, so this example is in the minor key because it has the small third.

The major melody has the larger third. For example:

This example closes again on D, but before the time-signature a sharp on F and another on C is written. The example is therefore written in the major key because the F, as the third from D has been raised by the ♯.

## § 3

You must know, however, that of each of the two keys there are six species which are only distinguished from each other by their pitch. Each major key has, reckoned upwards from the key note, the following intervals: the large second, the large third, the pure fourth, and common fifth, and lastly the large sixth and seventh. Each minor key has in its scale the large second and small third, the true fourth, and pure fifth, the small sixth, and small seventh: albeit nowadays, as an improvement when ascending, the large sixth and large seventh are used, and the small sixth, and small seventh only in descending. Yea, it often makes a far pleasanter harmony when ascending, if the small sixth be taken also before the large seventh. For example:

Does not this indeed sound better than the following example, and should not then this first example lead more correctly and naturally into the minor key than the following example?

66      THIRD CHAPTER

[musical notation]

To a voice, certainly, such a progression is not natural. But then one arranges the melody thus:

[musical notation]

§ 4

The above intervals of a major key lie already naturally in the scale of C major and the descending intervals of the minor key are found in the diatonic scale of A minor. The other species of the major and minor keys must, however, be formed by means of ♯ and ♭. For example:

[musical notation]

Here are the intervals of a major key in the diatonic scale:

[musical notation]

Here they are formed by the ♯s.    And here by the ♭

written at the beginning of the line.

  Now because it follows from this that the key of every piece must be recognized by the ♯s or ♭s written next to the clef, as well as from the final note; because of this I will here give the designation of all the species of major and minor keys, and in such fashion that at a glance two similarly marked keys can be seen one

THIRD CHAPTER 67

above the other. But it will be readily understood that, for example, a ♯ on C is to be retained on every C, in the high, middle, and low octave. The same will apply to a ♭ on H,[1] and so on.

[1 B.]

## THIRD CHAPTER

*[Musical examples: Eb Major, Bb Major, C Minor, G Minor, F Major, D Minor scales]*

The note a third below the key note of a major scale is the key note of a minor key, and both have the same signature. For example, the last species here is F major, but the third below is D minor, and both have a ♭ placed before the H,[1] in order to form the necessary intervals and therefore the key.

### § 5

Many believe that a violinist has learnt enough if he knows the large and small third, and generally the fourth, fifth, sixth, and seventh, without understanding the difference between the intervals. We see from the preceding that this knowledge is of great use to him; but when it comes to grace notes and other optional ornamentations, we see that it is even essential. I will therefore give all the simple intervals, large and small; well-sounding and ill-sounding. The notes on the lower line represent the foundation-note from which one counts up to the higher note.

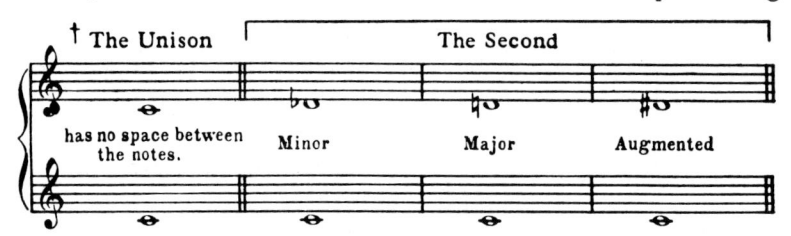

*[Musical examples: † The Unison has no space between the notes. The Second — Minor, Major, Augmented]*

[1] *Edition of 1787 reads*: 'placed before the B natural or H' in order....

[† *I have preferred here to use the English terms, major and minor, in dealing with intervals, rather than translate L. Mozart literally. He uses the words 'large, and small'.*]

## THIRD CHAPTER

*[Musical notation showing simple intervals:]*

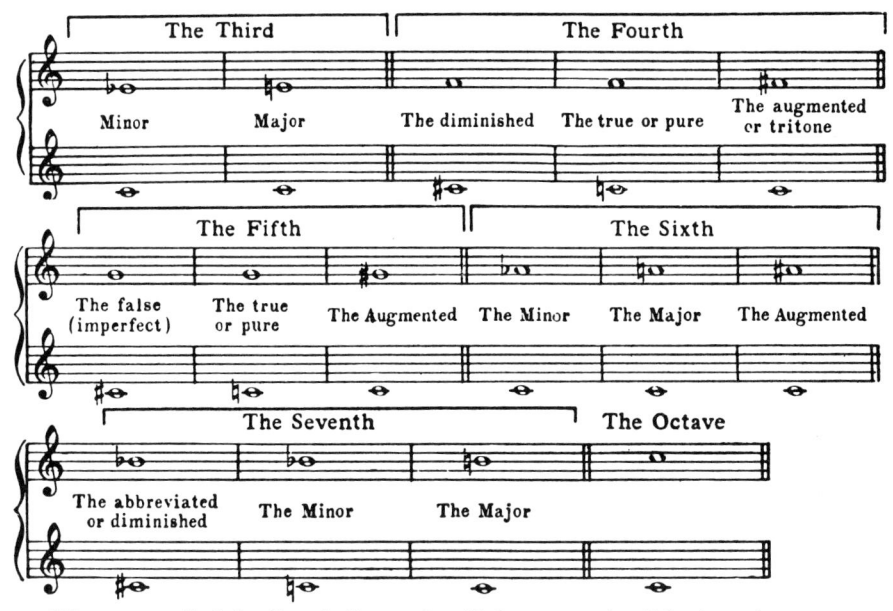

**The Third:** Minor, Major
**The Fourth:** The diminished, The true or pure, The augmented or tritone
**The Fifth:** The false (imperfect), The true or pure, The Augmented
**The Sixth:** The Minor, The Major, The Augmented
**The Seventh:** The abbreviated or diminished, The Minor, The Major
**The Octave**

These are called the Simple Intervals. If they ascend still higher, they are then called Compound Intervals. Here, for instance, are the compound intervals:

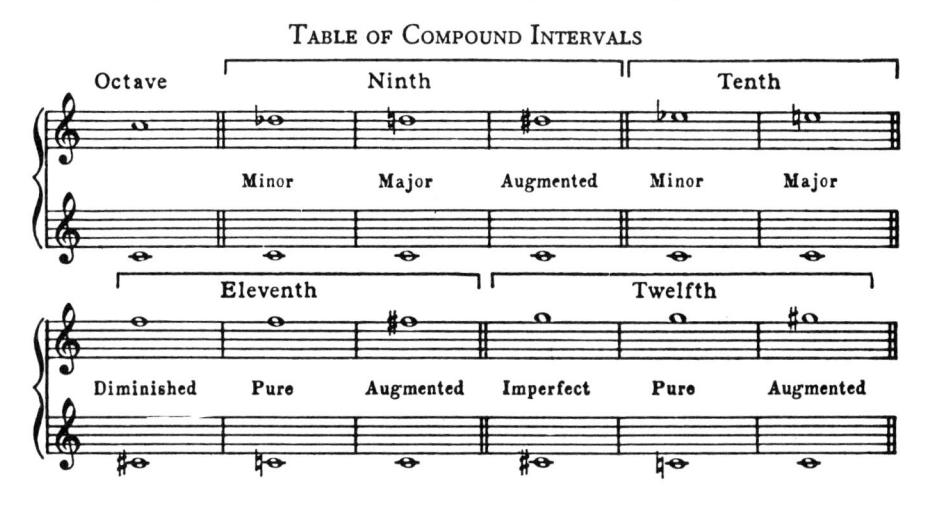

### TABLE OF COMPOUND INTERVALS

*[Musical notation showing:]*

**Octave**
**Ninth:** Minor, Major, Augmented
**Tenth:** Minor, Major
**Eleventh:** Diminished, Pure, Augmented
**Twelfth:** Imperfect, Pure, Augmented

70    THIRD CHAPTER

and so on. And yet they continue to be the large or small third, the perfect, diminished, and augmented fourth and so on, even though they be spoken of as tenths and elevenths. Yea, when the key note is low, they can be built with a high upper note into two, three, and four times compounded intervals which, however, still retain the nomenclature of the simple intervals.

§ 6

Now in order to enable a beginner to acquaint himself thoroughly with all the intervals and to learn to play them in tune, I will here write down a couple of scales for practice, of which one leads through the ♭, the other through the ♯.[1]

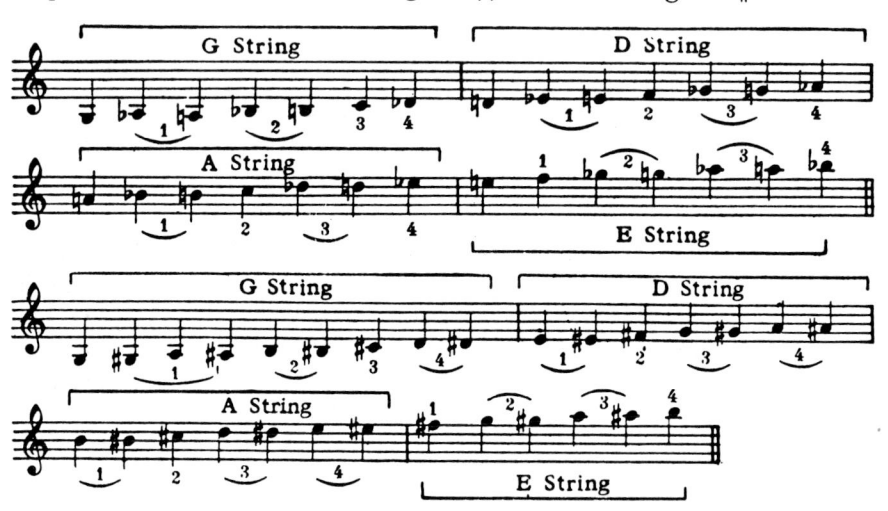

The strings are given above and the fingers indicated by numbers. The unmarked notes are to be played open, and now nothing remains to be explained excepting

---

[1] On the keyboard, G♯ and A♭, D♭ and C♯, F♯ and G♭, and so on, are one and the same note. This is caused by the temperament. But according to the right ratio, all the notes lowered by a ♭ are a comma higher than those raised by a ♯. For example: D♭ is higher than C♯, A♭ higher than the G♯, G♭ than F♯, and so on. Here the good ear must be judge, and it would indeed be well to introduce the pupils to the monochord.

[*The monochord is a very ancient instrument for deciding the mathematical relation between musical notes of varied pitch. It consisted of a sound-box, and a movable bridge over which strings were stretched. The bridge was placed according to the length of string desired.*]

why in the second scale the D♯, A♯, and E♯ are to be played by the fourth finger. It is true that some take these three notes with the first finger and in slow pieces it can be done quite well. But in quick pieces, and especially if the next notes, E, H,[1] or F follow immediately after, it is not feasible because in such cases the first finger notes follow too quickly one after the other. Try, for example:

Who will not see that it is too difficult in quick tempo to use the first finger here for three consecutive notes? The D♯, A♯, and E♯ are therefore taken by the fourth finger on the next lower string.

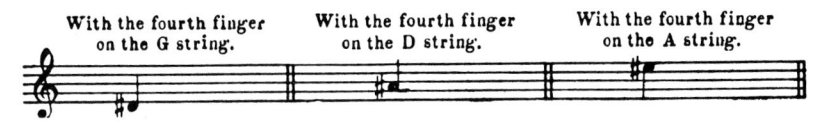

| With the fourth finger on the G string. | With the fourth finger on the D string. | With the fourth finger on the A string. |

## § 7

A beginner will act sensibly if he endeavours to take also the natural D, A, and E with the fourth finger on the next lower string. The tone is then more even; for the open strings are shriller than the stopped notes. And the little finger, which one should at all times be at pains to make as strong as the other fingers, becomes more useful and dexterous. At first the open strings can be played as well, in order to try if the fourth finger be in tune.

## § 8

Now if you understand thoroughly everything that has been said in this chapter, then play the first five lines of the table given in the third section of the first chapter, in order to put into practice the right division of minim-notes into crotchets, the crotchets into quavers, the quavers into semiquavers, and so on, in perfectly even time-measure. After that, repeat the instruction concerning dots, also in the third section of the first chapter, and try over and over again to play the eighth and ninth line of the table in strict time. Finally, take before you all the scales given in § 4 of this chapter and learn to play them in time and correctly. In order to make this more methodical and easier to understand, begin with C major and A minor, and

[1] B.

72 THIRD CHAPTER

continue the scales, the sharps of which increase in number up to six; after which, begin from the last two given scales (F major and D minor) for the beginning of the scales with flats, and play hereafter backwards through the scales of ever-multiplying flats up to six flats in number.

## § 9

At the close of this chapter I will add another little example which can be practised with great benefit, for there are many notes therein which, although they be played immediately after each other by the same finger, are not the same height or depth. The notes are marked (*), and it must be remembered what has been said in the previous chapter, § 9.

## CHAPTER IV

# Of the Order of the Up and Down Strokes

### § 1

As melody is a constant varying and mixing, not only of higher and deeper, but also of longer and shorter tones which are expressed by means of notes, which again are restricted by a definite time-measure, so must there necessarily exist rules which instruct the violinist how to use the bow properly and in such manner that by an orderly system of bowing the long and short notes will be played easily and methodically.

### § 2

In simple time, where the time-signature is four and two crotchet time, if even notes are to be played, there is no difficulty. For example:

The first note is played with the down stroke, but the second with the up stroke, and so on to the end.[1]

---

[1] *In the edition of 1787 the following footnote is added here*: 'I earnestly entreat you to keep Chapter Two constantly in mind, and to play everything slowly with long, sustained strokes. Also forget not that of which I have spoken in Par. 6 of the same chapter. Leave the fingers lying on each note, until they be needed for another note. Here, for example, the second finger remains lying on the minim C, until it is required to play the first note of the second bar, G. The third finger on the third crotchet of the second bar, D, remains lying until the second note of the third bar, C, is played, and so on. He who neglects to do this will achieve neither a good intonation nor facility in playing.'

## § 3

So the first and chief rule should be: if the first crotchet of a bar does not begin with a rest, whether it be even or uneven time,[1] one endeavours to take the first note of each bar with a down stroke, and this even if two down strokes should follow each other. For example:

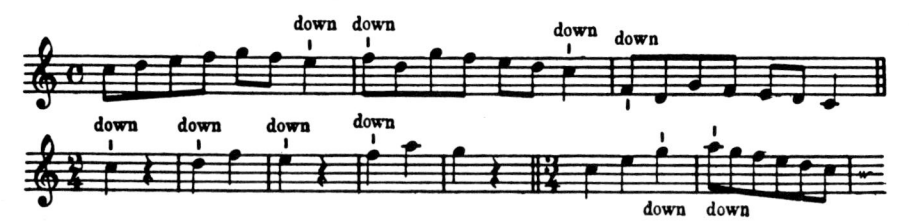

[One acquires, through this exercise, facility in changing the bow quickly.]

## § 4

To this rule only the quickest tempo necessitates an exception being made. But how to arrange the stroke so that a down stroke comes on the first crotchet of each bar, will be learnt from the ensuing rules. Such an arrangement of the bow-strokes is all the more necessary because in even or common time the third crotchet must also be taken at all times with a down stroke, as we have already seen in the first example. Here is another:

## § 5

After each of the following three rests (𝄾), (𝄿), (𝅀), if they stand at the beginning of a crotchet, an up stroke must be used. For example:

[[1] *Even or uneven time* = simple or triple time.]

FOURTH CHAPTER

[musical example marked "Adagio" with "up" bowing indications]

### § 6

But if a quaver-rest occurs before a whole crotchet, then the note following it must be taken with a down stroke. This shows itself in $\frac{3}{8}$, $\frac{6}{8}$, and $\frac{12}{8}$ time. For example:

[musical example with "down" bowing indications]

### § 7

In Allabreve, the crotchet rest is regarded as only half a crotchet. Therefore if it stands at the beginning of the bar, the note following it must be taken with an up stroke. For example:

[musical example with "up" bowing indications]

This happens also in minim and semibreve triple-time. For example:

[musical example]

### § 8

The second and fourth crotchet is usually played with the up stroke; especially if a crotchet rest be written before the first and third crotchet. For example:

## FOURTH CHAPTER

### § 9

Every crotchet is begun with a down stroke if it consists of two or four notes of equal value, whether it be in simple or triple time. For example:

### § 10

Here again a rapid tempo demands an exception. For in the first example of the previous paragraph it is better, if the tempo be quick, to take the two notes (E) in one stroke, but in such manner that each note, by the lifting of the bow, is clearly distinguishable from the other. In the same way, in the quickest tempo the four semiquavers in the second and third bar are better slurred together in an up stroke. For example:

### § 11

Two notes in the second and fourth crotchet, of which one is dotted, are always taken up stroke in one bow, but in such fashion that if the dot comes after the first note, the bow is lifted at the dot and the first note perceptibly separated from the last—the latter being deferred till the last moment. For example:

# FOURTH CHAPTER

### § 12

If, however, the last note be dotted and the first shortened, both of them are slurred together in a quick up stroke. For example:

### § 13

If four notes come together in a crotchet, be it the first or second, the third or fourth crotchet; and if the first and third note be dotted, each note is played separately and with a special stroke, in such manner that the three-stroked notes are played very late and the following note played immediately after it with a swift change of bow. For example:

### § 14

Should, however, the up stroke happen to occur on the first of four such notes, then the first two notes must be taken in one stroke and separated from each other by a lifting of the bow in order to bring the bowing back to its proper order. For example:

## FOURTH CHAPTER

### § 15

If four notes come together in one crotchet, of which the second and fourth are dotted, the notes are always taken together, in pairs, with one stroke. One must, however, neither let the dotted note fade away too quickly nor let the dot be accented, but let the same be sustained quite smoothly. This it is which must be particularly observed in § 12. For example:

### § 16

The last note of each bar, indeed of each crotchet, is usually taken in the up stroke. For example:

In the same way the so-called up beat begins each time with the up stroke. For example:

What the up beat is you will know from § 24, in the third section of the first chapter.

### § 17

If three unequal notes come together in a crotchet-value, of which one is slow and two are quick, the two quick notes are slurred in one stroke. But if one of the two quick notes be dotted, they are still taken in one stroke, but are separated. For example:

[musical notation examples]

But such figures are also played in quite a different manner, in order to provide a special musical flavour, as we shall see in the second section of the seventh chapter. Yea, there are cases when of necessity one has to perform them differently, so that the bowing may retain its routine, or rather so that the stroke may be brought back to the general rule.

§ 18

If, with three uneven notes, the two quick or short notes come first and a dot be placed after the long note following them, each of the two quick ones must be bowed with a separate stroke. For example:

[musical notation example]

§ 19

Note therefore a universal rule. If, with a long and two short notes, the first of the two short notes be taken in a down stroke, each of them is played with a separate stroke. For example:

[musical notation example]

But if the first of the two quick notes be played up stroke, then the rule of § 17 holds good. For example:

[musical notation example]

## FOURTH CHAPTER

This is an example of both cases. But I speak in every case of the figures where the long note comes before the two short ones, and this occurs most frequently in triple time.

### § 20

In simple time, a note following immediately after a minim is played down stroke. For example:

*[musical example: down down up down down up down down]*

### § 21

If three notes are to be played, of which the middle one is to be divided (which we have already mentioned in the third section of Chapter I), one must observe whether several such figures follow directly after each other. If there be several, then the bow is drawn up and down according to the notes before your eyes, and without regard to the rules given hitherto.

*[musical example: down up down up down up]*

Or in quick notes:

*[musical example: down up down up down up]*

We must, however, notice here that the middle note must be divided in thought but not in execution. That is, the middle, namely the longer note, must be attacked somewhat more strongly with the bow, but in no case may it be divided by a perceptible accent, but sustained according to the demands of the time-measure.

### § 22

It is a different matter if the composer himself marks the bowing by a slur. For example:

*[musical example: down up down up   down up down up]*

For here he binds the second note to the third, so that they are slurred together in an up stroke. But in such a case one must not only avoid letting the middle note be heard in two parts by means of an after-pressure of the bow, but must also bind the third note on to the second quite smoothly, and without any particular accent.

## § 23

If only one figure of this sort occurs, it is to be played at all times thus; for in this way, according to the general rule, the down stroke is reserved for the beginning of a bar, and the stroke remains therefore in order. For example:

You must not forget to attack the middle note rather more strongly with the up stroke; and to slur the third note smoothly on to it with a gradual fading away of the tone.

## § 24

If the second and third note cannot be played on one string they must still be taken in an up stroke, but the bow is lifted slightly after the second note. For example:

This also happens with notes which are on the same line or have the same pitch.

## § 25

A rest occurs frequently in place of the first note. In that case the second and third can be bound together or played separately. If one desires to bind them together, one avails oneself of the up stroke in order to regain the down stroke on the first crotchet of the following bar. For example:

82                    FOURTH CHAPTER

If, however, the notes are to be separated and each played with a special stroke, one begins with a down stroke. Here is the example:

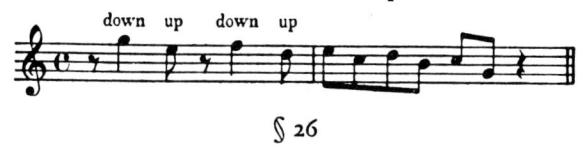

### § 26

If two short notes occur before and after the note which is to be divided, either the first two or the last two must be slurred in one stroke. For example:

### § 27

Frequently three, four, five, or even whole rows of such notes are slurred, which must be divided according to the time-measure. These notes are played up stroke and down stroke as they lie before your eyes, without regard to previous rules. Here are some examples:

† *The following footnote occurs here in the edition of 1787*: 'This is the only case in which it is customary to mark the division of the notes by a perceptible after-pressure of the bow. That is to say: when several such notes follow each other in a quick tempo.'

FOURTH CHAPTER 83

§ 28

A beginner finds the greatest difficulty in triple-time because, as the time-measure is uneven, the main rule of § 3 breaks down and special rules must be made in order to bring the down stroke back to its proper order. A new rule may read: When in triple time only crotchets occur, two notes of the three must always be taken together in one stroke. And this especially if one foresees quicker or other mixed notes coming in the next bar. For example:

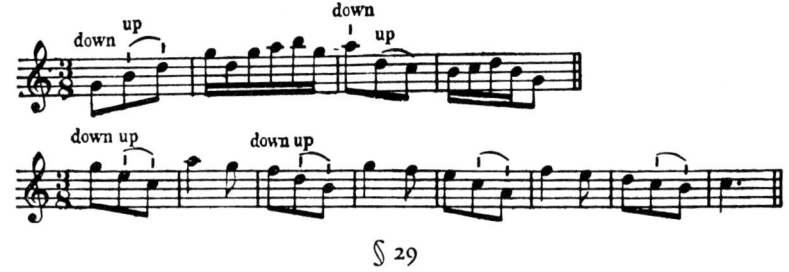

§ 29

Now the question is, whether the first or last two notes should be slurred together? And another question: If, and when they should be slurred or detached? Both depend on the cantilena of the piece and on the good taste and sound judgement of the performer, if the composer has forgotten to mark the slurs, or has himself not understood how to do so. Still, the following rule can serve to some extent: Notes at close intervals should usually be slurred, but notes far apart should be played with separate strokes and in particular be arranged to give a pleasant variety. For example:

## § 30

If it happens that each of the three crotchet notes has been played with its own special stroke, care must be taken immediately afterwards to bring the stroke back to its proper order. If in the following bars there are still too many notes, for example:

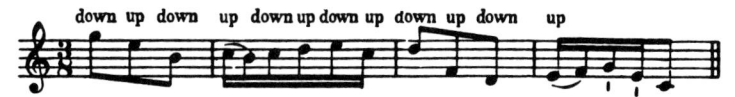

then the first two of the second bar must be taken in the up stroke, but the remaining notes played each with its own separate stroke.[1]

## § 31

If after three crotchets, each of which is taken with a separate stroke, two notes occur in the first crotchet of the next bar, whilst the other two crotchets are single notes, then the two notes of the first crotchet are played in an up stroke.[1] For example:

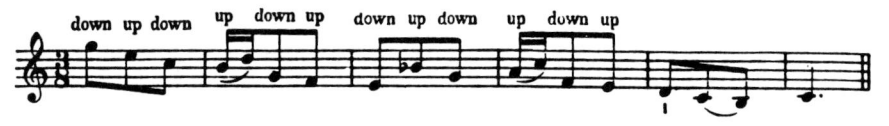

## § 32

It is customary to draw the bow up and down if several consecutive bars consist of crotchets. For example:

[1 *L. M.* speaks here, and in paragraphs 28 and 31, of $\frac{3}{4}$ but writes his example in $\frac{3}{8}$.]

## FOURTH CHAPTER

It is true that the up stroke always comes on the first crotchet of the second bar, but the stroke returns to its proper order in the third bar. The first note of each crotchet should be marked by a strong attack of the bow, and in $\frac{6}{8}$ time the attack comes also on the fourth quaver and again in $\frac{12}{8}$ time on the first, fourth, seventh, and tenth quavers.[1] For example:

§ 33

If in $\frac{3}{8}$, $\frac{6}{8}$, or $\frac{12}{8}$ time two quavers are filled up by four semiquaver notes and followed by a quaver note, the two quavers or the four semiquaver notes, are taken together in the down stroke, especially if the tempo be quick. For example:

§ 34

In the quickest tempo, particularly in $\frac{12}{8}$ time, such figures can even be taken in one stroke. For example:

§ 35

This figure is often reversed: that is to say, the quaver note stands before the four semiquaver notes. In such case the first two semiquavers are slurred together

---

[1] *In the edition of 1787 the following is added after 'quavers'*: 'This is not to say that all similar passages must be played in this fashion, but it is advisable to practise thus in order to achieve the ability to emphasize instantly when necessary.'

in an up stroke, whereas each of the last two are played with a separate stroke. For example:

§ 36

But if the tempo be very rapid, the four semiquavers are slurred together in the up stroke. For example:

§ 37

Now the pupil can learn to play the whole of the table given at the end of this book, in order to mould himself thoroughly to playing in time. For if he is in doubt about the stroke he can refer to these rules. But if he cannot quite manage the mixed note-values in right time, he must, at first, make out of two semiquavers one only. For example: supposing that these notes occurred in a piece of music:

he would play in the first and second quaver, instead of the two semiquaver notes, only the first of them, namely the note E, and in the second beat the note D. But he must make out of each a quaver note, and play them thus:

Let him observe the equality of the note-value carefully and, when repeating, slur the two notes together in such fashion that no more time be occupied by them than was necessary for the playing of the quaver note. In like manner must the pupil deal with the first and third crotchets of the eleventh line, and the second and fourth crotchets of the twelfth line of the table. Moreover, if a beginner will follow my advice, he will play the table not only in the order of the lines but play also the first bars one after another, through all the lines; then the second bars; after that the third bars and so on, so that he may make himself certain of the time of the constantly changing figures.

§ 38

But in order to give the pupil at once something on which to practise the prescribed rules of bowing, I will set down a few examples in various changes of time and begin with even notes which follow each other continuously through many bars. These running notes are the stumbling-block over which many a man trips who, blinded by his conceit, imagines that he knows how to progress rightly, at once, and with certainty. Many a violinist, who otherwise plays not too badly, falls into hurrying when playing such continuously running, equal notes, so that if they continue for several bars he is at least a crotchet in advance of the time. Such an evil must therefore be avoided and such pieces be played at first slowly, with long drawn-out strokes of the bow which remain throughout on the violin; not pressing forward but holding back, and in particular, not shortening the last two of four equal notes. If in this way all goes well, try it rather faster. Then detach the notes with shorter strokes and play them by degrees more and more rapidly, but in such fashion that you end always as you began. Here is the example:

## FOURTH CHAPTER

### § 39

In this and all following examples a second violin part is added below, so that the teacher and pupil together may play each part alternately. In order, however, to make everything quite clear, the different styles of bowing are marked with numbers, as can be seen in the table, and in the lower voice of the previous example. These numbers indicate the paragraph in which the rule for the style of bowing can be sought. If, however, the rule has once been given, it is never repeated in the same example. But I must again remind you that the teacher must on no account play the prescribed example to the pupil, for he would then play only by ear and would not learn to play according to the fundamental rules. The teacher should rather let the pupil divide each bar of the piece into the crotchets and later on beat time to these, telling him that while beating time he should picture in his mind the division of the crotchets by careful contemplation of the piece. After this he may begin to play while the teacher beats time and, only when necessary, plays with him and even then only plays the lower voice when the disciple can play the upper voice well and in tune.

Here are the pieces for practice. The more distasteful they are the more am I pleased, for that is what I intended to make them.

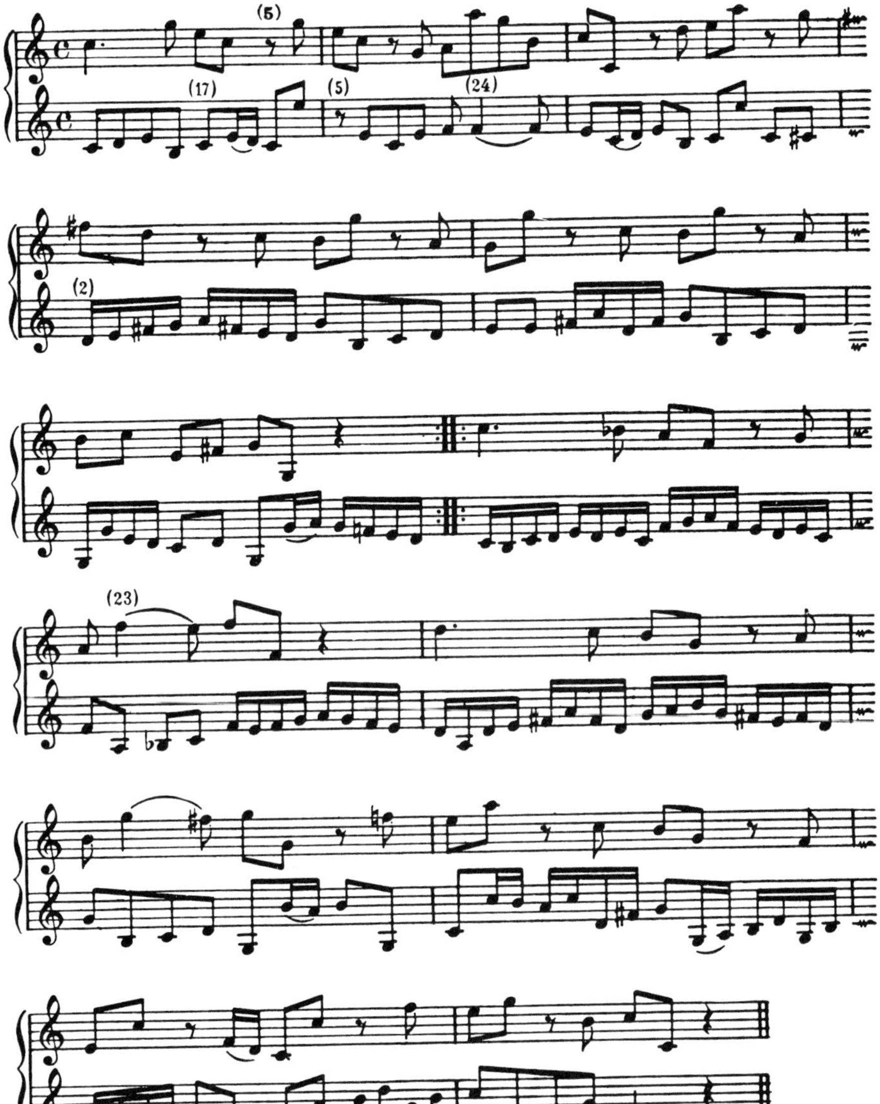
(5)
(17)
(5)
(24)
(2)
(23)

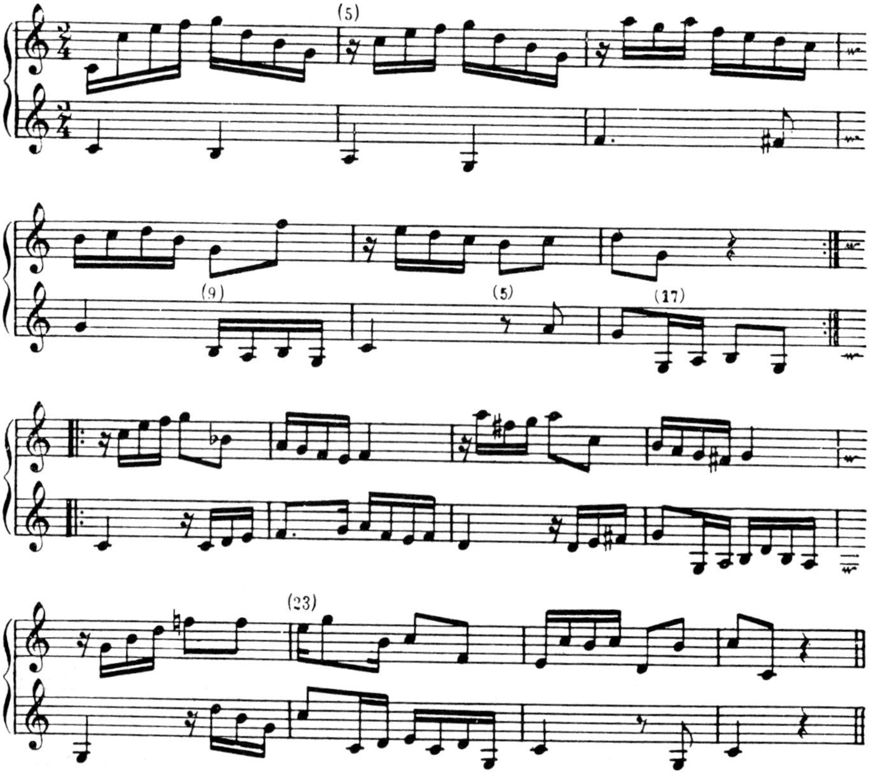
(5)
(9)
(5)
(17)
(23)

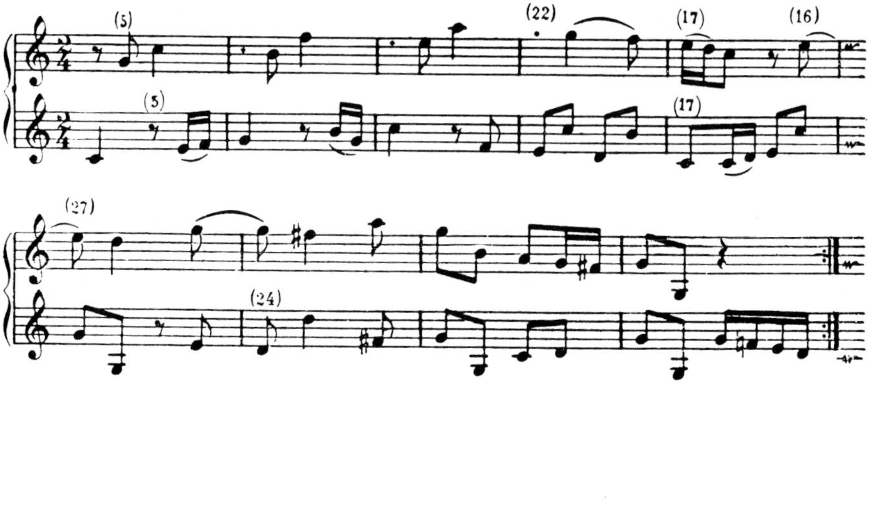
(5)
(22)
(17)
(16)
(5)
(17)
(27)
(24)

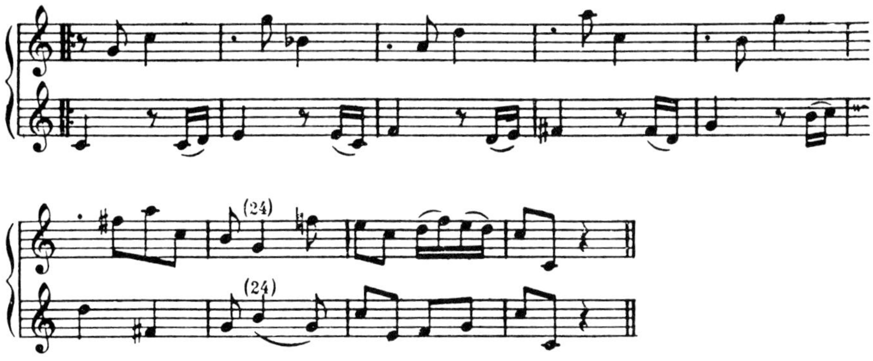
(24)
(24)

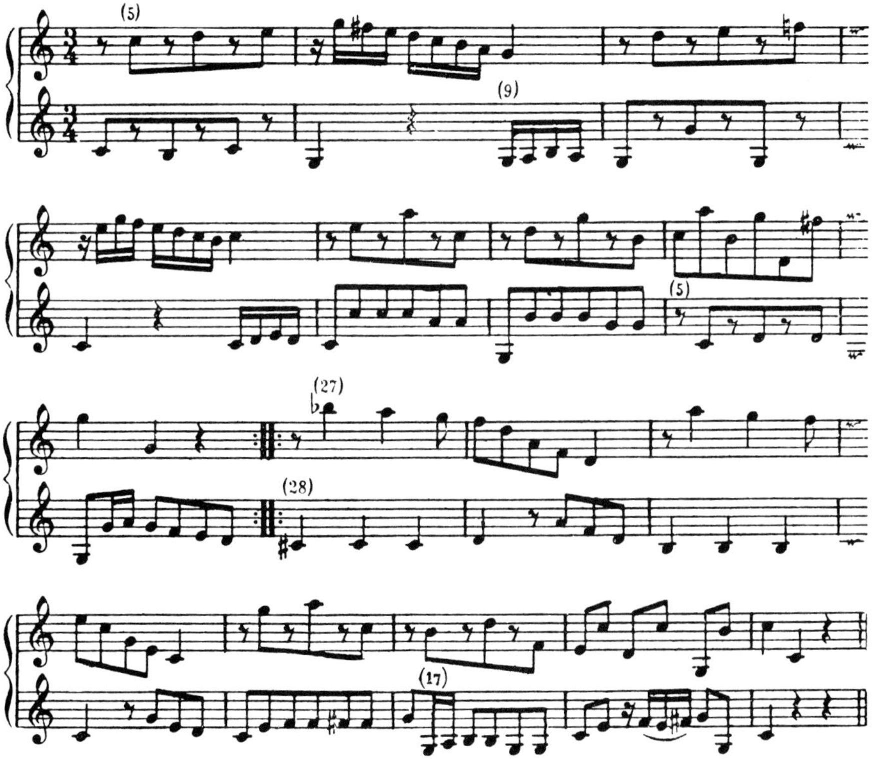
(5)
(9)
(5)
(27)
(28)
(17)

Allegro

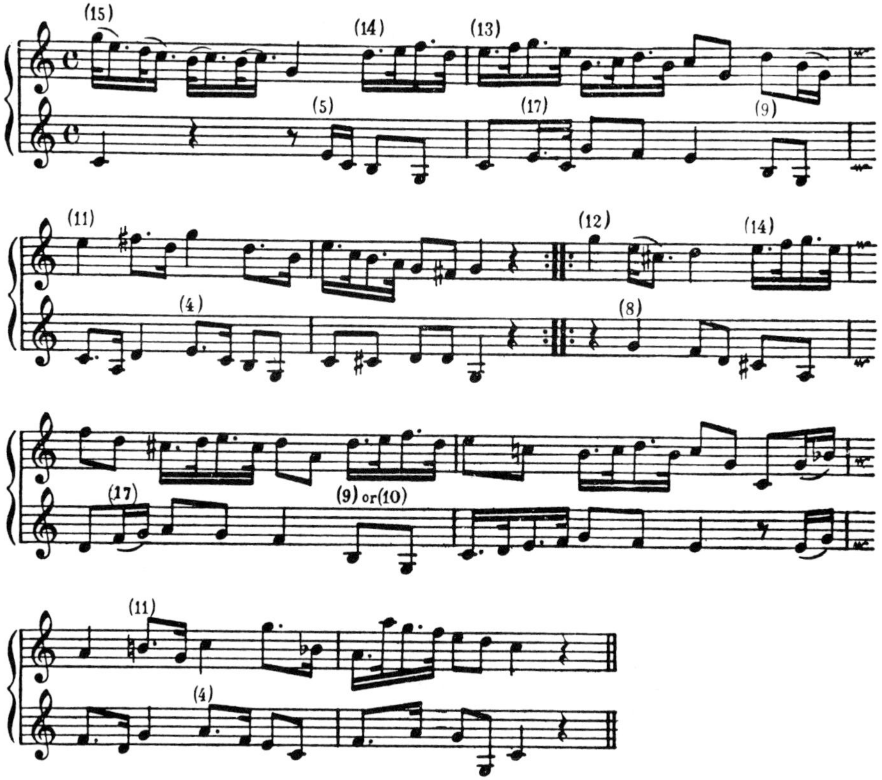


Allabreve

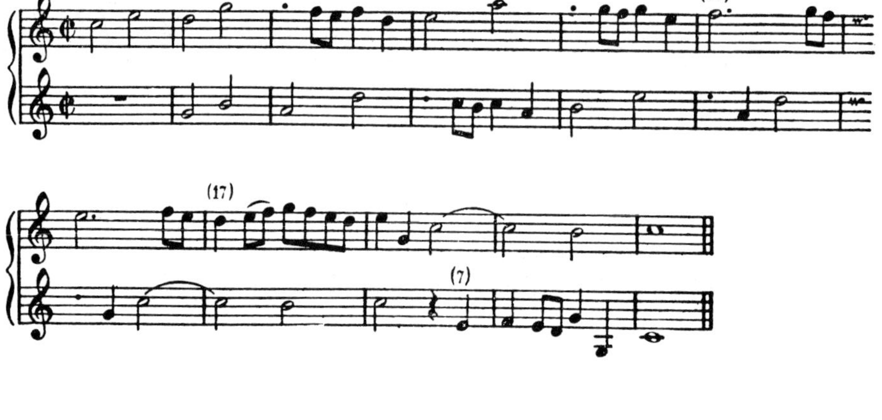

Such progressions are played throughout with the alternative down stroke and up stroke.

The fourth, fifth and sixth bars can also be played according to the rule of Par. 33. For example:—

This and the following species of time are usually used for slow melodies.

One can thus play all the notes with a long up and down stroke without thereby offending too greatly the rules of bowing.

CHAPTER V

# How, by adroit control of the Bow, one should seek to produce a good tone on a Violin and bring it forth in the right manner

§ 1

IT may perchance appear to some that the present treatment stands in the wrong place and should rather have been inserted near the beginning, in order to make the pupil dexterous in producing a pure tone as soon as he takes the violin in his hand. But when they consider that a beginner, in order to be able to play the violin, must also necessarily know something of bowing, and when they take into consideration that he has enough to do to observe exactly all the prescribed essential rules and with great care to look now at the bowing, now at the notes, and now at the time and at all other signs, they will not blame me for postponing this treatment until now.

§ 2

That the violin should at first be rather thickly strung has already been said in Chapter II, § 1, and for this reason: that owing to the strong down-pressure of the finger, and strong gripping of the bow, the joints become hardened and a strong, masculine stroke is achieved thereby. For what can be more insipid than the playing of one who has not confidence to attack the violin boldly, but scarce touches the strings with the bow (which is often held by two fingers only); and makes so artificial and whispering a sound right up against the bridge of the violin that only the hissing of a note here and there is heard and the listener knows not what is meant thereby; for everything is merely like unto a dream?[1] Therefore string

[1] Such hare-brained violinists are so wayward that they do not hesitate to improvise the most difficult pieces off-hand. Their whisperings, even if they miss or leave nothing out, are scarce heard; but this is called by them 'playing pleasantly'. They imagine the greatest inaudibility to be sweet. But should they have to play loudly and strongly, all their skill has suddenly fled away.

the violin more thickly; take pains always to play with earnestness and manliness; and finally strive, even when the tone is strong, to make it pure; to which end the right division of the bow and the changing from soft to loud contribute the most.

## § 3

Every tone, even the strongest attack, has a small, even if barely audible, softness at the beginning of the stroke; for it would otherwise be no tone but only an unpleasant and unintelligible noise. This same softness must be heard also at the end of each stroke. Hence one must know how to divide the bow into weakness and strength, and therefore how by means of pressure and relaxation, to produce the notes beautifully and touchingly.

## § 4

The first division can be thus: Begin the down stroke or up stroke with a pleasant softness; increase the tone by means of an imperceptible increase of pressure; let the greatest volume of tone occur in the middle of the bow, after which, moderate it by degrees by relaxing the pressure of the bow until at the end of the bow the tone dies completely away.

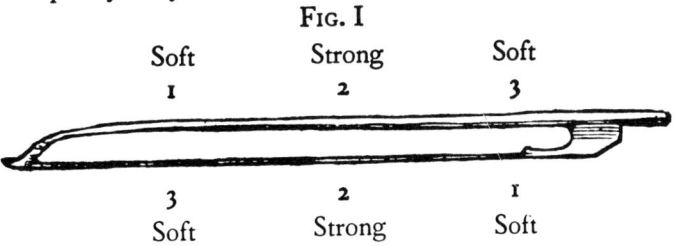

FIG. I

| Soft | Strong | Soft |
|------|--------|------|
| 1    | 2      | 3    |

| 3    | 2      | 1    |
|------|--------|------|
| Soft | Strong | Soft |

This must be practised as slowly and with as much holding back of the bow as possible, in order to enable one to sustain a long note in Adagio purely and delicately, to the great pleasure of the listener. Just as it is very touching when a singer sustains beautifully a long note of varying strength and softness without taking a fresh breath. But in this case there is something special to be observed; namely, that the finger of the left hand which is placed on the string should, in the soft tone, relax the pressure somewhat, and that the bow should be placed a little farther from the bridge or saddle; whereas in loud tone the fingers of the left hand should be pressed down strongly and the bow be placed nearer to the bridge.

## FIFTH CHAPTER

### § 5

In this first division in particular, as also in the following, the finger of the left hand should make a small slow movement which must not be sideways but forward and backward. That is, the finger must move forward towards the bridge and backward again towards the scroll: in soft tone quite slowly, but in loud rather faster.

### § 6

The second division of the bow may be made in the following manner. Begin the stroke strongly, temper it imperceptibly and gradually, and finish it quite softly.

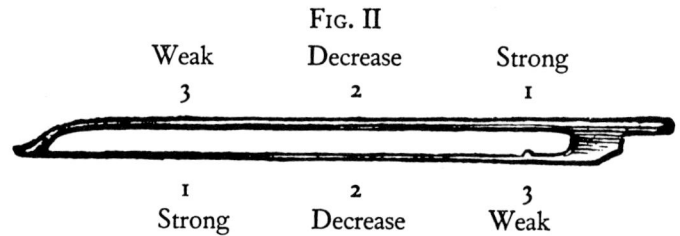

FIG. II

| Weak | Decrease | Strong |
|---|---|---|
| 3 | 2 | 1 |

| 1 | 2 | 3 |
|---|---|---|
| Strong | Decrease | Weak |

This applies as much to the up stroke as to the down stroke. Both must be practised diligently. This kind of division is used more in cases of shortly sustained tone in quick tempo than in slow pieces.

### § 7

The third division is as follows. Begin the stroke softly and increase the tone gradually and smoothly, finishing with strength.

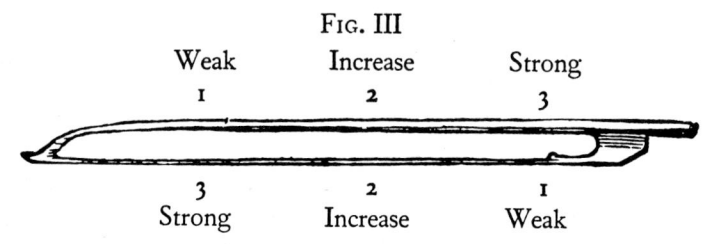

FIG. III

| Weak | Increase | Strong |
|---|---|---|
| 1 | 2 | 3 |

| 3 | 2 | 1 |
|---|---|---|
| Strong | Increase | Weak |

This also must be practised with down stroke and up stroke, which must be understood as applying to all divisions. But be it observed that the stroke in soft tone must be drawn very slowly; when increasing the tone, somewhat quicker; and in the final loud tone very quickly.

## § 8

Now try the fourth division with loud and soft twice in one stroke.

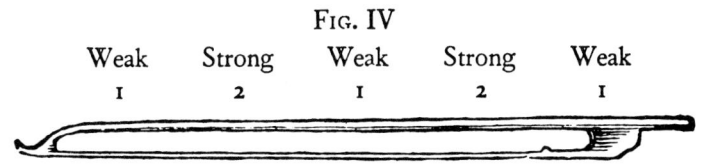

Fig. IV

| Weak | Strong | Weak | Strong | Weak |
|------|--------|------|--------|------|
| 1    | 2      | 1    | 2      | 1    |

Let it be practised up stroke and down stroke. The numeral (1) indicates soft and the numeral (2) loud. The latter has therefore each time a gentle softness before and after it. This example of a double loudness, alternating with softness, can obviously be performed four, five, and six times; yes, often even more in one stroke. One learns through practice of this and the preceding divisions to apply strength and weakness in all parts of the bow; consequently, it is of great use.

## § 9

But besides this, a very useful experiment may be made. Namely, to endeavour to produce a perfectly even tone with a slow stroke. Draw the bow from one end to the other whilst sustaining throughout an even strength of tone. But hold the bow well back, for the longer and more even the stroke can be made, the more you will become master of your bow, which is highly necessary for the proper performance of a slow piece.

## § 10

By diligent practice of the division of the stroke one becomes dexterous in the control of the bow, and through control one achieves purity of tone. The strings stretched on the violin are brought into movement by the bow: these divide the air and therefrom arises the tone and note given forth by the strings when touched. Now if a string be bowed again and again, and is therefore pushed each time from the old vibration into either similar or slower or quicker movement according to the strokes following each other, the stroke must necessarily be started gently with a certain moderation and, [without the bow being lifted, played with so smooth a connexion that][1] even the strongest stroke brings the already vibrating string quite

[1] *In the first edition, the following words occur at this point*: 'played in such manner that.'

imperceptibly from one movement into another and different movement. This is what I would have you understand by that softness of which something has already been said in § 3.

### § 11

If you would play in tune, much depends on tuning the violin carefully. If it be tuned to a low pitch, you must place the bow farther from the bridge, but if it be tuned sharp, you can approach the bridge more nearly. But in particular you must always play farther from the bridge on the D and G strings than on the A and E. The reason for this is quite natural. The thick strings are not so easily moved at their extremities where they are at rest, and if you use force they give forth a rough tone. I do not mean, however, a great distance. The distance is only slight, and as not all violins are exactly the same you must know how to seek carefully on each for that spot where the strings can be brought, with purity of tone, into gentle or rapid vibration in the melodious manner demanded by the Cantilena of the piece about to be played. Moreover, you can always grasp the thick and low strings more strongly without offending the ear, for they divide and move the air but slowly and weakly and sound thus less sharply in the ear. On the other hand the thin and tightly stretched strings are quick in movement and cut the air strongly and rapidly, and one must therefore moderate them more because they penetrate the ear more sharply.

### § 12

By means of these and similar useful precautions, great pains must be taken to obtain evenness of tone; which evenness must be maintained at all times in the changes between strong (*forte*) and weak (*piano*). For *piano* does not consist in simply letting the bow leave the violin and merely slipping it loosely about the strings, which results in a totally different and whistling tone, but the weak must have the same tone quality as the strong, save that it should not sound so loudly to the ear. We must therefore so lead the bow from strong to weak that at all times a good, even, singing and, so to speak, round and fat tone can be heard, which must be accomplished by a certain control of the right hand, but in particular by a certain alternate adroit stiffening and relaxing of the wrist. This can be better shown than described.

### § 13

Everyone who understands even a little of the art of singing, knows that an even tone is indispensable. For to whom would it give pleasure if a singer when singing low or high, sang now from the throat, now from the nose or through the teeth and so on, or even at times sang falsetto? Similarly an even quality of tone must be maintained on the violin in strength and weakness not on one string only, but on all strings, and with such control that one string does not overpower the other. He who plays a solo does well if he allows the open strings to be heard but rarely or not at all. The fourth finger on the neighbouring lower string will always sound more natural and delicate because the open strings are too loud compared with stopped notes, and pierce the ear too sharply. Not less should a solo-player seek to play everything, when possible, on one string, in order to produce consistently the same tone quality. They are therefore by no means to be praised who express *piano* so quietly that they can scarce be heard, and in *forte* start such a rasping with the bow that no notes can be distinguished, especially on the lower strings, but only an unintelligible noise be heard. When to this the perpetual intermingling of the so-called flageolet is added, there ensues a really laughable kind of music and, owing to the dissimilarity of tone, one which fights against nature herself and which becomes at times so faint that one must prick one's ears to hear it, but at others must stop one's ears against the abrupt and unpleasant clatter. With such performances those who associate with Carnival merry-makers would distinguish themselves excellently.[1]

§ 14

Not a little is added to evenness and purity of tone if you know how to fit much into one stroke. Yea, it goes against nature if you are constantly interrupting and changing. A singer who during every short phrase stopped, took a breath, and specially stressed first this note, then that note, would unfailingly move everyone to laughter. The human voice glides quite easily from one note to another; and a sensible singer will never make a break unless some special kind of expression, or the divisions or rests of the phrase demand one.[2] And who is not aware that

---

[1] He who wishes to make a flageolet heard on the violin, will do well to write his own Concerto or Solo thereon, and not to mix them with the natural violin-tone.

[2] The stops and pauses are the Incisiones, Distinctiones, Interpunctiones, and so on. But what sort of animals these are must be known to great grammarians, or better still, rhetoricians or poets. But here we see also that a good violinist must have this knowledge. For a sound composer this is indispensable, for otherwise he is the 'Fifth wheel on the wagon'. The Diastolica (from διαστολή) is one of the most necessary things in melodic composition. A natural disposition, it is true, often makes up for a lack of learning, and many a time a man with

singing is at all times the aim of every instrumentalist; because one must always approximate to nature as nearly as possible. You must therefore take pains where the Cantilena of the piece demands no break, not only to leave the bow on the violin when changing the stroke, in order to connect one stroke with another, but also to play many notes in one stroke, and in such fashion that the notes which belong together shall run into each other, and are only differentiated in some degree by means of *forte* and *piano*.

## § 15

These few remarks may suffice to enable a diligent thinker to achieve a dexterous control of the bow, and to produce by degrees a pleasant union of weakness and strength in one stroke. I should have added here certain useful remarks which would contribute not a little to the practice of enticing a pure tone from the violin, had I not preferred to postpone them on account of the double-stopping, and of the fingering necessary for the same, dealt with in the third section of Chapter VIII. They may be found in the twentieth paragraph.

the greatest talent has, alas, never had the opportunity of studying science. But when now someone, of whom you might think that he was well educated, gives marked proof of his ignorance, it is really too exasperating. What can one think of a man who cannot even arrange six clear words of his mother tongue and set them down intelligibly on paper, but nevertheless considers himself a trained composer? Just such a person, who had apparently run through the schools, to prepare himself for the position in which he now finds himself; just such a person once wrote to me an excessively badly written letter, both with regard to the merits of the matter and of the grammatical style, so that all who read it were convinced of the crass ignorance of the writer. He wished, in this letter, to settle a musical controversy and avenge the honour of one of his worthy friends. However, it so happened that the simple, silly bird caught himself in his own snare, and was exposed to public derision. His simplicity touched me; I let the poor writer go, although I had already written down an answer for the diversion of my friends.

## CHAPTER VI

# Of the so-called Triplet

### § 1

A TRIOLE, or so-called triplet, is a figure of three notes of the same value, which three notes, according to the time-measure in which they stand, must be regarded as only two notes and must be so divided among themselves that all three take up no more time than is needed for the playing of two of the same value. There is therefore in each triplet a superfluous note with which both the other two must so even themselves out that the length of the bar is not altered in the slightest degree.

### § 2

Charming as these triplets are when played well, they are equally insipid when not executed in the right and proper manner. Many fail in this, even those who pride themselves not a little on their musical knowledge and in spite of this are yet unable to play six or eight triplets in their relative equality, but play either the first or last two notes quicker, and instead of dividing such notes

evenly, play them in quite a different style, and mostly thus:

which surely expresses something totally different and goes directly against the meaning of the composer. These notes are specially marked with the numeral (3) to distinguish them more easily from others and to give them the necessary characteristic, and no other interpretation.

104  SIXTH CHAPTER

## § 3

Every figure can be varied in many ways by means of bowings, even if it consists of but few notes. These variations are usually indicated by a sensible composer and must be observed exactly in the playing of a piece. For if it be a piece in which more than one play together from the same part, this must be done for the sake of the unanimity which the players must observe among themselves. If, however, it be a solo, then the composer wishes thereby to express his affects,[1] or at the least, to make a desirable variety. The triplets, too, are subject to such changes, where the bow is responsible for all that is needed for the expression of this or that affect, without going against the nature of a triplet.

## § 4

At first each note can be played with a separate stroke, as can be seen from the previous bowing rules. Here is an example:

---

[1] See *Translator's Appendix*, p. 232.

§ 5

If, however, you wish to slur the first of the two triplets in the down stroke and the second in the up stroke, you have at once a variation. Examine the examples, which must at first be practised quite slowly, increasing the speed by degrees.

Not only in this example where the (*) is marked, but also in all similar cases, the next lower string must be grasped by the fourth finger instead of using the open string. You are hereby saved from the inconvenient movement of the bow and will produce a more even tone, as we know already from § 13 of the previous chapter.

## § 6

The triplet sounds very different if the first note be played quickly and by itself in the down stroke, while the other two are slurred together in the up stroke. But in this, as in the previous and all following variations, the equality of the notes must be the sole aim of the player. Here is the example:

SIXTH CHAPTER

Also in place of the first note there may be a rest. For example:

§ 7

Reverse the stroke and slur the first two notes in the down stroke, detaching the last in the up stroke according to the instructions in the following example:

Here I must remind you that the first note of a triplet in the previous example of the sixth paragraph, and the last note of each triplet in the present example, must indeed be played quickly, but not with exaggerated strength and even rasped at so foolishly that you make yourself laughable to the audience. Those who possess this fault are apt to err in this manner in certain figures, as in the following example:

and to jerk off the first note, or indeed anywhere else where they can catch a note alone, in so ludicrous a manner as to move everyone to laughter at the first glance.

§ 8

In quick pieces one often has to play two triplets, that is, six notes in one stroke. When therefore several triplets follow one after the other, the first six notes are taken with the down stroke, the other six with the up stroke. But the first of each six notes must be rather more strongly accented and the remaining five notes quite smoothly slurred on to them, thus differentiating, by means of a perceptible accent, the first from the other five notes. For example:

But this also happens frequently in slow pieces. For example:

## SIXTH CHAPTER

### § 9

But should you wish to play such a passage with energy and spirit, you must take the first note of the two triplets, or six notes, with the down stroke and slur the remaining five notes together in the up stroke. For example:

In order to accustom the beginner to playing triplets in divers time-signatures and also to the different modes of writing, two triplets are here slurred together, marked with the numeral 6, and written in allabreve time.

### § 10

If, in place of the first note of two triplets, a rest be written, the remaining notes may be slurred together in an up stroke with good result. In slow pieces this style sounds uncommon well, especially if the first two notes be attacked rather more strongly, and the remainder slurred quite quietly and smoothly on to them, without accents or lift of the bow. Here is an example:

Always with the up stroke.

You can also try taking the first crotchet with the up stroke and the second with the down stroke.

## SIXTH CHAPTER

### § 11

Further, a passage can be played in the foregoing manner and yet again be played quite differently; namely, if the five notes are detached in one up stroke separating each by means of a short pressure. Just as in the former style the example sounded touching and pathetic, so does this sound rather animated and has more spirit; especially if it be varied with strength and weakness. For example:

*Always with the up stroke*

### § 12

If, however, such a figure is to sound very disdainful and audacious, every note must be detached strongly and shortly with a separate stroke, which alters the whole style of performance and contrasts markedly with the former. For example:

### § 13

If two triplets, which are to be played singingly, begin with a rest, they can be performed very pleasingly and ingratiatingly with a kind of cross-bowing; namely, if the first, second, and third notes are slurred together in the up stroke, but the fourth and fifth in the down stroke. But the first in the up stroke must be attacked somewhat more strongly, and the remaining notes, even when you are changing the stroke, must be bound together, so as to let the tone gradually die away. For example:

### § 14

[1]In a medium tempo which is neither too slow nor too hurried, the first note of

[1] *Ed. 1787 reads*—'In a tempo which is', &c.

a triplet can be taken alone in the down stroke, and the second and third taken together in the up stroke, but in such fashion that each of the last two notes sounds detached. This effect must be obtained by lifting the bow. See the following example:

### § 15

A variation may be made which can be distinguished at once from all others. Namely, if indeed three notes be slurred together but not the usual three, and of each triplet the second and third notes are slurred on to the first of the following triplet or of another figure following it. Special care must be taken with regard to the evenness of the triplet, and the stress or accent must not be applied at the beginning but at the end of the bow; or otherwise this accent falls in the wrong place, namely, on the second note, while it should fall on the first. The example will make this clearer:

### § 16

For the purpose of imitation or for the expression and excitation of this or that emotion figures also are devised, by the means of whose characteristics one believes oneself to come closest to nature. If, for example, each triplet begins with a rest, a plaintive sighing cannot be better expressed than by slurring the remaining two notes together in the up stroke, alternating *forte* with *piano*. But the stroke must begin with very moderate strength and end quite quietly. Try it in the following example:

## SIXTH CHAPTER

### § 17

One can also slur many triplets together in one stroke: especially in a quick tempo. For example:

The first six triplets are played in the down stroke, the other six in the up stroke, but played so that the first note of each bar is strongly marked by an accent from the bow. It will, moreover, be well to remember what has been said in § 5 concerning the notes marked with an (*). In this example also are similar passages, and here in particular, because of the open strings, no string may be relinquished, but the fourth finger must be used in every case.

### § 18

If you desire to play it in a different manner, the first note of two triplets can be played alone, the following four slurred together, and the last again by itself. In this way you have a new variation. For example:

Adagio

### § 19

These now are the varied triplets which occur to me. They can be used in every kind of time-measure and, according to the demands of the circumstances, can be applied now separately, now mixed. I shall probably be reproached for having put most of the foregoing examples in C major. It is true that they are almost all given in this key. But then, is it not better that a beginner make himself thoroughly familiar with the diatonic scale, than that he begin to play in other scales without first understanding one of them thoroughly? Is it not easier for a pupil to practise in the scale where the intervals lie naturally and thus quickly get all the tones correctly in his ear, than to play first in one key, then in another; playing out of tune everywhere, becoming confused thereby, and even becoming so unfortunate as never to be able to distinguish the false from the true? Such people usually reach a stage where they finally even forget how to tune their violins correctly. There exist living examples hereof.

# CHAPTER VII

# Of the many varieties of Bowing

## I. Of the varieties of Bowing in even notes

### § 1

THAT bowing can greatly vary a phrase we have already become in some measure aware in the previous chapter. The present chapter will convince us entirely that the bowing gives life to the notes; that it produces now a modest, now an impertinent, now a serious or playful tone; now coaxing, or grave and sublime; now a sad or merry melody; and is therefore the medium by the reasonable use of which we are able to rouse in the hearers the aforesaid affects.[1] I mean that this can be done if the composer makes a reasonable choice; if he selects melodies to match every emotion, and knows how to indicate the appropriate style of performance suitably. Or if a well-skilled violinist himself possess sound judgement in the playing of, so to speak, quite unadorned notes with common sense, and if he strive to find the desired affect[1] and to apply the following bowings in the right place.

### § 2

Consecutive and continuous rapid notes are subject to many variations. I will here set down a single passage which from the first can be played quite smoothly and easily, and in which each note may be performed with its own separate stroke. Great pains must be taken with their exact equality, and the first note of each crotchet must be marked with a vigour which inspires the whole performance. For example:

[1] See Translator's Appendix, p. 232.

## SEVENTH CHAPTER—FIRST SECTION

### § 3

If notes are slurred in pairs with the down stroke and up stroke, we have at once another variation. For example:

The first of two notes coming together in one stroke is accented more strongly and held slightly longer, while the second is slurred on to it quite quietly and rather late. This style of performance promotes good taste in the playing of the melody and prevents hurrying by means of the afore-mentioned sustaining of the first notes.

### § 4

Take the first note alone in the down stroke but slur the following three together in the up stroke and here you have a second variation. For example:

But the equality of the four notes must not be forgotten; for otherwise the last three notes might easily sound like triplets, and be played as follows:

### § 5

If the first three notes be taken together in the down stroke and the fourth detached and alone in the up stroke, there appears a third variation. But the equality of the notes must always be kept in mind. For example:

### § 6

A fourth variation arises if the first two notes be slurred together in the down stroke, but the following two, on the contrary, be played with separate strokes quickly and accented. This style is mostly used in quick tempo; and is to be regarded as an exception to the rule of bowing given in § 9 of Chapter IV, for although the first crotchet begins with the down stroke, the second, on the contrary, begins with the up stroke, and so on. For example:

## § 7

If now the third and fourth notes be taken together in one stroke, but in such manner that the first two notes (as in the preceding paragraph) be slurred, but the last two of the up stroke be separated by lifting the bow, you have a fifth variation. For example:

## § 8

A sixth variation is obtained if the first note be detached quite by itself, but quickly, in the down stroke; the second and third slurred together in the up stroke; and the fourth again separated quickly in the down stroke. Here, too, the second and fourth crotchets begin, contrary to the rule given in § 9, Chapter IV, with the up stroke. The first and last notes of each crotchet are to be played with a quick stroke, for otherwise an unevenness of time-measure will ensue.

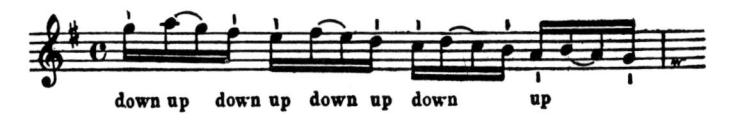

## § 9

A similar passage can also be played pleasingly if the first note be detached in the down stroke; the second and third slurred in the up stroke, and the last bound to the first of the next quarter-bar by means of a slur in the down stroke and so

## SEVENTH CHAPTER—FIRST SECTION

continued in the same style, so that even the last note is slurred on to the last but one. This can be the seventh variation.

§ 10

Further, the four semiquavers of the first quarter of the bar can be slurred together in the down stroke, and the four of the second quarter in the up stroke, and so on. This gives an eighth variation. But one must differentiate the first note of each crotchet by means of an accent.

§ 11

A new and ninth variation is obtained at once if you slur the first and second crotchet, namely eight notes, in the down stroke; the third and fourth crotchet as the other eight notes in the up stroke, but in such fashion that the first note of each crotchet be marked by a strong emphasis of the bow, and thus distinguished from the others. The evenness of the time-measure is furthered in this way; the performance becomes clearer and much more lively, and the violinist accustoms himself to a long stroke. Here is the example:

§ 12

In a very quick tempo, and in order to make a new exercise and a tenth variation, one can even play a whole bar in one stroke. But here also, as in the previous style, the first notes of each crotchet must be marked by an emphasis. For example:

## SEVENTH CHAPTER—FIRST SECTION

### § 13

Now if you wish to accustom yourself to a really long stroke of the bow; if you wish to learn to play many notes in one bow, with expression, clarity, and evenness, and therefore make yourself really master of your bow, you can play with great profit this whole passage first in an up stroke, then in a down stroke. But do not forget to apply on the first note of each crotchet the emphasis which must distinguish one crotchet clearly from the other. This is the eleventh variation.

### § 14

Now when you are thoroughly practised in slurring so many notes together in one stroke, you must also learn to lift the bow and play several notes detached from each other in one stroke; which gives a twelfth variation. For example:

down up   down up

The first two notes are, it is true, taken in the down stroke and the other two in the up stroke, but they are not slurred but are separated from each other and detached by means of lifting the bow.

### § 15

In the same manner you can take the first note in the down stroke, but the other three on the contrary in the up stroke, which can be the thirteenth variation. For example:

down up

### § 16

If you wish to vary it a fourteenth time, you need only slur the four notes of the first crotchet together in the down stroke but play the four notes of the second crotchet detached in the up stroke. But do not forget the evenness of the time-measure, for in the second and fourth crotchets, you may easily be betrayed into hurrying. Here is the example:

### § 17

When you have practised playing, in § 11, § 12, and § 13, a whole or even two bars in one slur, you must also learn to detach many notes in one stroke. Slur the first crotchet in the down stroke but play the twelve notes of the remaining three crotchets in the up stroke, separating them by a quick lift of the bow. Here we have a fifteenth variation.

This style of performance will be somewhat difficult to the beginner. A certain relaxing of the right hand is necessary for it, and a retarding of the bow. This is more easily shown or discovered by oneself by practice than can be explained with words. The weight of a violin bow contributes much, as does also in no less degree its length or shortness. A heavier and longer bow must be used more lightly and retarded somewhat less; whereas a lighter and shorter bow must be pressed down more and retarded more. Above all, the right hand must here be made a little stiff, but the contracting and relaxing of the same must be regulated according to the weight and length, or the lightness and shortness of the bow. The notes must be played in an even tempo, with even strength, and not over-hurried or, so to speak, swallowed. But in particular you must know how to hold back and guide the bow in such fashion that towards the end of the second bar so much strength remains over, that the crotchet note (G) at the end of the passage in the same stroke can be distinguished by a noticeable accent.

### § 18

Finally, a sixteenth variation can also be made: namely, if the first note be played alone in the down stroke and the following three taken together in the up stroke. But whereas the second and third are slurred together, the fourth is detached by a quick lift of the bow. For example:

*down up*

But this style of performance sounds more effective when the notes are at a greater distance from each other or, so to speak, are written 'springingly'. For example:

§ 19

You must not believe, however, that these variations can be applied only to simple time. In triple time the same and many more can be made. I will set down what occurs to me: but I hope that so much may have been learnt from the preceding numerous examples and their indications that there will be no difficulty in playing the following examples according to the signs attached to them, and without further explanation. For the rest I will add that every unmarked note is played with its own stroke; the notes marked with little strokes are played shortly; the notes marked with a half-circle are slurred together in one stroke; and those marked with both half-circle and little strokes are taken in one bow but must be detached by lifting the bow.

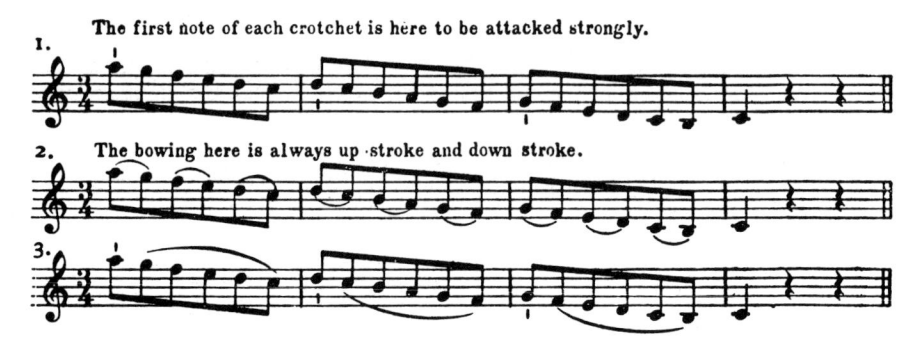

1. The first note of each crotchet is here to be attacked strongly.

2. The bowing here is always up-stroke and down stroke.

3.

4.
5.
6.
up
down
7.
8.
9.
10.
11.
down up
down up
12.
down
up
down
up
13.
14.
In an up-stroke or down-stroke.
up
down
15.

16.
up
down
17.
18.
19.
up
down
20.
up
down
21.
22.
up
down
23.
up
down
24.
up
down
25.
up
down
down
26.
up
down
down
27.

§ 20

But it is not enough to play such figures just as they stand, according to the bowing indicated; they must also be so performed that the variation strikes the ear at once. It is true the question of tasteful performance should be given special treatment under 'Good taste in Music'. But then why should one not, when opportunity offers, help oneself to some of this good taste and accustom the pupil to a singing style of performance? A beginner will thereby become better able to grasp the rules of the good taste of his day; and the teacher has then but half the trouble in instilling the same into his pupil. Now if in a musical composition two, three, four, and even more notes be bound together by the half circle, so that one recognizes therefrom that the composer wishes the notes not to be separated but played singingly in one slur, the first of such united notes must be somewhat more strongly stressed, but the remainder slurred on to it quite smoothly and more and more quietly. Let it be tried in the foregoing examples. It will be seen that the stress falls now on the first, now on the second, or third crotchet, yea, frequently even on the second half of the first, second, or third crotchet. Now this changes indisputably the whole style of performance, and it will be wise to practise these and similar passages, and in particular the thirty-fourth, very slowly at first, in order to become thoroughly familiar with the style of each variation, but later by diligent practice to gain greater fluency.

## II. Of variations of Bowing in figures which are composed of varied and unequal notes

### § 1

That a melodic piece is not composed purely of equal notes only is known to all. One must learn accordingly how to play the compound figures consisting of unequal notes according to the indications of a rational composer.[1] There exist, however, so many of these figures that it is not possible to remember all of them. I will set down in consecutive order as many as occur to me. If a beginner plays them all correctly, he will easily find his way in other similar phrases. Here they are:

[1] There exist, unfortunately, enough of such would-be composers, who themselves either will not indicate the style of a good performance, or 'put a patch by the side of the hole'.* We are not talking of these bunglers; in such cases everything depends on the good judgement of the violinist.

*[A tailor's expression and means a person, who does not understand his craft. The patch must be set over the hole!]

3.
(a)
down up
(b)
p f p f p f
down up down up
4.
(a)
down up
(b)
(better) down up down
5.
(a)
down up
(b)
f p f p f p f p
down up down up
6.
(a)
(b)
down up
(c) in still more singing style.
down up
7.
(a)
down up
(b)
down up
(c)
down up down up down up
8.
(a)
down up
At the dot the bow is lifted.
(b)
This is performed without lifting the bow, and slurred in sustained style.
(c)
down up
After the dot, the note following it is long delayed.
(d)
down up
At the dot the bow is lifted.

9.
(a)
down up
(b)
p
f
p
f
down up
down
10.
(a)
(b)
11.
(a)
(b)
down up
down
up down
12.
(a)
(b)
At the dot. not detached.
down up down
down up
13.
(a)
(b)
down up down up
down up down up
(c)
(d)
down up
down up
14.
(a)
(b)
up down up
up down u. d. u.
15.
(a)
(b)
down up
down up
(c)
down

16.

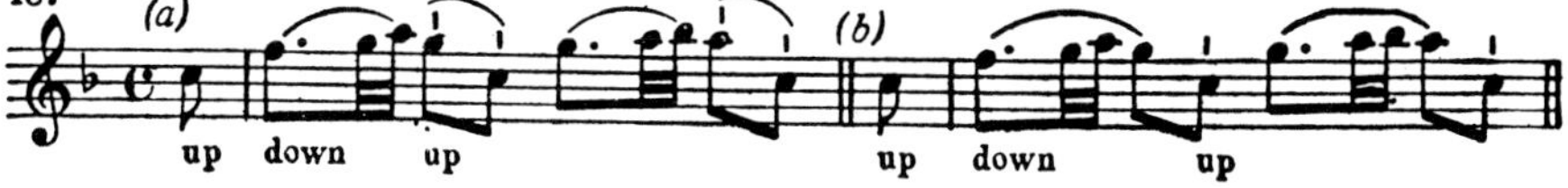


17.

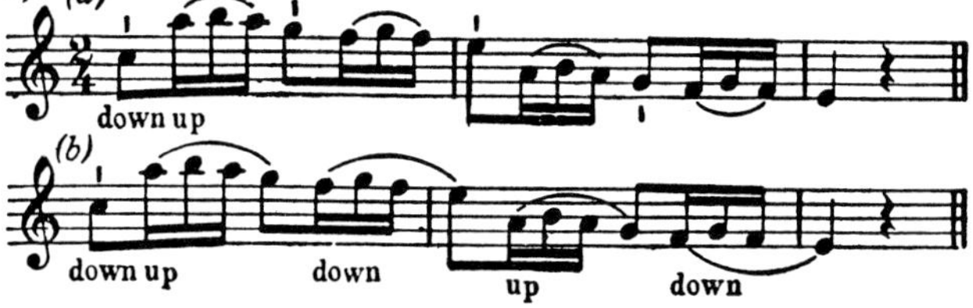


18.

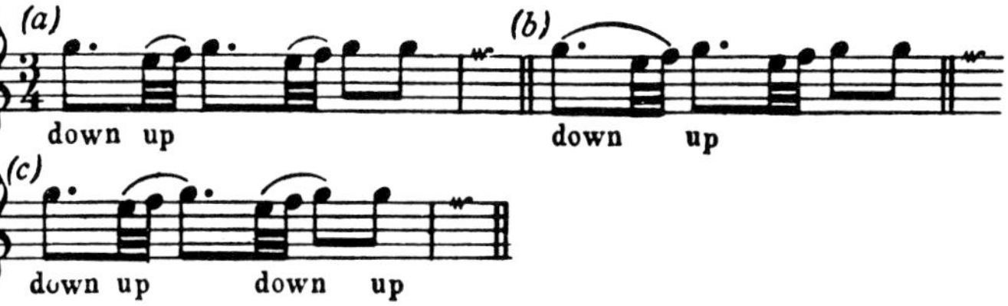


19.

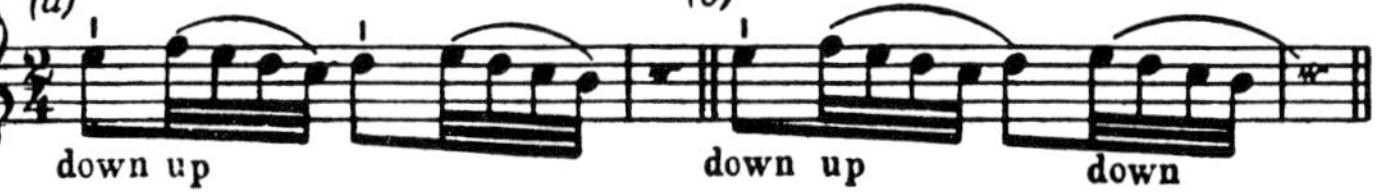


20.

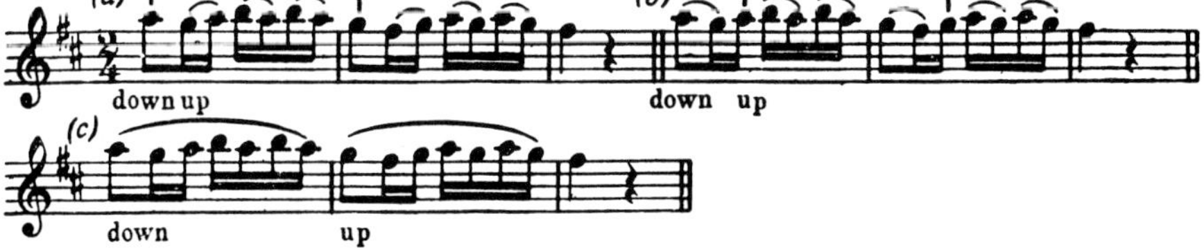


21.

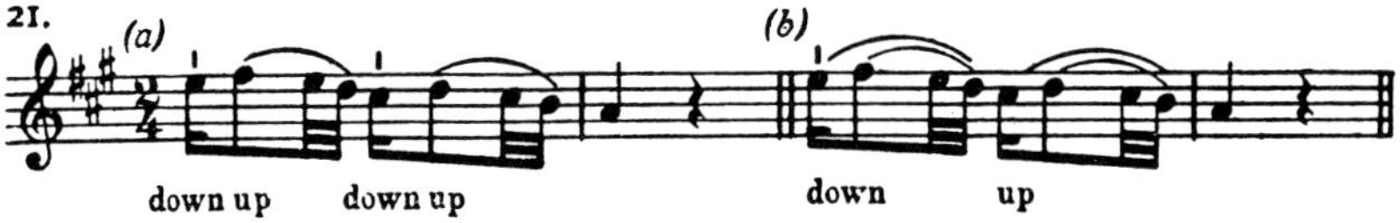

22. (a) (b) (c)
down up
down up down up down up
23. (a) (b)
down up down up
24. (a) (b)
3 3
down up down up
25. (a) (b)
down up down down up down up
26. (a)
down up
(b)
down up down up
27. (a) (b) (c)
down up down up
28. (a) (b)
down up down up down up down up down up
29. (a) (b) (c)
down up down up down down up

Here several notes are played in one stroke of the bow.

## § 2

In all these passages and their variations I recommend, as always, evenness of time-measure. It is only too easy to err in tempo, and nothing is more easy than to hurry in dotted notes if the value of the dot be not held out. It is therefore always better if the note following the dot be played somewhat late. For by means of the notes which are detached by a lift of the bow, the style of performance becomes more enlivened; as at 2, *c*; 4, *a* and *b*; 8, *a*, *c*, and *d*; 12, *a*; and 24, *a* and *b*. 26, always at the second dotted note in *a* and *b*. Slurred notes, on the contrary, make the style of performance satisfying, melodious, and pleasant. Not only must the dotted note be prolonged, however, but it must also be attacked somewhat strongly, slurring the second decreasingly and quietly on to it, as at 8, *b*; 12, *b*; 22, *b* and *c*; and the first dotted note in 26, *a* and *b*. Further, in 29, *c*, and in 30, *c*.

## § 3

The same must be observed with dotted notes followed by two quick notes which are slurred together; as, for example, in 15, *a*, *b*, and *c*; 16, *a* and *b*; 18, *a*, *b*, and *c*; 23, *a* and *b*; 25, *a* and *b*; and 27, *a*, *b*, and *c*. The dot must rather be held too long than too briefly. In this manner hurrying is avoided and good taste promoted; for that which is added to the dot will be subtracted imperceptibly from the following notes. That is, the latter are played more rapidly.

## § 4

If the second note be dotted, then must the first be quickly slurred on to the dotted note. The dot, however, is not to be accented but played warmly with a sustained yet gradually decreasing tone, as for example at 34 and 10, *a* and *b*. The same occurs, it is true, at 30 in *b*, but only fortuitously. In itself this figure is played as indicated in *a* and *c*, but in consequence of the varying of the stroke, which alters the style, the figure comes under the rule of this paragraph.

## § 5

The first of two, three, four, or even more notes, slurred together, must at all times be stressed more strongly and sustained a little longer; but those following must diminish in tone and be slurred on somewhat later. But this must be carried out with such good judgement that the bar-length is not altered in the smallest degree. The slight sustaining of the first note must not only be made agreeable to the ear by a nice apportioning of the slightly hurried notes slurred on to it, but must even be made truly pleasant to the listener. In such fashion are to be played examples: 1, *a*; 6, *b* and *c*; 7, *a* and *c*; 9, *a* and *b*; 11, *a* and *b*; 13, *a*, *b*, *c*, and *d*; 14, *a*; 17, *a* and *b*; 20, in the second beat of both bars; 22, *b*; 28, *a* and *b*; and 33, *a*, *b*, and *c*.

§ 6

In the same way, when uneven notes occur which are slurred together, the longer notes must not be made too short but rather sustained a little over-long, and such passages shall be played singingly and with sound judgement, according to the style indicated in the preceding paragraph. Such are for example: 2, *b* and *c*; 4, *a* and *b*; 5, *b*; 7, *b*; 8, *c* and *d*; 13, *c* and *d*; 14, *b*; 20, *b* and *c*; 21, *a* and *b*; 32, *a* and *b*.

§ 7

A short note followed by a long one must frequently be slurred on to it, in which case the short note is always played quietly; not hurried, but so slurred on to the long note that the whole weight falls on the latter. For example, at 1, *b* from the E to F, and in the second bar from the C to D; at 3, *b* from the D to C; from the B to A, and from the G to F. 30, *b* from the A to F, and so on.

§ 8

This now is what occurs to me readily concerning such passages. Diligent practice of these few examples will be very useful to a beginner. He will gain thereby facility in playing all other similar figures and variations according to the instructions of a wise composer, in tempo, with spirit and expression, correctly and in tune, and will be able to change and guide the strokes in such fashion, that even when these take the most complicated course he will be in a position to bring all into order again by the application of the teachings of Chapter IV.

# CHAPTER VIII
# Of the Positions
## I. Of the so-called Whole Position[1]

### § 1

IT lies in the nature of the violin that if on the E string a yet higher note than B 𝄞 should be played, a good tone can still be produced; which same is to be understood with regard to the other three strings. As nowadays in most pieces there are constantly to be seen, besides the five lines, two, three, four and more added to them, there must necessarily be also a rule according to which the notes over the five lines shall be played. And this is what is called position playing.

### § 2

Three reasons there be which justify the use of the positions. Necessity, convenience, and elegance. Necessity manifests itself when several lines are drawn over the usual five lines. Convenience requires the use of the positions in certain passages where the notes are set so far apart that they cannot be played otherwise without difficulty. And finally the positions are used for the sake of elegance when notes which are Cantabile occur closely together and can be played easily on one string. Not only is equality of tone obtained thereby, but also a more consistent and singing style of delivery. Examples hereof will be seen in the course of this chapter.

### § 3

The positions are threefold: the Whole Position, the Half Position, and the Compound or Mixed Position. There may, perchance, be some who look upon

[1 *Leopold Mozart's 'Whole Position' includes what we now call the 3rd, 5th, and 7th Positions; the 'Half' includes the 2nd, 4th, and 6th; the 'Compound or Mixed' is a combination of the 2nd and 3rd Positions, and the 'Natural Position' is the 1st. I shall use L. M.'s names for the positions throughout.*]

this my third species as superfluous because it consists of the whole and half put together. But I know with certainty that after more careful inspection they will not only find it useful, but even necessary.

## § 4

In the present section we speak of the common or so-called whole position. The note A on the E string, which is otherwise taken by the third finger, is now taken by the first finger, in order to be able to play the notes ascending still higher above the usual B with the second, third, and fourth fingers. This little alphabet must therefore be practised:

in which at the note A* the first finger must again be used which was previously on the note F. The common name for this is: 'Placing'. It is, namely, customary to say: 'Here must the first finger be placed', or 'one must place the first finger'.

## § 5

This manner of placing the fingers is called the common or whole position, by reason that it lies nearest to the general rules of violin playing. The first and third fingers are used at all times on the notes which occur on the lines: the second and fourth fingers, on the contrary, fall on the notes which fill the space between the lines. From this it can be most quickly recognized when to avail oneself of this position. If namely the uppermost or highest note be in a space, it is almost always an infallible sign that no other than the whole position shall be used.

## § 6

But notes occur frequently which are placed very far apart; where one has to leap downwards from the E string directly to the D or even the G string and immediately back again. No less do quick notes occur which proceed so quickly from the heights to the depths and from the depths to the heights, that without the use of the positions they can scarcely be produced. For this reason one must know how to use the positions on all four strings and must therefore learn to play the given alphabet in tune.

The C on the G string (*) is now taken with the first finger instead of the third, the hand remaining fixed in the same position: the open string is therefore heard no more, because the notes, otherwise played on the open string, are now taken with the second finger on the lower neighbouring string. For example:

## § 7

One cannot sooner make oneself skilful in this position than by taking the next-best pieces which one can play glibly, and for the sake of practice play them throughout in the whole position.[1] In this manner the placing of the fingers becomes thoroughly familiar and an extraordinary facility is achieved thereby. It is not really difficult if a little trouble be taken, for the placing of the fingers can be sought in the alphabet.

## § 8

If in a passage the highest note surpasses the high D by only one tone and therefore ascends no higher than E, the passage is played in the whole position and the note E taken with the fourth finger. In such cases the fourth finger is often used twice consecutively. Here are examples:

[1] *In the edition of 1787 there is a footnote (a) here, as follows:* '(a) Take now the pieces in the Fourth Chapter, after Par. 39, and play them in the positions.'

But in the forward movement of the little finger, neither the whole hand nor any of the fingers may move with it but the hand must be left unmoved in its position, only the fourth finger being extended. This is best achieved, if the finger with which the note immediately before the E is played be pressed down firmly and not relaxed during the extension of the fourth finger. In the first example it is the second finger*, in the second example it is the first*, and in the third it is the third* finger.

§ 9

If several notes be written above the note E, then the hand must be moved. With even notes ascending consecutively tone for tone, beginning with the first finger on A, the changes of position must be made each time with the first and second fingers. For example:

And if there be ascending notes, one of which, however, descends previously each time by a sixth, then such notes should usually be taken with the first finger. For example:

But look carefully whether the passage progresses still farther into the heights or whether perchance it returns again; and whether the first finger has to be moved up once more; or whether the highest tone can be reached by the fourth finger. It would be an error if in the first example the note G (*) were taken with the first finger, for it can be foreseen that the third and fourth fingers can, in any case, reach the highest two notes. However, the passage returns again at the two quaver notes

F and E, and just for this reason it would also be an error if, in the second example, the note D (*) were taken with the first finger and the hand had therefore to move up once more, as the passage in the fifth bar never ascends, but always descends.

## § 10

And even if it ascends by yet another note, which from its appearance would demand either a further continuation of the positions or a fifth finger, but the passage after such a note immediately descends again, then the hand is left in its position, and the uppermost or highest note is taken with the fourth finger. The

fourth finger is frequently used twice consecutively. But here also, that which was first remarked at the end of paragraph 8 must be well observed.

## § 11

But passages do not all begin with the first finger. In many of them the third finger must be placed and continued with alternate use of the third and fourth fingers. For example:

## § 12

Many begin with the second finger. That is: the second finger is placed first and is used alternately with the third. For example:

## EIGHTH CHAPTER—FIRST SECTION 137

It is true, one could go up with the first finger to the note A, but because the alternating of the second with the third finger is much more usual and natural it is therefore better to continue upwards with the second and third fingers at the notes B and C as was done before in the natural position at the notes G and A. Yea, if it ascends in such order still higher than the note D, then the second and third fingers must always be used alternately. For example:

### § 13

Passages exist which, without the use of the positions, are very inconvenient to play, but which on the contrary, in the positions lie, so to speak, in the hand. In such passages one avails oneself of positions partly from necessity, partly for convenience. For example:

### § 14

Many double-stoppings cannot be played otherwise than in the positions. For example:

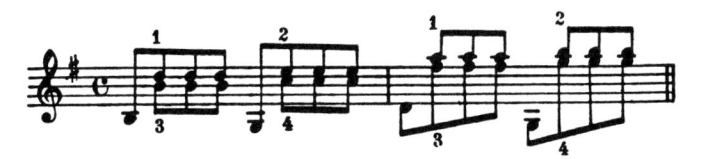

It is true that in the present example the second and third beats of the first bar could be played without going into the positions, but because of the sequel it is necessary to remain up in the whole position; for all unnecessary backward and forward movement of the hand must be most carefully avoided.

## § 15

Very often one must move up on the spur of the moment into the positions; now with the second, now with the third or even with the fourth finger. It demands, therefore, great practice to be able always to grasp the notes in tune and play them neither too sharp nor too flat. Practise yourself therefore in the following and similar passages.

## § 16

One must remain in the position as long as it is at all necessary. One must always foresee whether one or the other high note occurs, or even a different passage which necessitates the use of the position. If, however, one is no longer constrained to remain in the position, one must not instantly run headlong down but await a good and easy opportunity to descend in such fashion that the listener does not perceive the change. This can be most conveniently achieved if you wait for a note which can be taken on the open string, when the descent can be made quite comfortably(*).

## § 17

It is also very easy to descend if similar passages be played with similar fingering. The example will make this clearer.

## EIGHTH CHAPTER—FIRST SECTION

The descent is made here on the note G. It is a natural progression which lies very conveniently to the hand, because the alternation of the second and first fingers occurs more frequently and facilitates the descent of the hand. The passage can be practised with benefit, gradually increasing the speed thereof.

### § 18

When two similar notes occur consecutively, they afford very good opportunity for descending. The first note must be taken in the upper position while the second note is played in the natural position. For example: (*)

In this manner the note, already heard in the higher position, will not be so easily played out of tune in the ensuing change, but on the contrary, the fourth finger will in its course be placed the more certainly on the second B, in consequence of the second finger having previously indicated its place in the whole position.

### § 19

After a dot, too, the descent can be made very conveniently.

At the dot the bow is lifted, during which the hand is moved and the note F taken in the natural position.

### § 20

In order, however, to establish thoroughly the ascent and descent in the whole position in various ways, I will add an example which must be practised conscientiously according to the given rules.

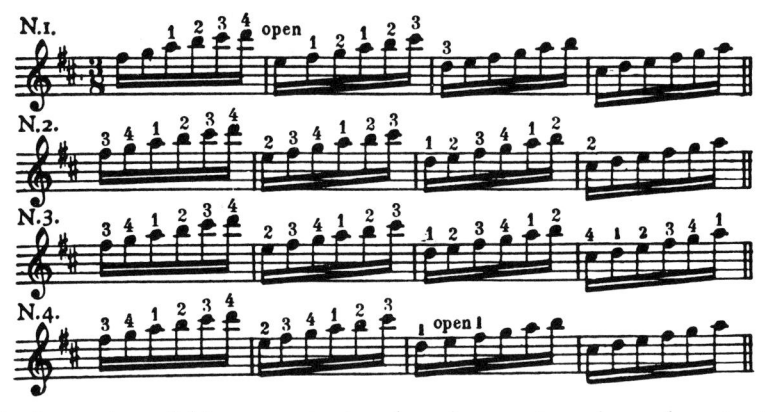

The first variety of this passage is given here for practice only, so that a beginner may achieve, by means of playing this and other such examples, facility in ascending and descending. The descent on the note E in the first beat of the second bar is unnecessary; because on the H in the third beat of the same second bar it is necessary to ascend again. It is therefore only an example for practice. The variation No. 2 is better. You begin straightway in the whole position and remain there till the fourth bar, when you return on the first note of the fourth bar, C, to the natural position. Variation No. 3 can, for the sake of practice, be played throughout in the whole position. No. 4, on the contrary, is the best and most usual kind. The first two bars are played in the whole position; the first note of the third bar remains still in the whole position but on the second, that is the open E, the descent is made and the rest is played in the natural position without further change.

## II. Of the Half Position

### § 1

The Half Position is: when the C on the A string, which is otherwise taken with the second, is now taken with the first finger in order to reach the note C on the E string with the fourth finger. It is called the half position because it is not subject to the usual rule. Whereas in the whole position the notes which are on the lines (as in the common musical stave) are taken with the first or third fingers, they are now on the contrary taken in the half position with the second and fourth fingers.

# EIGHTH CHAPTER—SECOND SECTION

According to the usual manner of playing, the notes which occur in the spaces are taken with the second and fourth fingers, but are now taken with the first and third. Here is the alphabet. Practise it diligently and forget not to play the H (*) well in tune and not too flat; but to set the fourth finger immediately against it for the C (*). The same is to be observed with the notes E and F under the third and fourth fingers on the A string (*).

### § 2

As the whole position includes all strings, so also is the half position used on all strings. But the third finger must be specially watched, for there is always a danger of playing out of tune with it. Here is the alphabet on all strings:

In order to avoid playing out of tune with the third finger, the note played by it in the half position can be compared with the similar note on the upper, neighbouring open string. For example:

### § 3

This half position is mostly used in pieces which are written in C or E, with the major or minor third, and also with those in F, B♭, and A; but especially in the last two because of the modulation to the relative keys. In particular is to be noticed whether the course of a passage oversteps the upper C ; whether also the middle C be present and whether the fifth thereof, namely the G occurs also in the composition. In these three cases the use of the second position is wellnigh obligatory. Here is an example:

## § 4

In the half position too the ascent can often be made with the second finger in the same manner as in the whole position, of which mention has been made in § 12 of the previous section. In particular: if the passage runs up still higher, then the interchange of the second and third fingers is necessary. For example:

## § 5

Especially is the first finger used in passages which are set in E. For example:

Here the ascent is made, step by step, by the first finger. In the following example, however, where the upper note falls every time to a sixth below, each lowest note is taken with the first finger a third higher.

## § 6

All such passages are easy to play at sight if it be quickly observed whether the highest and lowest notes are an octave apart. In the whole position this is recognizable if the lower note is on a line; the other, on the contrary, being placed in a space. This can be seen at once at D, F, A, and D in the second example given in § 9 of the previous section. In this half position exactly the opposite happens. The lower note lies always in the space while the upper, on the contrary, is always on the line. We see it in the aformentioned example, C, E, G, and C, and so forth.

## § 7

But in this half position, as in the whole position, one must also look at the height of the passage: whether the passage ascends still higher, or whether the highest note can be reached without a change. But read what is said at the end of § 9 of the previous section; for just that has to be carefully observed in this position also if one desires that the fingers should not lose their way.

## § 8

In this position too the ascent is made sometimes with the first, sometimes with the second, third, or fourth fingers quickly and boldly. Here are examples thereof:

### EIGHTH CHAPTER—SECOND SECTION

### § 9

For the sake of convenience quite ordinary passages are often played in this half position. For example:

But best of all is it to begin from the first bar in the position. For example:

### § 10

In slow pieces the fourth finger is often used, not from necessity but for the sake of equality of tone and therefore also for the sake of elegance. For example:

The minim F could, it is true, be taken on the E string with the first finger. But as the E string sounds far too shrill against the A string, the tone is made more level if the F be taken indeed with the fourth finger but without the hand changing its position, and the note E be also taken with the fourth finger. Yea, the passage hangs better together and is rendered thereby more melodious.

### § 11

In double-stopping, the half position is used partly from necessity but also partly for convenience. See the example:

## EIGHTH CHAPTER—SECOND SECTION

### § 12

Many passages which seem to fit the half position perfectly, can and must often be played in the whole position. For example:

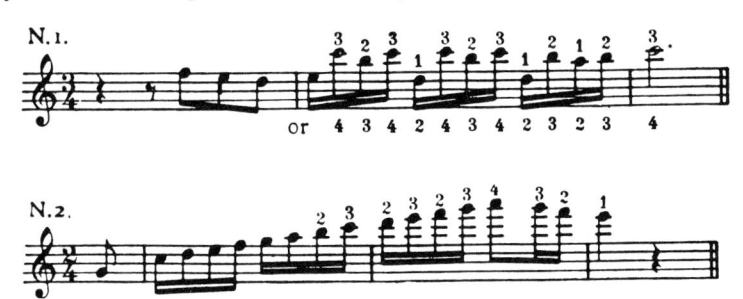

[musical example N.1 and N.2]

The first example, it is true, can also be played in the half position. The second example, on the contrary, must always be played in the whole position throughout.

### § 13

When in a passage the note C occurs on the E string, and moreover with a leap of a third, fourth, fifth, or sixth after it, one does not avail oneself of the position, but leaves the hand in the natural position and takes the note C by extending the fourth finger. For example:

[musical example]

Oft-times the fourth finger occurs even twice, and that in not very slow pieces. For example:

[musical example]

And many pieces can be played either in the upper position or in the natural position. Here is an example. Let it be played in the half position but practised also in the natural position, in which case the admonition in § 8 of the previous section must be borne in mind.

## EIGHTH CHAPTER—SECOND SECTION

§ 14

In returning from this position into the natural position, just those rules must be observed which I have laid down in § 16, § 17, § 18, and § 19 of the previous section. It is much easier to descend from this position than from the whole because it is nearer to the finger position of the natural manner of playing. The whole position is raised a whole third, while the half position lies only a tone higher. For this reason the descent can be made in rapidly running notes, at any time and on any note. I will here give a single passage as a basis. If it be practised according to the instruction, then will you be able to descend on any note, at your pleasure.

The whole of this to be played in the half position

It is clear to the eye that at N.1 the descent has already been made on the second note, and that the fourth finger must be used twice. At N.2 the third finger occurs twice and descends on the A. At N.3 the note G occurs on the second finger. At N.4 the return is made on the second A. At N.5 the descent is made on the G of the second half of the bar, but in N.6 on the first finger. And, finally, at N.7 the first note of the second bar is taken in the natural position. But above all, the attached bowings must be observed. Throughout, those notes must at first be slurred together on which the descent is made from the upper position back into the natural position, in order thereby to deceive the ear of the listeners; that is, so that they may not perceive the change and swift descent of the hand. Similarly, the first bar can be played entirely in the half position, and only in the second bar the descent made in as many ways as in the first bar. I will write it down, albeit only for practice, and then proceed to the mixed position.

## III. Of the Compound or Mixed Position

### § 1

I will call the Compound or Mixed Position that manner of playing when now the whole, now the half position is used; either from necessity, for convenience, or for charm, according to the demand of circumstances. One could put forward countless examples thereof which, to a conscientious violinist, when undertaking divers musical pieces, will appear in different styles. For who indeed would put down here all the passages so often studied with great pains? Are there not indeed violinists who insert into the solos or concertos compiled by themselves all imaginable kinds of jugglers' tricks? Do not others exist who, in the most incomprehensible passages, wander through every scale; who insert the most unexpected, most curious, and wonderful capers: yea, mix these offensive passages together which have neither method nor consistency? The rules which I can give here are for the most part aimed at rational, well-written compositions. The examples are written down plainly and simply, and borrowed, one or the other, from good concertos.

## § 2

When a passage is repeated only one tone higher or lower, it is customary to play it each time with the same fingering as was used in the first; particularly if the passage runs through a whole octave or, at least, if the use of the first and fourth finger be necessary to the passage. For example:

In this, as well as in all the following examples, the fingering is indicated by numbers, but only the first time: afterwards, however, only that note is marked where the finger is to be placed, or where the hand is to return. Here is another similar example in which one begins to move up and down on the second finger (*).

## § 3

Often a passage begins again on the same note with which the previous one ended, but in such a case a different finger is used. For example (*):

But the descent can also be made thus. For example:

## § 4

Very often the passage remains the same but does not progress by steps, but by leaps. For example:

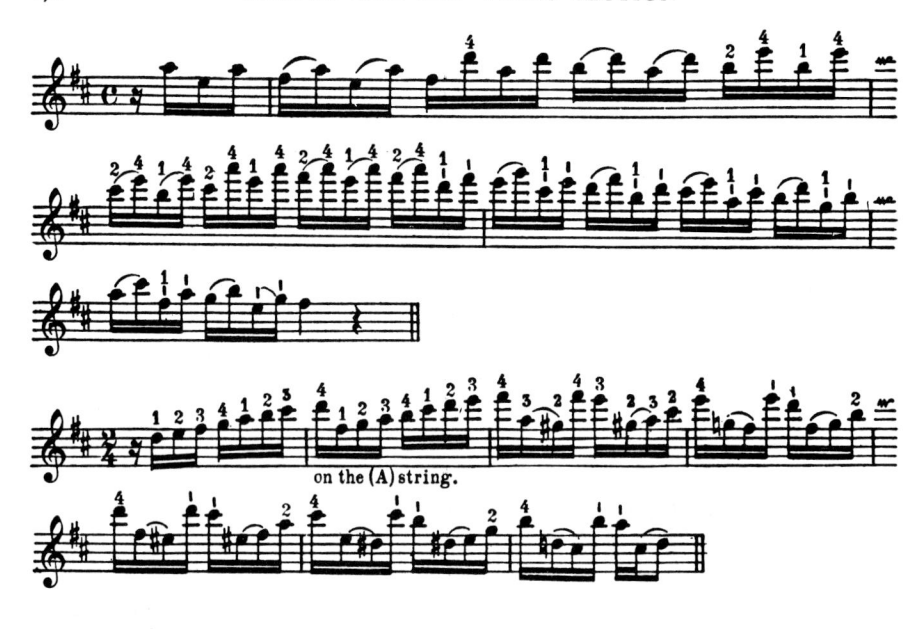

## § 5

But there are also passages in which the notes cannot be taken by means of the usual interchange of the fingers. These are the most difficult passages. The notes occurring therein must be arrived at by the rapid moving up of the hand, partly by extending the fourth finger, but mostly by reaching them at a venture. Now he who would in time bring to light something special on the violin in difficult pieces must acquire concertos of fine masters; study them deeply, and practise them diligently. I will here set down a few examples:

But at the minim note of the second bar (\*) the minim can be taken in the whole position. For example:

He who has a large fist does well to remain in the whole position and by means of expansion of the hand take the note D with the third finger, and the note F with the fourth. For example (\*\*):

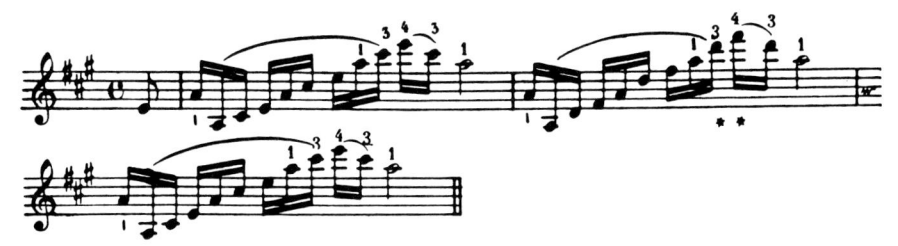

One can even jump with the second finger on to the note D; yea a large hand may reach it without moving the first finger from the note A. I set down such things for practice. One learns therefrom to stretch out well with the fingers; and he who practises playing a passage in many different ways, gives himself more certainty of bringing it off safely in one way or the other.

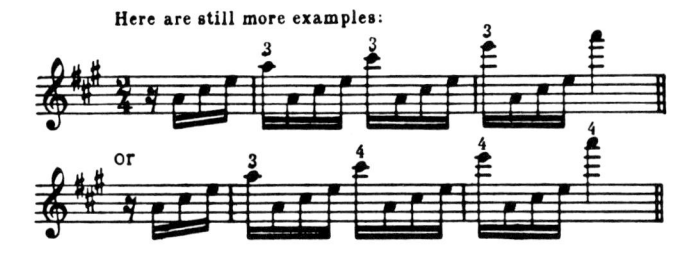

Here are still more examples:

[Musical notation]

*This passage begins on the (D) string.*

[Musical notation]

Now in the usual course, the first crotchet of the first and second bar would be played in the natural position without the use of the whole position, but even so one must not come to a standstill. For example:

[Musical notation]

And why then should one not practise it also in the following manner? It is not without advantage if it be continued thus:

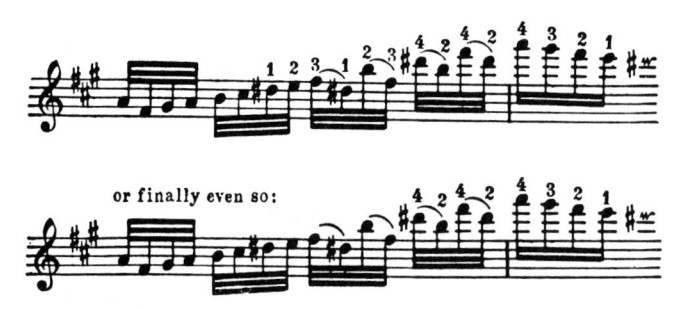

[Musical notation]

or finally even so:

[Musical notation]

It is confessedly best to remain in the position. The first manner of performance is therefore the most natural, but the others must also be practised for utility's sake, for similar rapid jumps are often unavoidable, and what would happen to him who had not practised them? The same applies to the extension of the fingers. Here are more examples for practice:

## § 6

In the same way that the fourth finger must very often be extended in all the varieties of the positions, just so, in the mixed position, the first finger must often be stretched backwards without changing the position of the other fingers. Here the fourth finger in particular, which must be pressed down firmly and not lifted, must be watched when presently the first finger moves downwards. Observe this example:

## EIGHTH CHAPTER—THIRD SECTION

### § 7

The key in which a passage is written must be particularly observed. And, according to whether a passage remain in the key or pass on to other keys, just so must the hand according to the change of circumstances, now move, now remain stationary. It is clear as day from the given examples, that the fourth finger is chiefly used for the highest note and the first finger for the lowest. The remaining fingers must be arranged accordingly. If one observes the compass of the octave this is not difficult. For example:

I will here put down a few examples and, for the sake of greater clearness, explain them in some degree at the close.

N.1.

N.2.

In the first example the highest note in the third bar is, according to rule, taken with the fourth finger, but the whole hand is changed in the third crotchet of the same bar and moved downwards because the passage closes on A, and in order to take the remaining notes with comfort, the first finger is indispensable.

In the second example the change is made with the second and third fingers in the last crotchet of the first bar, and the hand is moved up in order to take the highest note A correctly. In returning, however, the first finger springs back each time to the lowest notes, E, C, and A.

The highest note in the third example is again taken with the fourth finger and, without changing the position of the hand, you pass from the C through the small seventh to the F.[1] Because, however, the first and second bars can also be played otherwise, I will here set it down for practice.

[[1] *L. M.'s point here is obscure.*]

156 EIGHTH CHAPTER—THIRD SECTION

In the fourth example the first finger is used for the middle and high D♯, to make the ascent easier and to reach the highest note by means of an extension of the fourth finger. As, however, the first finger must be taken on the last note but one, for it is, at the close of the passage, the lower note, so, in stretching upwards with the fourth finger, the hand must in nowise move after it, but the fourth finger be merely extended to the A; the F being taken with the third finger.

§ 8

There are also occasions when the mixed position is indispensable. For example: in double-stopping it is at times unavoidable. Here are examples:

## EIGHTH CHAPTER—THIRD SECTION

### § 9

In double-stopping too the fourth finger is often extended, but the hand remains fixed in its position. For example: (*)

The lower notes are played throughout in the natural position.

### § 10

The first finger is also moved backwards, while the third or fourth finger either remains in its proper place or must in its turn be moved down. For example:

Here the fourth finger remains lying on the upper note.

One must take pains here to place the fourth finger in tune.

The third finger glides down.

## EIGHTH CHAPTER—THIRD SECTION

### § 11

Yea, often two fingers have to be extended without the hand changing. As, for instance in the following two examples, only the second and fourth fingers move out of one position into another, returning immediately afterwards, while the first finger remains ever in its own position.

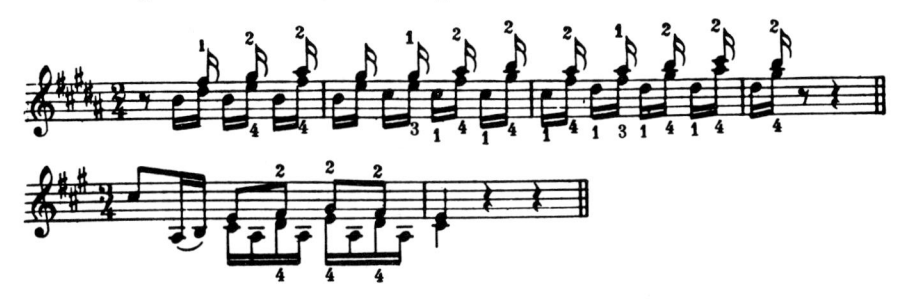

### § 12

With one or two notes in double-stopping the open string can often be used, but to speak the truth it pleases me not greatly. The tone of the open strings contrasts too sharply with that of the stopped notes, and the inequality arising therefrom offends the ears of the listener. Make the experiment yourself. Here is an example:

### § 13

But one avails oneself also of the mixed position for convenience' sake, namely, in order to arrange everything nearer to the hand and to avoid unnecessary ascending and descending. For example:

## EIGHTH CHAPTER—THIRD SECTION

### § 14

Many passages could, it is true, be played straightway without use of the upper position, but they are used for the sake of equality of sound and charm. For example:

The descent could already be made at the note G (*), but not only do you remain up there, but after the descent in the fifth bar you re-ascend in the sixth. The same happens in the seventh and eighth bar. As now from the fourth bar onward everything is played on one string, a pleasing result is obtained owing to the equality of the tone.

### § 15

To this section belongs also that exchange of fingers which in common parlance is called overlapping. One has to avail oneself very frequently of this kind of fingering in double-stopping, or also in rapidly running passages in which notes occur together or follow directly one after the other, which it is true should, according to the position, be taken by the same fingers, but owing to sharps or flats lie so awkwardly that each of them must be played with a separate finger. In such cases the fourth instead of the third finger; the third instead of the second; and the second instead of the first finger is used, the one above the other. From this comes then the word 'overlapping'. They must, however, be played carefully in tune. Here are examples:

## § 16

There are still a few more figures in which occur three notes standing above each other, which must be taken together at the same time and in one stroke. Here even the whole hand frequently has to move backward, below the natural position. Observe the example:

## § 17

These chords consisting of three notes are for the most part subject to the rules of the mixed position. For example:

N.1.

N.2.

The first example is taken throughout the whole passage with the first, second, and fourth fingers. The other two examples at N.1 pass through the mixed position. At N.2, the overlapping of the fingers is used, the which was previously mentioned in § 15. The two examples under N.3 deal with the extension of the fourth finger on which we have already touched in § 9. And finally in example N.4, the first finger is stretched back after the style given in § 10.

§ 18

Now we arrive at yet another style of playing in which one must avail oneself for the most part of the mixed position, namely, those broken chords called Arpeggio,[1] the performance of which, however, is called Arpeggiare. The style of performing these broken chords is partly indicated by the composer; partly carried out by the violinist according to his own good taste. I will here take this opportunity to put down one or two variations which occur to me at the moment. Here they are:

[1] It comes from the word harp (*arpa*). It also means playing Arpeggi (from *arpeggiare*) in a harp-like manner; that is, that the notes be not played together but separately.

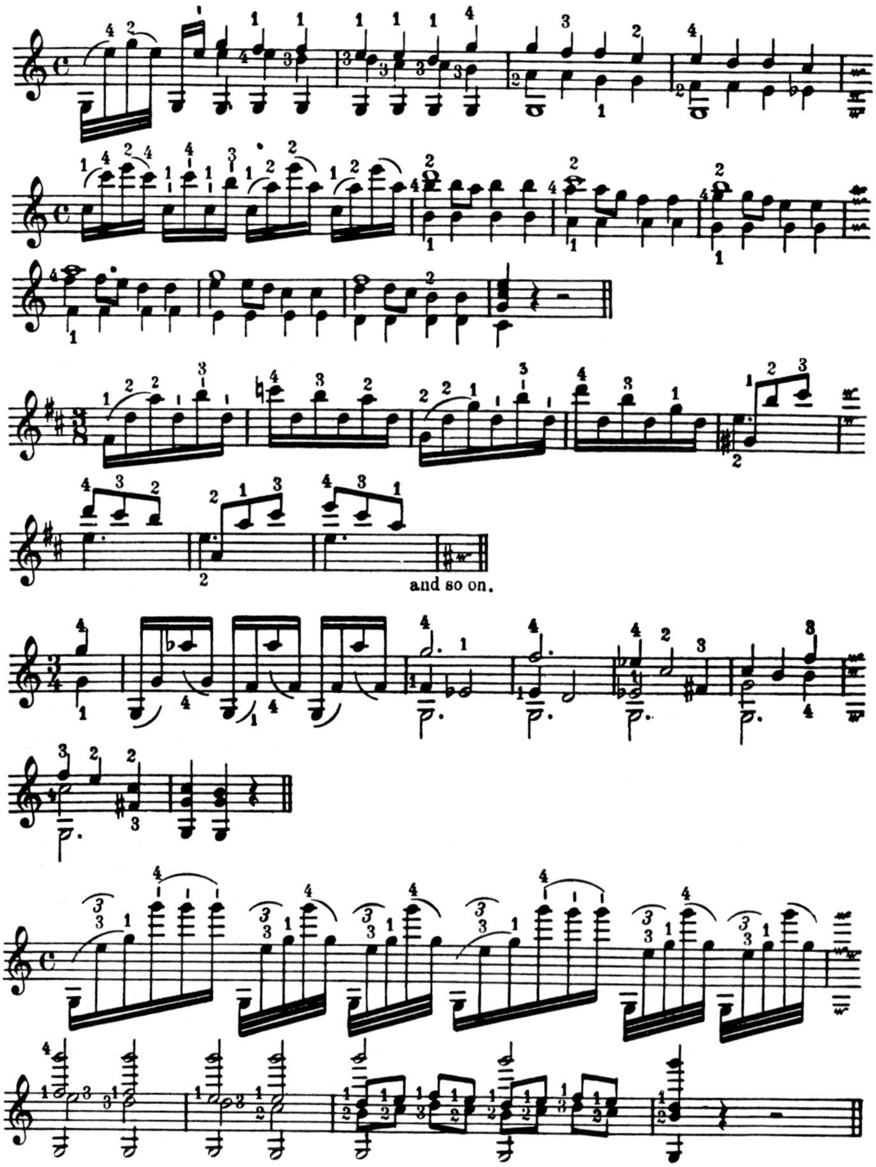
and so on.

## § 19

In these examples are to be found the overlapping of the fingers and the extension and drawing-back of one, or often two fingers simultaneously. Further there is to be found the usual ascent and descent through the mixed position; and finally we find some variations in Arpeggio-playing. As the Arpeggio is indicated in the first bar of each example, so must the following notes, written one above the other, be continued in the same manner. It is true that these few examples are only an outline of all possible variations both of this position and of broken chords, but when a beginner can play these in tune he has laid so good a foundation that he will find little difficulty in playing everything of a similar nature correctly and in tune.

## § 20

In concluding this chapter, I must insert yet another useful observation, of which a violinist can make use in playing double-stopping, and which will help him to play with good tone, strongly, and in tune. It is irrefutable that a string, when struck or bowed, sets in motion another string tuned in unison with it.[1] This, however, is not enough. I have proved that on the violin, when playing two notes simultaneously, the third, now the fifth, now even the octave, and so on, make themselves heard of their own accord in addition thereto and on the same instrument. This serves then as undeniable proof, which everyone can test for himself,

---

[1] That this was a matter already known to the Ancients, Aristides Quintilianus tells us in his Lib. 2 *de Musica* in these words: 'Si quis enim in alteram ex duabus Chordis eundem Sonum edentibus parvam imponat ac levem stipulam: alteram autem longius inde tentam pulset, videbit Chordam stipula onustam evidentissime una moveri.' Still another test can be made. Hang a stringed-instrument, the strings of which are not stretched too tightly, near an organ, and if the notes to which the open strings of the string-instrument are tuned be touched on the organ, those strings will immediately, although not touched, sound also, or will at least show a strong movement. Or on a violin, not too thickly strung and tuned rather low, play the G with the third finger on the D string, and the open G string will at once vibrate of its own accord.

if he be able to play the notes in tune and correctly. For if two notes, as I will indicate below, be so to speak drawn well and rightly out of the violin, one will be able at the same moment to hear the lower voice quite clearly, but as a muffled and droning sound. If on the contrary the notes be played out of tune, and one or the other be stopped even in the slightest degree too high or too low, then will the lower voice be false. Try it patiently, and he who cannot succeed at all therein, let him begin by playing also the black fundamental note and hold the violin nearer to the ear; then will he, while playing the two upper notes, hear this lower black note droning in addition. The nearer the violin is held to the ear, the more the stroke may be moderated. But above all, the violin must be well strung and well tuned. Here are a few proofs thereof. It can be seen herefrom how powerful is the harmonic triad (*trias harmonica*). For example: if two notes lie a minor third apart, the major third or tenth is heard in addition below. They produce therefore a concordant triad.

When, on the contrary, the two notes make a major third, the octave to the lower note is to be heard.

If the two notes lie a perfect fourth asunder, the fifth to the lower note will be heard.

If the two notes be a minor sixth apart, one hears the major third or tenth.

With the major sixths, the lower fifth is heard.

It is heard still more clearly if a few double-stoppings be played directly after each other, for then the interchange of these droning tones strikes the ear more sharply. For example:

CHAPTER IX

# Of the Appoggiature, and some Embellishments belonging thereto

§ 1

THE Appoggiature[1] are little notes which stand between the ordinary notes but are not reckoned as part of the bar-time. They are demanded by Nature herself to bind the notes together, thereby making a melody more song-like. I say by Nature herself, for it is undeniable that even a peasant closes his peasant-song with grace-notes [music] for, after all, it only means fundamentally [music]. Nature herself forces him to do this. In the same way the simplest peasant often uses figures of speech and metaphors without knowing it. The appoggiature are sometimes dissonances;[2] sometimes a repetition of the previous note; sometimes an embellishing of a simple melody and an enlivening of a sleepy phrase; and finally they are that which binds the performance together.

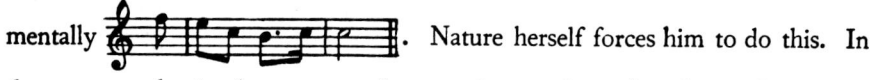

Here is now a rule without an exception: The appoggiatura is never separated from its main note, but is taken at all times in the same stroke. That the following

[[1] *Appoggiatura (German: Vorschlag)* meaning '*Fore-beat*' *or suspended note.*]
[2] To him who knows not what a dissonance is, I will say that I will first tell him of the consonances. The consonances are the unison, the large third and the small third, the fifth, the sixth, and the eighth. The dissonances are all the other intervals, which can be looked up in § 5 of Chapter III. The division of the consonances and dissonances and all the rest belongs to the art of composing.

## NINTH CHAPTER

and not the preceding note belongs to the appoggiatura will be understood from the word *Vorschlag*.

### § 2

There are both descending and ascending appoggiature, which, however, are divided into accentuated appoggiature and passing appoggiature. The descending appoggiature are the most natural, for according to the most correct rules of composition they possess the true nature of an appoggiatura. For example:

### § 3

The descending appoggiature are of two kinds: namely, the Long and the Short. Of the long there are two kinds, of which one is longer than the other. If the appoggiatura stands before a crotchet, quaver, or semiquaver, it is played as a long appoggiatura and is worth half of the value of the note following it. The appoggiatura is therefore sustained the length of time equivalent to half the note and is slurred smoothly on to it. What the note loses is given to the appoggiatura. Here are examples:

**Is played thus:**

It is true that all the descending appoggiature could be set down in large print and divided up within the bar. But if a violinist, who knows not that the appoggiatura is written out, or who is already accustomed to befrill every note, happens on such, how will it fare with melody as well as with harmony? I will wager that such a violinist will add yet another long appoggiatura and will play it thus:

which can surely never sound natural but only exaggerated and confused.[1] It is a great pity that beginners acquire this fault so readily.

## § 4

The second kind of the long appoggiature which may be called the longer appoggiature are found firstly before dotted notes; secondly before minims if they occur at the beginning of a bar in $\frac{3}{4}$ time; or if in $\frac{2}{4}$ time or $\frac{4}{4}$ time only one, or at the most two occur, of which one is marked with an appoggiatura. In such cases the appoggiatura is held longer. With dotted notes the appoggiatura is held the same length of time as the value of the note. In place of the dot, however, the written note is taken first, and in such fashion as if a dot stood after it. Then the bow is lifted and the last note played so late that, by means of a rapid change of stroke, the note following it is heard immediately after.

Thus is it written:

So is it played:

If, however, one desires to play a minim with an appoggiatura in the above-mentioned two examples, then the appoggiatura receives three parts of the minim note, and only at the fourth part is the note of the minim taken. For example:

[1] Neu desis Operae, neve immoderatus abundes. Horat. Lib. III. Sat. V.

Thus is it written:

So is it played:

### § 5

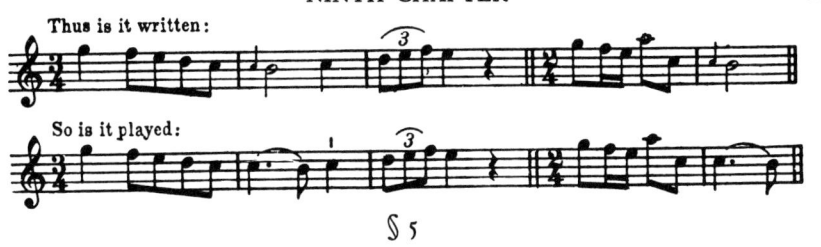

There are yet other cases in which the longer appoggiatura is used, but these all belong to the same subject of how to play dotted notes. For example, in $^6_4$ and $^6_8$ time two notes are often tied together as one note, of which the foremost has a dot after it. In such cases the appoggiatura is held out the whole value represented by the note together with the dot. For example:

Thus is it written:

And so it is played:

Just in the same manner is the appoggiatura in the following example sustained throughout the whole of the first crotchet and only at the second crotchet is the principal note taken; the remaining notes being then played immediately after it. This is, however, not always feasible with the minims, as we shall see with the short appoggiatura.

So is it written:

So is it played:

And sometimes a rest or even a pause occurs, when the note should surely still be heard. If now the composer has overlooked this, the violinist must be more clever and must sustain the appoggiatura as long as the value of the following note, and only at the pause bring in the written note. For example:

**Thus should it be written and also thus played.**

But thereto belongs either insight in composition or sound judgement, and these, my precepts, refer chiefly to playing alone; for in pieces of several parts the composer could, on account of the progression of the lower or middle voice, require it to be played thus:

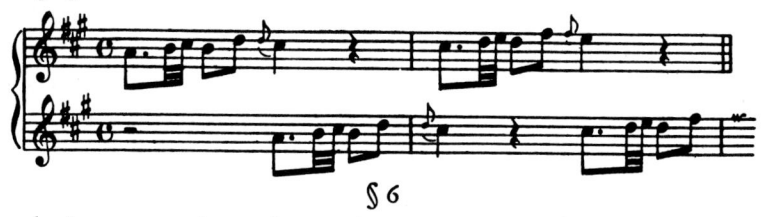

§ 6

But the long appoggiature do not always arise out of the previous note. They can also be used freely. For example:

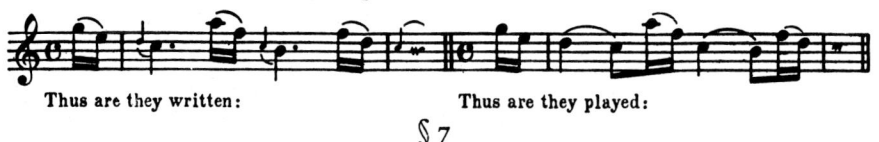

**Thus are they written:**        **Thus are they played:**

§ 7

Neither do they always come from the neighbouring note but from all degrees. And here they make[1] the figure of a suspension on the previous note.

[1] This is, it is true, Figura Retardationis, but the first example is also a repetition which must be reckoned among the Figures of Rhetoric, and called by their right name: 'Anaphora'.

## § 8

Above all things must be observed: firstly, that for the descending appoggiature the open string must never be used, but that when an appoggiatura occurs on such a note, the same must always be taken with the fourth finger on the next lower string. Secondly, the accent must, in the long and longer appoggiature, always be on the appoggiatura itself, the softer tone falling on the melody note. But this must be carried out with a pleasant moderating of the stroke. Also the accent must have a softer tone preceding it. In the long appoggiatura, of which we speak here, it is quite easy to accent somewhat gently, letting the tone grow rapidly in strength and arriving at the greatest volume of tone in the middle of the appoggiatura; but then so diminishing the strength, that finally the chief note is slurred on to it quite *piano*. In particular, however, beware of after-pressure of the bow on the chief note. Only the finger with which the appoggiatura is made is to be lifted, while the bow is allowed to move smoothly on its way.

## § 9

Now there be also short appoggiature with which the stress falls not on the appoggiatura but on the principal note. The short appoggiatura is made as rapidly as possible and is not attacked strongly, but quite softly. The short appoggiatura is used: (1) when several minims follow each other, of which each is marked with a little appoggiatura note; (2) or if at times only one minim be present which, however, occurs in such a passage as is imitated immediately by a second voice in the fourth above, or in the fifth below; (3) or else if it be foreseen that the regular harmony, and therefore also the ear of the listener, would be offended by the use of a long appoggiatura; (4) and finally, if in an allegro or other playful tempo, notes descend in consecutive degrees or even in thirds, each being preceded by an appoggiatura; in which case the appoggiatura is played quickly in order not to rob the piece of its liveliness by the long-sustained appoggiatura. Here follow the examples, where the use of the long appoggiatura would make the style of performance much too sluggish.

In these suspended sevenths, indeed, one should move from the appoggiatura to the principal note only at the quaver (*), as has been said in § 5: but if there be a second voice the result pleases me not at all. For firstly, the seventh occurs with the principal note, and has not its proper preparation; although perhaps someone might say that the ear will be deceived by the chromatic of the appoggiatura and, by means of this delay, will still be pleased by it as a charming suspension; secondly, the notes in the first half of the bar sound so offensive together that if they be not played right quickly, the dissonance will be intolerable to the ear. For example:

§ 10

The ascending appoggiature are in general not as natural as the descending, particularly those which originate from the next note, and that a whole tone, for they are always[1] dissonances. But who does not know that dissonances must not be resolved upwards but downwards?[2] It is therefore reasonable if a few passing

[1] See Ed. *1787*—'*mostly* dissonances'.
[2] *The following footnote is added here in the edition of 1787*: 'When the bass-part remains always on the same note one need not, it is true, proceed so carefully but can introduce all ascending grace-notes.'

notes be added which please the ear by the right resolution of the dissonances and improve both melody and harmony. For example:

*[musical notation: Thus is it written. / So is it played. / The regular resolution of the dissonance. / The bass-part.]*

In this fashion the stress falls on the first note of the appoggiatura, and the two little notes, together with the following principal note, are slurred smoothly thereon as taught in § 8. But here too there must be no after-pressure of the bow on the principal note.

### § 11

It is frequently the custom to make the ascending appoggiatura from the third below, even if it should appear to flow from the neighbouring note. But in such cases one makes it mostly with two notes. For example:

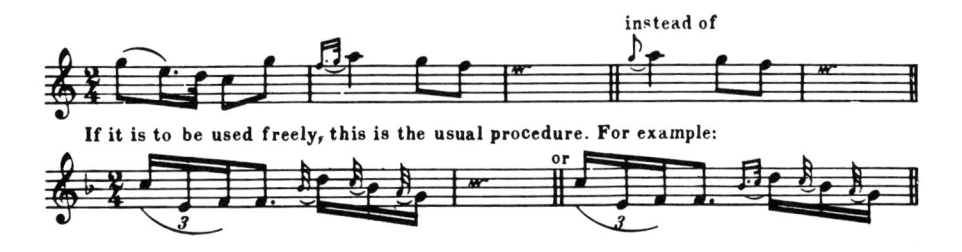

*[musical notation with "instead of"]*

If it is to be used freely, this is the usual procedure. For example:

*[musical notation with "or"]*

The first note of this appoggiatura of the third with two notes is dotted, whereas the second is shortened. And just so must this appoggiatura be played. Namely

## NINTH CHAPTER

the first note must be sustained somewhat longer, but the other, together with the principal note, must be slurred smoothly on to it without after-pressure of the bow.[1]

§ 12

An appoggiatura of two notes can also be made between two neighbouring notes if the note above the principal note be added.[2] Here are the examples:

§ 13

If one desires to make an ascending appoggiatura of only one note and up to the one lying next to it, it sounds well if it be raised to a semitone below the principal note. For example:

For the same reason it sounds very well before a concluding note. For example:

---

[1] See *Translator's Appendix*, p. 232.

[2] *The following is added here in the edition of 1787*: 'From this style of ascending appoggiature arise the so-called Anschläge, which even repeat the distant note; only then softly taking the note above the principal note and slurring both on to the principal note.'

*After the illustration, the edition of 1787 concludes with the following paragraph*: 'But it must be well observed that the Anschlag of two equal notes in examples 1 and 3 is played softly and only the principal note played strongly; while in the dotted Anschlag in examples 2 and 4, on the contrary, the dotted note is played louder, sustained longer, and the short note is slurred softly on to the principal note.'

And the major seventh, accompanied by the second and fourth, fits in well with the ascending half-tone appoggiatura and makes a good impression on the mood of the listener; in particular, if the appoggiature be placed also in the other parts and be observed with exactitude while performing them. For example:

But the augmented fifth is added thereto; justifying the use of the half-tone appoggiatura. For example:

But let it not be forgotten that the stress must fall on the appoggiatura and the softer tone on the principal note, which manner of appoggiatura has been explained in § 8.

§ 14

Reason and hearing convince us therefore that a long appoggiatura consisting of a rising whole tone, played as it is written, rarely sounds well, but that the semitone appoggiatura always does so—because, whether it flows from the major third, the three-toned fourth,[1] or the augmented sixth; or through the augmented fifth, the augmented second, or through the major seventh; it is resolved according to rule. He exposes the slightness of his acquaintance with the rules of composition, who writes an ascending whole-tone appoggiatura in a passage which more

[1 *Tritone*.]

naturally leads him downwards, and where everyone, without explicit indication, would of his own accord make a descending appoggiatura. For example:

Now is this not, so to speak, a case of dragging the ascending appoggiatura right clumsily 'by the hair'?—when it should surely conform itself to nature, thus:

For the appoggiature are not invented to cause confusion and harshness of performance, but rather are they intended to bind it properly together, thereby making it smoother, more melodious, and more pleasing to the ear.

§ 15

Ascending appoggiature, too, are often taken from distant lying notes, as also happens with descending appoggiature, of which § 7 has spoken. Here is an example:

Retardatio

Anaphora

Here, too, the stress always falls on the appoggiatura and it is performed according to the instruction given in § 8.

§ 16

Now these were purely Anschlag appoggiature which the composer must indicate, or at least should and can indicate, if he desires to have reasonable hope of a good performance of the pieces he has written. And even then many a good composition is martyred miserably. Now we come to the passing appoggiature, intermediate appoggiature, and other similar ornamentations in which the stress falls on the principal note, and which are rarely or never indicated by the composer. They are therefore such ornamentations as the violinist must know how to apply in the right place according to his own sound judgement. They follow here.

§ 17

The first are the passing appoggiature. These appoggiature do not belong to the time of the principal note to which they descend but must be played in the time of the preceding note. It is true, one could indicate the style by means of a little note, but it would look very unusual and strange. He who wishes to express it in print, sets it down in properly distributed notes. It is customary to use these passing appoggiature in a series of notes lying a third apart. For example:

Without embellishment.   Thus could it be written.

But they are played thus, and are better written so.   down up   down

The semiquaver is taken quite smoothly and quietly, the stress always falling on the quaver.

§ 18

The passing appoggiature can also be used with notes which ascend or descend by conjunct degrees. For example:

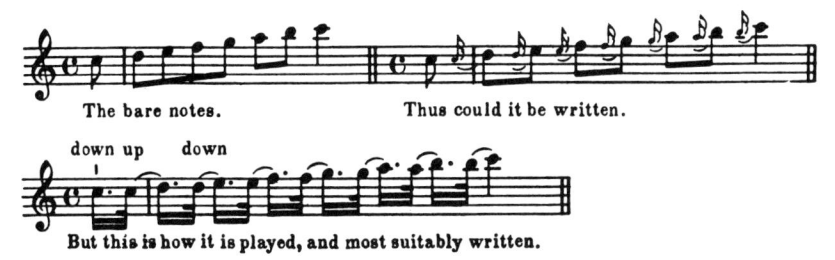

The bare notes.   Thus could it be written.

down up   down

But this is how it is played, and most suitably written.

## NINTH CHAPTER

*Without embellishment.*     *The manner of indicating how to perform it.*

*Thus is it played, and also best written.*

§ 19

To the passing appoggiature belong also those improvised ornamentations which I will call 'uebersteigende and untersteigende Zwischen-Schläge'[1] They occur between the appoggiatura and the principal note, descending quite smoothly from the appoggiatura to the principal note. See here their form and origin. Here are those which descend:

*The foundation thereof.*

*With the Appoggiatura written out.*

*Embellished with the Zwischenschlägen.*

*Thus must it be played.*

If one desires, however, to play it still better and very vivaciously, one must attack the first note of each crotchet strongly and slur the remaining notes smoothly on to it; dotting the last note but one; bringing the last one late; and taking each crotchet in one stroke. For example:

[1 *These may be translated as rising and falling Intermediate Grace-notes.*]

# NINTH CHAPTER

## § 20

The ascending Zwischenschläge are played in the same manner and the same rules must be observed. For example:

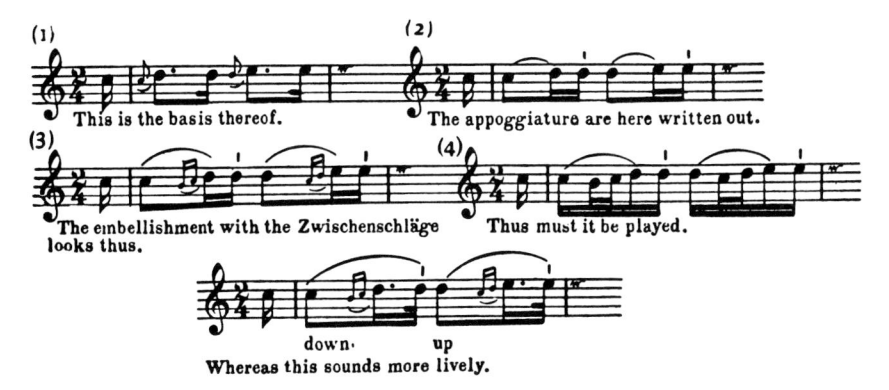

(1) This is the basis thereof.
(2) The appoggiature are here written out.
(3) The embellishment with the Zwischenschläge looks thus.
(4) Thus must it be played.

down. up
Whereas this sounds more lively.

That these ascending Zwischenschläge come to the aid of the appoggiatura which ascends a whole tone, we know from § 10.

## § 21

It is clear as daylight that a violinist must know well how to decide whether the composer has intended any ornamentation, and if so, what kind. We see it as clearly as the sun, in the examples of § 19 and § 20. For how badly would it sound if the violinist were to honour the appoggiature, written down by the composer and divided up into the bar, by adding yet another descending long appoggiatura. That is, for instance:

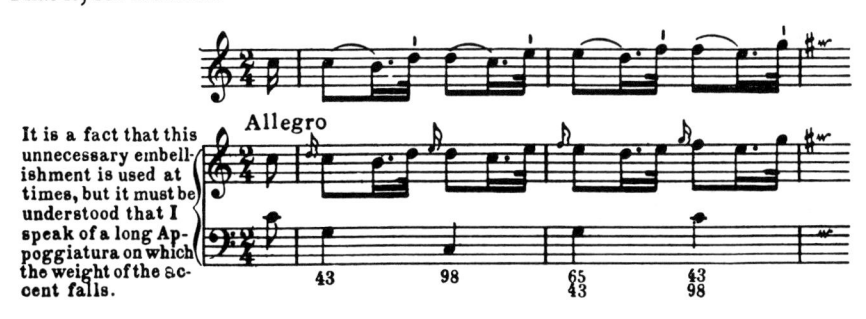

It is a fact that this unnecessary embellishment is used at times, but it must be understood that I speak of a long Appoggiatura on which the weight of the accent falls.

Allegro
43   98   65/43   43/98

Those unmusicianly violinists who wish to befrill each note, can see here the reason why a sensible composer is indignant when the notes set down by him are not played as they are written. In the present examples the descending appoggiature are written down and divided into the bar. They are dissonances which resolve themselves beautifully and naturally, as we see from the lower voice and the numbers written below it, which we will call by their real name: the Signatures.[1] Who then does not grasp with both hands at the fact that it is a pitiful mistake to spoil the natural appoggiatura with yet another long appoggiatura—if one omits the dissonance which has already been prepared according to rule, and plays in its stead an unsuitable note—yea, if one actually throws the stress of the tone on the unnecessary additional appoggiatura, and in addition to this, quietly slurs the dissonance together with the resolution thereof; seeing that the dissonance should surely sound strongly and only lose itself by degrees in the resolution?

But how can the pupil help it if the teacher himself knows no better; and if indeed the teacher himself plays at random without knowing what he does. Yet in spite of this, such a haphazard player often calls himself a composer. Enough!—let us make no embellishments, or only such as spoil neither the harmony nor melody. And in pieces where more than one play from the same part, take all notes in such manner as the composer has prescribed. Finally, learn to read well before trying to take liberties with embellishments, for many a one can play a half-dozen concertos in a wonderfully neat and finished manner; but when it comes to having to play something straight off, he is unable to perform three bars according to the composer's intention, even if the style of performance be indicated in the most exact manner.[2]

§ 22

There are still some embellishments belonging to this chapter, of which I will call one the Ueberwurf, another the Rückfall or Abfall, the third the Doppelschlag,

[1] *Signatures = numbers and signs of a figured bass.*]

[2] I am zealous for the purity of style of performance. Be therefore not offended with me that I speak the truth. 'Quid verum atque decens curo, & rogo, & omnis in hoc sum.' Horat.

the fourth the Half-triller, and the fifth the Nachschlag. The Ueberwurf is a note which is slurred quite quietly on to the note preceding the appoggiatura. This Ueberwurf is always made upwards; sometimes on to the note above, sometimes on to the third, fourth, and so on; and also on to other notes. It is used partly in order thereby to exchange the rising appoggiatura for the falling, as a better kind of appoggiatura, but also partly to make a note more lively. For example:[1]

The bare notes.

With the rising and falling appoggiatura

The first note must be played thus with an Ueberwurf.

Not only is the performance made thereby more animated, but one sees also that both harmony and melody are improved; the former by a regular phrase; the latter by a singing style. Compare it with the lower part, where one will find that by means of the Ueberwurf the regular preparation for the seventh or the sixth and so on is made; namely, according to the bass used. For example:

[1] *In the edition of 1787, the paragraph continues as follows:*

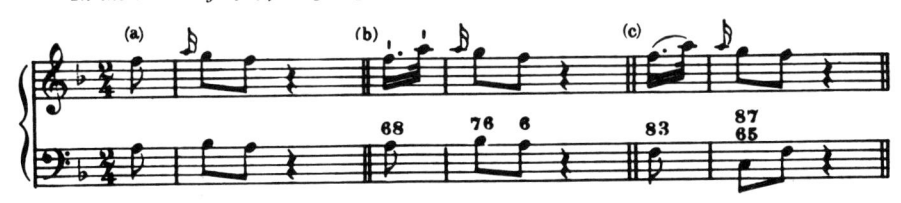

'The example (*a*) shows us the falling appoggiatura. In example (*b*) we see that the performance becomes more lively, and in example (*c*) more *cantabile*; but in particular we shall also find in the changed lower part (*b*) the regular preparation of the seventh, and in (*c*) the preparation of the sixth.

'One can also make this Ueberwurf on the note next to it, and also on more distant notes. I will here set down a few(\*):'

*[Here follows the concluding illustration of § 22.]*

One can also make this Ueberwurf on the note next to it, and on other notes. I will here set down a few (*):

§ 23

The Ueberwurf, however, does not please me at all if the upper voice moves with the bass from the large third into the perfect fifth. For out of this arise two fifths which, as you know, are banished from good music. For example:

It is true that a long appoggiatura from E to the semitone D can obscure it to some extent; but it pleases me better thus:

## NINTH CHAPTER

### § 24

Just as the Ueberwurf rises, so in the same manner the Rückfall or Abfall falls to the note next to the one following it, or to the appoggiatura following it. This occurs when the note standing immediately before the appoggiatura is so remote, or is placed so dryly or dully that by means of this embellishment the figures may be made to hang better together or made more lively. For example:

*Thus can it be played.*

One descends to the next note above the appoggiatura, or even on to the note of the appoggiatura itself in order to make a preparation for the dissonance. For example:

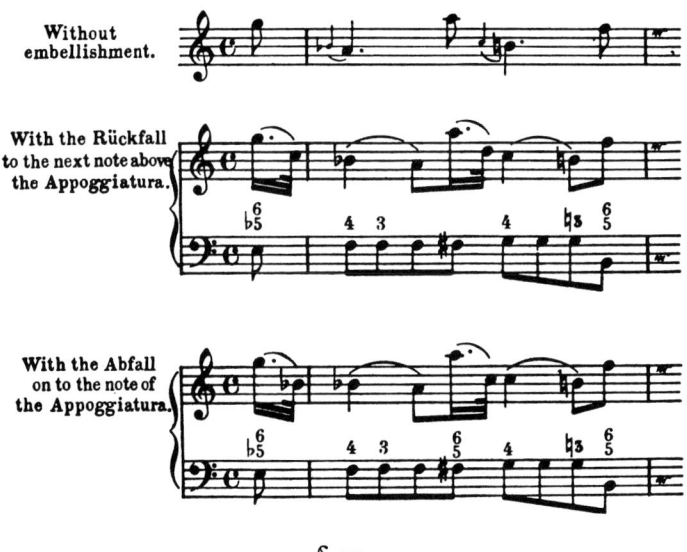

Without embellishment.

With the Rückfall to the next note above the Appoggiatura.

With the Abfall on to the note of the Appoggiatura.

### § 25

One can always make an Abfall on to the descending appoggiatura itself. But on to the next note above the same it is not always possible. It depends on the bass note. For example:

If one made an Abfall from the first note on to D; for example: [music]; it would be in truth the Rückfall to the next note above the appoggiatura, but it would sound very feeble against the bass note C, and spoil both melody and harmony. At the second note, namely at the * D it is, on the other hand, very good; because the Rückfall to G makes the sixth to the bass note. Now just as in order not to spoil the harmony one must fall from the first note not to D, but to C, that is to the note of the appoggiatura, so one may descend also from the second note to the imperfect fifth, namely, to F, in order thereby to make the preparation for the perfect fourth. Now let everyone decide for himself whether for an orderly manner of playing, either insight into composition or an uncommonly good natural judgement be not necessary.

## § 26

The Doppelschlag is an embellishment of four rapid little notes, which occur between the ascending appoggiatura and the note following it, and which are attached to the appoggiatura. The accent falls on the appoggiatura; on the turn the tone diminishes, and the softer tone occurs on the principal note. We shall see in the example how to apply the turn.

## NINTH CHAPTER

### § 27[1]

The Doppelschlag is exactly the same in appearance, except that it is inverted. It is used between the appoggiatura and the principal note, but is played so rapidly that it sounds exactly like the beginning of a trill; whence its name. Here too the accent falls on the appoggiatura, the remainder diminishing in tone. Here is an example:

With only an Appoggiatura.

With the half-trill.

Thus must it be played.

### § 28

Now, for the close of this chapter, I will name yet another kind of embellishment belonging hereto, which I will call Nachschläge. These are a couple of rapid little notes which one can hang on to the principal note; in order, in slow pieces, to enliven the performance. For example:

Without embellishment.

With the Ueberwurf and the turns written out in notation.

Played thus.

These Nachschläge, Zwischenschläge and all the passing Appoggiature and Ornamentations given here must in no way be strongly attacked, but slurred smoothly on to their principal note; in which they differ wholly from the anschlagende appoggiature which are accented; and in only one particular are they alike—namely, that they are slurred in the same stroke on to the principal note.

[1] *See Translator's Appendix*, p. 233.

## CHAPTER X

# On the Trill

### § 1

THE trill is a common and pleasing alternation of two neighbouring notes which are either a whole-tone or a half-tone apart. The trill therefore is mainly of two kinds: namely the major second and the minor second. They err who would distinguish[1] the trill of the minor second with the word trilletto, from the trill of the major second called the trill (trillo); for surely trilletto means only a short trill, but trillo means at all times a trill, whether it be made with a whole or a half-tone.

### § 2

That the note on which a trill is to be applied is marked with the little letter (*t.*),[2] we know from the third section of the first chapter. Now one must press down strongly the finger with which one plays such a note marked with the (*t.*), and play with the next finger the neighbouring higher note of a whole or a half-tone, letting the finger fall and lift in such wise that these two notes are always heard alternately. For example: . Here the first finger is held down strongly and immovably on B, while the second or trilling finger lifts and falls quite lightly on the pure note C; which must be practised quite slowly thus:

### § 3

But as the trill is made with either the major or the minor second, exact attention must be given to the key of the piece.[3] Neglect herein is a shameful fault of which

---

[1] *In Edition 1787 it reads*: 'And I cannot see why some distinguish. . . .'
[2] *In Edition 1787* = (*tr.*).
[3] *Added in Edition 1787*: 'and the additional modulations to the incidental keys.'

# TENTH CHAPTER

many are guilty, who not only never look whether they have to trill with the major or minor second; but make the trill haphazard either on the third or even on an intermediate note. The trill must be played neither higher nor lower than the key of the piece demands. For example:

*With the major second, or whole-tone trill.*

*With the minor second, or half-tone trill.*

## § 4

There is only one case where it seems as if the trill might be made out of the minor third or augmented second, and a great Italian master[1] teaches his pupils thus. But in such case it is better if the trill be wholly omitted and in its place a different embellishment be used. For example:

Adagio

Here it sounds very feeble.    Is better without a trill with a different embellishment.

I do not indeed see at all why, in this case, the trill should not be made with the pure, natural D. Make the experiment yourself.

## § 5

The beginning and the end of a trill can be made in various ways. It can begin at once from the upper note downwards. For example:

[1 *This was Tartini.*]

188  TENTH CHAPTER

But it can also be prepared by a descending appoggiatura which is suspended rather longer; or by an ascending appoggiatura with an Ueberwurf or some such zurückschlagende movement, which is called Ribattuta and which it is customary to use at the close of a cadenza, where one may never bind oneself to strict time.

The preparation by means of the descending appoggiatura.

By means of the ascending appoggiatura with Ueberwurf.

By means of the Ribatutta or Zurückschlag.

§ 6

In the same way one can either close simply with the trill or with an embellishment:

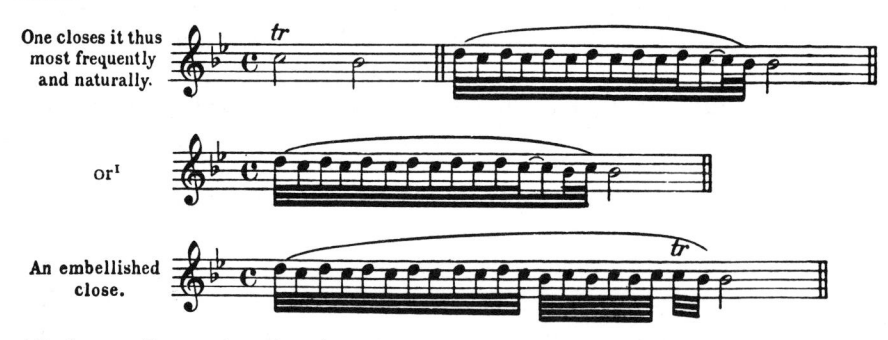

One closes it thus most frequently and naturally.

or[1]

An embellished close.

All short trills are played with a quick appoggiatura and a turn. For example:

[1] *Edition 1787 reads*: 'or with the Nachschlag.'

## § 7

The trill can be divided into four species according to its speed: namely into slow, medium, rapid, and accelerating. The slow is used in sad and slow pieces; the medium in pieces which have a lively but yet a moderate and gentle tempo, the rapid in pieces which are very lively and full of spirit and movement, and finally the accelerating trill is used mostly in cadenzas. This last is usually adorned with *piano* and *forte*, for it is most beautiful when performed in the manner given here:

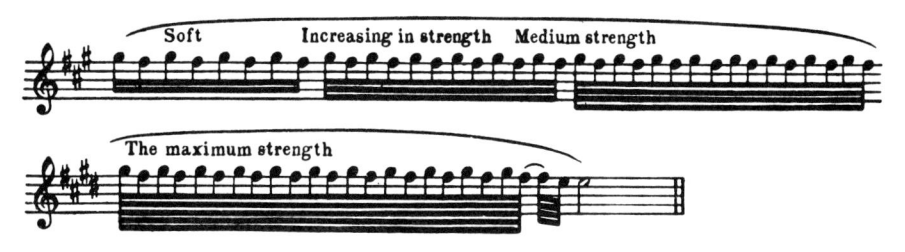

## § 8

The trill must above all things not be played too rapidly, for otherwise it becomes unintelligible and bleating, or a so-called 'Goat's trill'. Further, one can play a more rapid trill on the finer and higher-tuned strings than on the thick and low-pitched strings, since the latter move slowly, while the former move very rapidly. And finally, when one plays solo, attention must be given to the place in which it is intended to perform the pieces. In a small place, which is perhaps also carpeted, upholstered, and curtained or in which the listeners are too near, a rapid trill will have a better effect. On the other hand, if one plays in a large hall which is very resonant or the listeners are fairly far away, it is better to make a slow trill.

## § 9

Above all, one must accustom oneself to make a long trill with a restrained bow. For it often happens that a long note marked with a trill has to be sustained, and it would be just as illogical to change the bow and disconnect it as it would be if a singer took a breath in the middle of a long note.[1] There is nothing in worse taste

---

[1] *The following footnote is added here in the 1787 edition*: 'It is true that everything can become a matter of fashion, and I have actually seen some who, in the Cadenza-trill, change the bow several times in order to make a horribly long trill, and to receive thereby a bravo. This pleases me not.'

than in a cadenza, where one is not tied to strict time, to break off the trill so abruptly and unexpectedly that the ears of the listeners are more offended than entertained. In such case the ear is bereft of something and one remains in consequence displeased, because a longer sustaining of the trill was expected; just as it surely hurts the listeners sorely if they are aware that a singer is short of breath. On the other hand, nothing is more laughable than a trill held beyond bounds. Therefore the middle road must be chosen, and a trill must be made which comes closest to good taste.

§ 10

All the fingers must, by means of honest practice of the trill, be made equally strong and dexterous. This cannot be achieved more quickly than by practising the trill through all tones, and especially by not allowing the fourth finger to be idle. This finger, because it is the weakest and shortest, must by unremittingly earnest practice be made stronger, a little longer, more expert, and more useful. A trill is never made between the first finger and the open string, with the exception of the double-trill of which we shall hear later, where naught else can be done. With the simple trill, the second finger is always taken on the next lower string in the whole position instead of the open string. For example:

§ 11

One must know how to apply the appoggiatura both before and after the trill, in the right place, and of appropriate length or brevity. If a trill occurs in the middle of a passage; for example:

then not only is an appoggiatura made before the trill, but the appoggiatura is held through half the value of the note, while the trill [with the turn] is not begun till the other half, as given here:

But if a passage begins with a trill the appoggiatura is hardly heard, and is in such case naught but a strong attack on the trill. For example:

### § 12

The note following directly after a trill must never be preceded by an appoggiatura. In a formal cadenza, especially one occurring at the end of a piece, and one which, without binding oneself to strictness of time, can be played according to one's pleasure, an appoggiatura is never made after the trill in a full close, even if afterwards the note descend from the fifth downwards, or ascend from the major third upwards. For example:

### § 13

In the long, descending intermediate cadences, too, it is always better by means of a few little notes which are slurred on to the trill as a turn, and which are played somewhat slowly, to fall directly to the closing note rather than make the performance sleepy by playing an appoggiatura before the closing note. But I speak of long, not of short notes, to which at all times the appoggiatura can be applied. Here are long intermediate cadences:

192    TENTH CHAPTER

It sounds, however, more beautiful and *cantabile* if to the last of the two little turn-notes a passing appoggiatura be given, which is slurred smoothly on to it. For example:

§ 14

On the other hand, in the long, ascending intermediate cadences one must enter into the closing note immediately at the close of the trill; or one must make the turn with two short notes only and then make an appoggiatura of two notes from the third upwards; which is to be seen from the bass note.

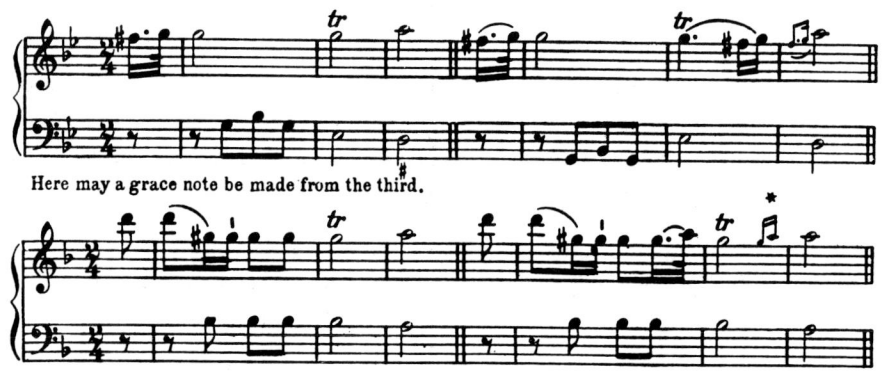

Here may a grace note be made from the third.

Here must one apply at the end of the trill an anticipation or forestalling of the concluding note.(*)

§ 15

Now I admit that some rules should be given, when and where to make the trills. But after all, who could instantly remember all the possible occasions which may arise in so many kinds of melody? I will, however, attempt it and here set down some rules.

As a principal rule it must be well observed, never to begin a melody with a trill if it be not expressly written down, or if some special expression be not demanded.

# TENTH CHAPTER

193

Here it is wrong if one begins with the trill.

But here it is right.

## § 16

Above all, do not overload the notes with trills. In the case of many quavers following each other step by step, or of semiquavers, be they slurred or detached, the trill[1] can always be brought in on the first of a pair. In such cases the trill occurs on the first, third, fifth, seventh notes of the bar, and so on. For example:

down up

But if the trill begins outside the bar on the note of the up stroke, then the trill comes on the second, fourth, sixth notes of the bar, and so on. This style of performance sounds still more effective if it be played, as it should be, with separate strokes. This, however, is used only in lively pieces.[2]

down up down up down up down up    down    up

## § 17

If four notes are shown, of which the first is detached and the other three are slurred together, the trill comes[1] on the middle note of the slurred three. For example:

up down up    down up

[1] *In 1787 edition is added* 'without a turn'.
[2] *The following is added in the 1787 edition*: 'and all these trills are without turns'.

## TENTH CHAPTER

### § 18

The first of four equal notes can be differentiated from the others by the trill [without an appoggiatura], if the first two be slurred together in one stroke, each of the other two being played with separate strokes. For example:

### § 19

If one desires to perform dotted notes without an appoggiatura, one can insert a little trill at each dot.[1]

### § 20

But also with dotted notes, either the first or last can be played with a trill without a turn. For example:

This style of performance belongs only to the instrumental melodies.

In the first example it is customary not to play each note separately, but to take each crotchet in one stroke, but in such fashion that on the dot the bow is lifted and the short note is taken at the end of the bow just before the change and in the same

---

[1] If one desires to perform dotted notes without an appoggiatura, one can, in a slow tempo, insert a little trill at each dot.—*Edition 1787.*

bow. But in the second example the bow must leave the violin wholly at the dot, as I will here make clear. For example:

down up  down up  down up  down up

§ 21

Among the embellishments of which one avails oneself nowadays, one sees also ascending and descending trills, most of which have already been indicated. These are a sequence of progressively ascending and descending notes, of which each is ornamented with a trill. Attention must be given to the following: firstly, that all the notes be taken in one stroke, or, if there be too many, that the bow must be changed at the beginning of the bar; or, in common time, changed at the third crotchet. Secondly, that the bow must never leave the violin entirely, but that the trilling notes must be carried through evenly by means of a scarcely noticeable accent. Thirdly, that the co-operation of the bow and the moving of the fingers must be so unanimous that they not only progress always together but also that the trill never weakens, for the open strings would otherwise be heard in between.

The finger with which the note is stopped is therefore left throughout on the string; the whole hand moves after it, and the notes are bound well together. The finger on the contrary, with which the trill is made, is lifted continuously and lightly.

§ 22

These ascending and descending trills can be made with either the first or second fingers, [but always without a turn]. For example:

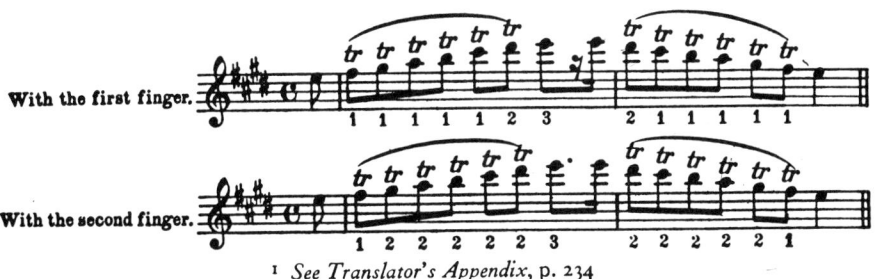

With the first finger.

1 1 1 1 2 3   2 1 1 1 1

With the second finger.

1 2 2 2 2 3   2 2 2 2 1

[1] See *Translator's Appendix*, p. 234

## TENTH CHAPTER

### § 23

But one must also know how to play them with a change of finger. For example:

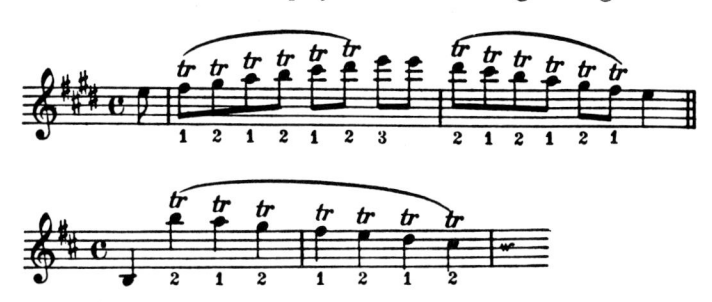

And in this way a right useful study of the ascending and descending trills can be practised through all the scales and with changes of fingers on all four strings, up and down. Yea, I would recommend such a useful exercise very earnestly to a pupil.

### § 24

But it is also necessary that the ascent and descent through the semitones be learnt. For example:

Here the second and first fingers (*) must change imperceptibly both in moving down and moving up; but the trilling finger must continue to rise and fall.

### § 25

With notes lying far apart, it is true, one can always continue with a trill, but it is rarely possible in a lively allegro, and then only as a rule in cadenzas. Here are some examples to practise.[1]

---

[1] *The following paragraph concludes Par. 25 in the 1787 edition*: These continuous trills through notes lying far apart are better made with the turn. And the rising and falling trills indicated in paragraphs 22, 23 and 24, can, when the tempo is very slow, be played also with turns. But, in such a case, one must proceed throughout with the second or third fingers, so

# TENTH CHAPTER

§ 26

There is a kind of ascending and descending trill where each note has, in place of the turn, a rapid fall to the open string below it. For example:

In such passages the trill must be made as long as if there were only one note, and the descent made quite late and hardly audible. Moreover, one can begin each trill with a separate stroke, or in the case of rapid notes, take several figures together in the same stroke. For example:

§ 27

It often occurs that two notes stand one above the other, on each of which a trill is to be made. In such cases the trill must be made on two strings and with two fingers simultaneously. For example:

that the first and second fingers can be used for the turn: But the turn must be quick and fiery. For example:

## TENTH CHAPTER

[musical notation]

Here the first finger on the E string, namely on F♯, and the third finger on the A string, namely D, are pressed down firmly, and the trill on the D string is made with the second finger, but on the A string with the fourth finger at one and the same moment. And this is called a double-trill. It can best be practised in the following manner:

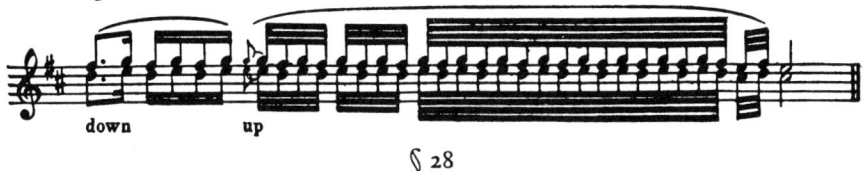

[musical notation: down ... up]

### § 28

In the double-trill the first finger is frequently obliged to make a trill on the open string. For example: [musical notation]. Such a trill is to be practised in the following way:

[musical notation: down ... In the up stroke]

In the double-trill special care must be taken not to play out of tune, and that the notes be taken by the two fingers at the same moment. Here are a few notes which can be practised with great advantage. But let pains be taken to play by degrees more and more quickly, so as to achieve facility with all the fingers.

[musical notation]

### § 29

The double-trill is used on all four strings and through all notes. Therefore it must be known how to play it in tune in the position where at all times the notes are held with the first and third fingers, while the second and fourth fingers are

### TENTH CHAPTER

used for the trill. I will here put down for practice the closes with the double-trill in most of the keys. [One closes, however, very rarely with a turn of two notes.]

## TENTH CHAPTER

§ 30

The double-trill [without a turn] can, however, be carried on step by step through many notes. It is dealt with in the same way as with the ascending and descending trill. Here is an example: the first and third fingers continue throughout, excepting when an open string occurs on the higher note, where the trill is then made with the first finger.

## § 31

There exists yet another double-trill which is played, not in thirds but in sixths. It is called a trill in sixths. It is rarely used, and then only in cadenzas as a change and as something special. It is shown at (*):

In the present example the trill is made in the first half of the bar on B only, and the note E is simply sustained with it. But in the second half of the bar the trill is made with the second finger from B to C♯ and below with the first finger from D to E. As, however, in such a case the first finger has to play with the rapidity of a trill and in quick succession, first a trill on the B on the A string, and then on the E on the D string, it is only too palpable that to play the trill in sixths in tune, special and diligent study is highly necessary. But it must be remembered that the first finger must never be lifted, but must be brought across to the D string by means of a movement of the whole hand, with the foremost part only and with a slight sideways movement. Here it is, as far as possible, expressed also in notes:

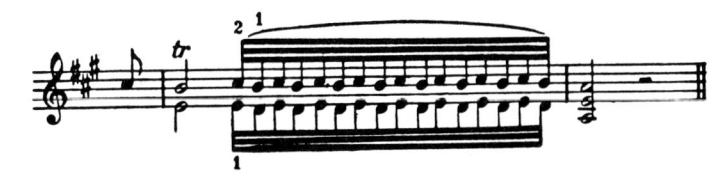

## § 32

Now we come again to a trill which I will call the accompanied trill (Trillo Accompagnato); because it is accompanied by the violinist[1] with other notes which move along their simple course. There is no doubt at all that for the execution of this accompanied trill in tune no little industry is demanded. I will put down a few examples which are drawn from the pieces of one of the most celebrated violinists of our time.[2] The lower notes must be taken with such fingers as will allow the continuance of the trill to remain unhindered. For example:

[1] *'by the violinist' is omitted in edition 1787.*
[2 *Tartini.*]

## TENTH CHAPTER

**N. 1.**

**N. 2.**

The fingers are here always, when necessary, indicated by numerals. In the first example the fingers are changed already in the fourth bar, in order that the progress of the lower notes may not interrupt that of the trill, which begins at the minim and must be continuous. In the second example the last quaver-note E in the first complete bar must be taken on the G string by extending the fourth finger, while the second finger continues to make the trill over the note E on the D string. The same occurs in the seventh, ninth, and fifteenth bars. In the third bar, on the minim F, the fingers must be changed on the second part of the first crotchet and the first finger taken in place of the second finger as soon as the first note D of the lower notes is taken by the third finger, in order not to interrupt the trill in the upper note; which occurs also in the eleventh bar. Again in the fourth and twelfth bars a quick change must be made; and the lower crotchet note could not be taken, if on the higher note the first finger were not exchanged for the second.

CHAPTER XI

# Of the Tremolo, Mordent, and some other improvised Embellishments

§ 1

THE Tremolo[1] is an ornamentation which arises from Nature herself and which can be used charmingly on a long note, not only by good instrumentalists but also by clever singers. Nature herself is the instructress thereof. For if we strike a slack string or a bell sharply, we hear after the stroke a certain wave-like undulation (*ondeggiamento*) of the struck note. And this trembling after-sound is called tremolo, also tremulant [or tremoleto].[2]

§ 2

Take pains to imitate this natural quivering on the violin, when the finger is pressed strongly down on the string, and one makes a small movement with the whole hand; which however must not move sideways but forwards toward the bridge and backwards toward the scroll; of which some mention has already been made in Chapter V. For as, when the remaining trembling sound of a struck string or bell is not pure and continues to sound not on one note only but sways first too high, then too low, just so by the movement of the hand forward and backward must you endeavour to imitate exactly the swaying of these intermediate tones.

§ 3

Now because the tremolo is not purely on one note but sounds undulating, so would it be an error if every note were played with the tremolo. Performers there are who tremble consistently on each note as if they had the palsy. The tremolo

[1] *In the 1787 edition there is a footnote here as follows*: 'I do not mean Tremulant as it is used in organ-works, but an oscillation (Tremoleto).'

[[2] *Tremolo = Vibrato*.]

must only be used at places where nature herself would produce it; namely as if the note taken were the striking of an open string. For at the close of a piece, or even at the end of a passage which closes with a long note, that last note would inevitably, if struck for instance on a pianoforte, continue to hum for a considerable time afterwards. Therefore a closing note or any other sustained note may be decorated with a tremolo [tremoleto].

### § 4

But there is also a slow, an increasing, and a rapid oscillation. They can be distinguished by the following signs.

The slow.

The increasing.

The rapid.

The larger strokes can represent quavers, the smaller semiquavers, and as many strokes as there be, so often must the hand be moved.

### § 5

The movement must, however, be made with strong after-pressure of the finger, and this pressure must be applied always on the first note of every crotchet; and in rapid movement on the first note of every half-crotchet. For instance, I will here put down a few notes which can very well be played with the tremolo; yea, which in truth demand this movement. They must be played in the third position.

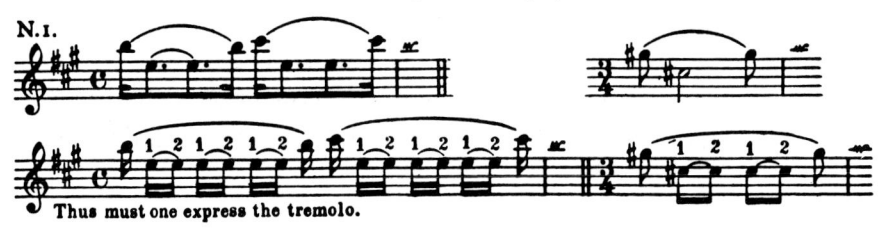

N.1.

Thus must one express the tremolo.

# ELEVENTH CHAPTER

[N.2 musical example]

Thus does one make the movement.

In the two examples, in No. 1 the strong part of the movement falls ever on the note marked by the numeral (2), for it is the first note of the whole or half-crotchet. In example No. 2, on the contrary, the stress falls, for the same reason, on the note marked with the numeral (1).

## § 6

The tremolo can also be made on two strings, and therefore with two fingers simultaneously.

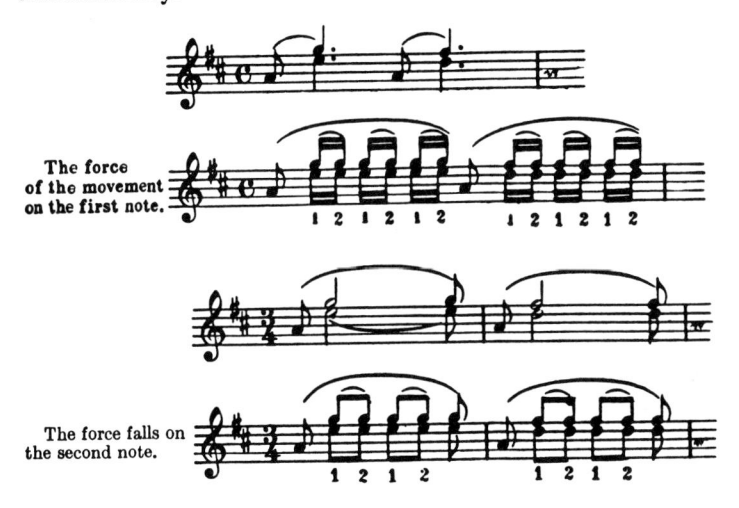

The force of the movement on the first note.

The force falls on the second note.

## § 7

Before beginning a cadenza which at the end of a solo is improvised thereto, it is customary to sustain a long note either on the key-note or on the dominant. On such a long-sustained note an increasing tremolo can always be used. For example: At the close of an adagio, one can play thus:

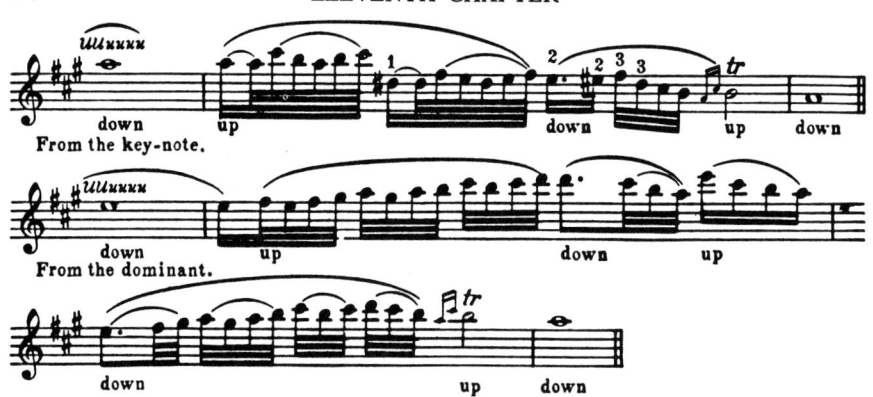

[musical notation: From the key-note. / From the dominant.]

But the stroke must commence softly and gather strength toward the middle, in such fashion that the greatest strength falls at the beginning of the more rapid movement; and finally the stroke must end again softly.

§ 8

Now we come to the Mordent. By mordent is meant the two, three, or more little notes which quite quickly and quietly, so to speak, grasp at the principal note and vanish at once, so that the principal note only is heard strongly.[1] In common parlance this is called the Mordent; the Italians call it *Mordente*; the French, *Pincé*.

§ 9

The mordent is made in three different ways. Firstly, it comes from the principal note itself. Secondly, from the two next higher and lower notes. Thirdly, it is made with three notes when the principal note falls between the two neighbouring notes. Here are all three:[2]

[1] If others make merry over this mordant or mordent, according to etymology from *mordere* (to bite), and because of the word 'bite', they call it a 'biter', I may be allowed to say of the French *pincé*, which means to twitch, pluck or pinch, that the mordent or the French so-called *pincé* clings closely to the principal note, quietly and rapidly, 'bites', tweaks, or pinches the same slightly, and at once releases it again.

[2] *In the 1787 edition, after the illustration, Par. 9 concludes as follows*: 'I know full well that as a rule only the first kind, or so-called French *pincé*, has the real right of citizenship as mordent, but as these, my second and third kinds, are also "biters", and have therefore the characteristics of a mordent, why should they not also be allowed to run with and among the mordents? Can there not exist polite and impolite "biters"? It is true that my second kind looks rather

[Musical examples labeled 1., 2., 3.]

Some, indeed, refuse to reckon the second kind among the mordents, but differentiate these two little notes from the mordent by the word *Anschlag*. But in truth they have all the characteristics of a mordent. They bite at the principal note quickly and quietly, and vanish so rapidly that one hears the principal note only. And are they therefore not mordents? They are, it is true, somewhat gentler than the others; perchance one could call them the courteous biters. One can also perform with only two notes the mordent arising out of the principal note itself, as we see above; and the performance becomes thereby much milder. But is it, because of this, no longer a mordent?

§ 10

The third kind of mordent can be used in two different ways, namely, ascending and descending. If the last note before the mordents be lower than the one following, where the mordent occurs, then is it played upwards; but if the note stands higher, it is played downwards. For example:

[Musical example]

§ 11

But the notes must not be overloaded with this kind of mordent, and there are only a few special cases where an up stroke can begin with a mordent. For example:

like the Anschlag and the third seems like a slide. But the execution thereof is entirely different. There are dotted and undotted Anschläge, and both these and the glide belong to melodious performance and are used interchangeably, only in slow or moderate tempo, for the filling out and binding together of melody. These second and third kinds of mordents, on the other hand, are unchangeable; are played with the greatest rapidity; and the stress falls at all times on the principal note.'

[Musical example: "Here it is good." ... "But here it is bad."]

### § 12

In the case, too, of a sequence of mordents descending step by step, it is better to play the note of the up stroke without a mordent. For after the up stroke the accent must fall only on the note following it.

[Musical example]

### § 13

Above all, the mordent must only be used if it be desirable to give special emphasis to a note. For the stress of the tone falls on the note itself, while the mordent, on the contrary, is slurred quite softly and very quickly on to the principal note; for, otherwise, it would no longer be called a mordent. It makes the note lively; it makes it different from the others, and gives to the whole style a different aspect. It is therefore generally used for unequal notes, mostly at the beginning of a crotchet, for it is here that the emphasis really belongs. For example:

[Musical example]

### § 14

Finally it must be remembered that, as with the appoggiature, so also here the descending mordent is always better than the ascending; and indeed for the same reasons which we have applied to the appoggiature. Moreover, the good performance of a mordent consists in its rapidity: the more rapidly it is played, the better it is. But rapidity must not be driven to the point of unintelligibility. Even in the quickest performance the notes must be expressed comprehensibly and very crisply.

§ 15

There are still a few other embellishments which are mostly named from the Italian. The Battement only is of French origin. The Ribattuta, Groppo, Tirata, Mezzo Circulo, and other such, are of Italian birth. And even though one now rarely hears them mentioned, I will, in spite of this, set them down here, for they are not without use and may well be used still. Yea, who knows if they may not rescue many from confusion, and at the least, kindle a light as a guide to playing with more method in the future? It is surely wretched always to play haphazard and without knowing what one is doing.

§ 16

The battement is a prolonged mordent of two neighbouring half-tones, which prolonged mordent from the lower half-tone to the upper is repeated a number of times, one after the other with the greatest rapidity. The battement or this prolonged mordent must not be mistaken for the tremolo or the trill, nor yet with the mordent flowing from the principal note. The tremolo looks in some respects like the prolonged mordent, but the latter is much quicker; is made with two fingers; and does not surmount the principal tone or principal note; whereas the tremolo oscillates also above the principal note. The trill comes from above to the principal note; but the prolonged mordent from below, and that always from the half-tone. And the mordent begins on the principal note, whereas the battement, on the contrary, begins on the next lower semitone. This prolonged mordent looks like this:

One uses this battement in lively pieces in place of the appoggiatura and mordent, in order to perform certain otherwise empty notes with more spirit and very gaily. The example given may be proof hereof. The battement, however, must not be used too often; nay, very seldom, and then only for the purpose of variety.

ELEVENTH CHAPTER

§ 17

The Zurückschlag (Italian *Ribattuta*) is used in the sustaining of a very long note and generally before a trill. Turn back to the fifth paragraph of the previous chapter, where in the double-trills I have preceded each by a short Ribattuta. The Zurückschlag can also be used pleasingly, for example, in an adagio:

**Thus it is written.**        **And thus can one play it with a Ribattuta.**

But the Ribattuta must begin with a strong tone which diminishes by degrees. Here is yet another example:

**Thus can one embellish it with the 'Zurückschlag.'**

§ 18

The ornament which is called Groppo is a combination of notes lying at a slight distance from each other, which combination is made by means of a few rapid notes. When these rapid notes, before ascending or descending, retreat each time by one tone, making this delay only in order not to arrive at the principal note too soon, then they have the appearance of so knotty a figure that some derive the word Groppo from the French and English *grape*, and figuratively after the old German *Kluster* (cluster); but others ascribe this nomenclature to the Italian *groppo*, a knob or button; *groppare* = to button. This ornamentation is shown thus:

ELEVENTH CHAPTER 211

Without embellishment.

With the Groppo upwards.

Without embellishment.

With the Groppo downwards.

This embellishment must, however, be used only when playing solo, and even then only for the sake of variety if such passages be repeated immediately one after the other.

§ 19

The circle and half-circle are little different from the groppo. If they be only four notes, they are called the Half-Circle; but if there be eight notes, then is it a Whole Circle. It is customary to name this figure thus because the notes present the shape of a circle. For example:

Without ornamentation.

The Circle.
Ascending. Descending.

Without embellishment.

The Half-circle.
Ascending. Descending.

§ 20

Those who are very intent on etymology have another bone of contention in the word Tirata, which some deduce from the Italian *tirare*, which means 'to pull', and which can be used for the formation of manifold and varied phrases. Others, however, give the derivation from *tirata*, a shot, or *tirare*, to shoot; which is understood figuratively and is in reality an Italian form of speech. Both are right. And as the tirata is no other than a sequence of step-wise ascending or descending notes, which are extemporized on the spur of the moment between two other notes which lie at some distance apart, there can be also a rapid and a slow tirata, according to whether the tempo be rapid or slow, or whether the two notes be far apart. Is the tirata slow—then is it called a 'pull' and comes from *tirare*, to pull; for one draws melody through many tones from one note to another, and unites the two notes lying apart by means of the other intervals lying between them. But is the tirata rapid—then the same combination takes place, it is true, but happens so rapidly that it could be likened to the flight of an arrow or a shot.[1] Here are examples:

[1] What? Banish the 'shot' from the kingdom of music? I myself should not venture to do that; for it has forced its way not only into the fine arts, but everywhere besides. Yes, even where one would have naught to do with it, there does it reek most strongly of gunpowder. 'Quisque suos patimur Manes . . . Virgil.'

ELEVENTH CHAPTER 213

Without ornamentation. *Adagio*

With a slow ascending Tirata. *Adagio*

Molto allegro
Without ornamentation.

Molto allegro
With a quick, ascending Tirata.

§ 21

But the tirata can also be used in many other ways. I will here set down one or two of these. For example:

Without ornamentation. *Adagio*

A slow Tirata with triplets. *Adagio*

Without ornamentation. *Adagio*

With a quick Tirata through the semitones.

Without ornamentation.

Through passages of thirds.

## § 22

All these decorations are used, however, only when playing a solo, and then very sparingly, at the right time, and only for variety in often-repeated and similar passages. And look well at the directions of the composer; for in the application of such ornaments is one's ignorance soonest betrayed. But in particular, guard against all improvised embellishments when several play from one part. What confusion would ensue, if every player should befrill the notes according to his own fancy? And finally one would not understand then aught of the melody, by reason of the various clumsily inserted and horrible 'beauties'? I know how it frightens one, when one hears the most melodious pieces distorted so pitifully by means of unnecessary ornamentations. I shall speak further thereof in the following chapter.

CHAPTER XII

# Of Reading Music correctly, and in particular, of Good Execution

§ 1

EVERYTHING depends on good execution. This saying is confirmed by daily experience. Many a would-be composer is thrilled with delight and plumes himself anew when he hears his musical Galimatias played by good performers who know how to produce the effect (of which he himself never dreamed) in the right place; and how to vary the character (which never occurred to him) as much as it is humanly possible to do so, and who therefore know how to make the whole miserable scribble bearable to the ears of the listeners by means of good performance. And to whom, on the other hand, is it not known that the best composition is often played so wretchedly that the composer himself has great difficulty in recognizing his own work?

§ 2

The good performance of a composition according to modern taste is not as easy as many imagine, who believe themselves to be doing well if they embellish and befrill a piece right foolishly out of their own heads, and who have no sensitiveness whatever for the affect[1] which is to be expressed in the piece. And who are these people? They are mostly those who, hardly at ease with time, get straightway to work on concertos and solos, in order (in their foolish opinion) to force themselves straight into the company of virtuosi. Many succeed so far that they play off with uncommon dexterity the most difficult passages in various concertos or solos which they have practised with great industry. These they know by heart. But should they have to perform only a couple of minuets melodiously according to the instructions of the composer, they are unable to do so; yea, this is to be seen even in their studied concertos. For so long as they play an allegro, all goes well: but when it comes to an adagio, there they betray their great ignorance and bad judgement in every bar of the whole piece. They play without method and without

[1] See *Translator's Appendix*, p. 232.

expression: the *piano* and *forte* are not differentiated; the embellishments are in the wrong place, too overloaded, and mostly played in a confused manner; and often the notes are far too bare and one observes that the player knows not what he does. For such people there is rarely any more hope of improvement, for they, more than anyone, are taken up with self-esteem and he would be in their great disfavour who would candidly attempt to convince them of their errors.

## § 3

To read the musical pieces of good masters rightly according to the instructions, and to play them in keeping with the outstanding characteristics of the piece, is far more artistic than to study the most difficult solo or concerto. For the latter, but little sense is necessary. And if one has enough wit to think out the appoggiature, one can learn the most difficult passages for oneself if energetic practice be added. The former, on the contrary, is not so easy. For, not only must one observe exactly all that has been marked and prescribed and not play it otherwise than as written; but one must throw oneself into the affect to be expressed and apply and execute in a certain good style all the ties, slides, accentuation of the notes, the *forte* and *piano*; in a word, whatever belongs to tasteful performance of a piece; which can only be learnt from sound judgement and long experience.

## § 4

Decide now for yourself whether a good orchestral violinist be not of far higher value than one who is purely a solo player? The latter can play everything according to his whim and arrange the style of performance as he wishes, or even for the convenience of his hand; while the former must possess the dexterity to understand and at once interpret rightly the taste of various composers, their thoughts and expressions. The latter need only practise at home in order to get everything well in tune, and others must accommodate themselves to him. But the former has to play everything at sight and, added to that, often such passages as go against the natural order of the time-division,[1] and he has, mostly, to accommodate himself to others. A solo player can, without great understanding of music, usually play

---

[1] Contra metrum musicum. Of this I have already made mention in the second footnote of the second section of Chapter I, Par. 4. And I know not what to think when I see arias of many very renowned Italian composers which err so greatly against the musical metre that one might think they had been composed by an apprentice.

his concertos tolerably—yea, even with distinction—but a good orchestral violinist must have great insight into the whole art of musical composition and into the difference of the characteristics; yea, he must have a specially lively adroitness to be prominent in his calling with honour, in particular if he wishes in time to become the leader of an orchestra. Perhaps there are, however, some who believe that more good orchestral violinists are to be found than solo players. They are mistaken. Of bad accompanists there are certainly enough; of good, on the other hand, but few; for nowadays all wish to play solo. But what an orchestra is like which is composed entirely of solo players, I leave to be answered by the composers whose music has been performed by them. Few solo players read well, because they are accustomed to insert something of their own fantasy at all times, and to look after themselves only, and but rarely after others.[1]

§ 5

Therefore one must not play solo before one can accompany right well. One must first know how to make all variants of bowings; must understand how to introduce *piano* and *forte* in the right place and in right measure; one must learn to distinguish between the characteristics of pieces and to execute all passages according to their own particular flavour; and in a word one must be able to read the work of many artists correctly and gracefully before one begins to play concertos and solos. It can be seen at once from a painting whether he who has executed it be a master of drawing; and in the same manner, many a one would play his solo more intelligently if he had ever learnt to perform a symphony or a trio according to the good taste required by it; or to accompany an aria with the right effect and according to the character thereof. I will attempt to set down a few rules of which you can avail yourself with advantage in the performance of music.

§ 6

That an instrument must be well in tune with the others goes without saying, and therefore my reminder seems in this case somewhat superfluous. But then, as even many people who wish to play first violin, frequently do not tune their instruments together, I find it highly necessary to remind them of it here; all the more

---

[1] I speak here nowise of those great virtuosi who, besides their extraordinary art in the playing of concertos, are also good orchestral violinists. These are the people who truly deserve the greatest esteem.

so as all the others have to tune to the leader. When one plays with an organ or piano, then the tuning must adjust itself to them; but if neither be present the pitch is taken from the wind instruments. Some tune first the A string; others, on the contrary, the D string. Both do rightly if they but tune carefully and perfectly. I will merely add the reminder that stringed-instruments always flatten in a warm room, and sharpen in a cold one.

## § 7

Before beginning to play, the piece must be well looked at and considered. The character, tempo, and kind of movement demanded by the piece must be sought out, and carefully observed whether a passage occurs not therein which often at first sight seems of little importance, but on account of its special style of execution and expression is not quite easy to play at sight. Finally, in practising every care must be taken to find and to render the affect which the composer wished to have brought out; and as sadness often alternates with joy, each must be carefully depicted according to its kind. In a word, all must be so played that the player himself be moved thereby.[1]

## § 8

From this it follows that the prescribed *piano* and *forte* must be observed most exactly, and that one must not go on playing always in one tone like a hurdy-gurdy. Yea, one must know how to change from *piano* to *forte* without directions and of one's own accord, each at the right time; for this means, in the well-known phraseology of the painters, Light and Shade. The notes raised by a ♯ and ♮ should always be played rather more strongly, the tone then diminishing again during the course of the melody. For example:

In the same way a sudden lowering of a note by a ♭ and ♮ should be distinguished by *forte*. For example:

---

[1] It is bad enough that many a one never thinks of what he is doing, but plays his notes merely as one who dreams; or as if he were playing just for himself only. Such a performer is not aware if presently he run a few crotchets in advance of the time, and I wager that he would finish the piece a few bars earlier than the others, did not his neighbour or the leader himself draw his attention to it.

It is customary always to accent minims strongly when mixed with short notes, and to relax the tone again. For example:

Yea, many a crotchet is played in the same manner. For example:

And this is in reality the expression which the composer desires when he sets *f* and *p*, namely *forte* and *piano*, against a note. But when accenting a note strongly the bow must not be lifted from the string as some very clumsy people do, but must be continued in the stroke so that the tone may still be heard continuously, although it gradually dies away. Read once more what I have written in the footnote, Ch. I, § 18, p. 46.

§ 9

Generally the accent[1] of the expression or the stress of tone falls on the ruling or strong beat, which the Italians call Nota Buona. These strong beats, however, differ perceptibly from each other. The specially strong beats are as follows: In every bar, the first note of the first crotchet, the first note of the half-bar or third crotchet in $\frac{4}{4}$ time; the first note of the first and fourth crotchets in $\frac{6}{4}$ and $\frac{6}{8}$ time; and the first note of the first, fourth, seventh, and tenth crotchets in $\frac{12}{8}$ time. These may be called the strong beats on which the chief stress of the tone always falls if the composer has indicated no other expression. In the ordinary accompaniment to an aria or a concert piece, where for the most part only quavers or semiquavers occur, they are now usually written detached, or at the least, a few bars at the beginning are marked with a small stroke. For example:

[1] I mean here by the word 'accent' by no means 'Le Port de Voix' of the French, of which Rousseau gives an explanation in his *Méthode pour Apprendre à Chanter*, p. 56; but an expression, accent, or emphasis, from the Greek ἐν, in, and φάσις, *apparitio, dictio*.

One must therefore continue to accent the first note strongly in the same manner, until a change occurs.

### § 10

The other good notes are those which, it is true, are at all times distinguished from the remainder by a small accent, but on which the stress must be applied with great moderation. They are, namely, crotchets and quavers in allabreve time, and crotchets in the so-called minim-triplet; further, there are quavers and semiquavers in common and also in $\frac{2}{4}$ and $\frac{3}{4}$ time: and finally, semiquavers in $\frac{3}{8}$ and $\frac{6}{8}$ time, and so on. Now if several notes of this kind follow each other, over which, two by two, a slur be placed, then the accent falls on the first of the two, and it is not only played somewhat louder, but it is also sustained rather longer; while the second is slurred on to it quite smoothly and quietly, and somewhat late. An example hereof can be seen in the first section of the seventh chapter, § 3; but read particularly § 5 of the second section of Chapter VII, and study the examples. But often three, four, and even more notes are bound together by such a slur and half-circle. In such a case the first thereof must be somewhat more strongly accented and sustained longer; the others, on the contrary, being slurred on to it in the same stroke with a diminishing of the tone, even more and more quietly and without the slightest accent. Let the reader remind himself frequently of the seventh chapter, and especially of what has been said in § 20 of the first section thereof.

### § 11

Similarly, from the sixth and seventh chapters is to be seen how greatly the slurring and detaching distinguishes a melody. Therefore not only must the written and prescribed slurs be observed with the greatest exactitude but when, as in many a composition, nothing at all is indicated, the player must himself know how to apply the slurring and detaching tastefully and in the right place. The chapter dealing with the many varieties of bowings, especially the second section, will serve to teach how an attractive change should be made, which however must be in keeping with the character of the piece.

## TWELFTH CHAPTER

### § 12

There are nowadays certain passages in which the expression of a skilful composer is indicated in a quite unusual and unexpected manner, and which not everyone would divine, were it not indicated. For example:

For here the expression and accent falls on the last crotchet of the bar, and the first crotchet of the following bar is slurred on to it quite quietly and without accent. These two notes, therefore, are on no account to be differentiated by an after-pressure of the bow, but are to be played as if they were merely a minim. Refer here to the eighteenth paragraph of the third section of the first chapter, and the footnote.

### § 13

In lively pieces the accent is mostly used on the highest note, in order to make the performance right merry. So it may happen here that the stress falls on the last note of the second and fourth crotchet in simple time, but on the end of the second crotchet in $\frac{2}{4}$ time; especially when the piece begins with the up stroke. For example:

But in slow, sad pieces this cannot be done, for there the up stroke must not be detached, but sustained singingly.

### § 14

In three-crotchet and three-quaver time the accent can fall also on the second crotchet. For example:

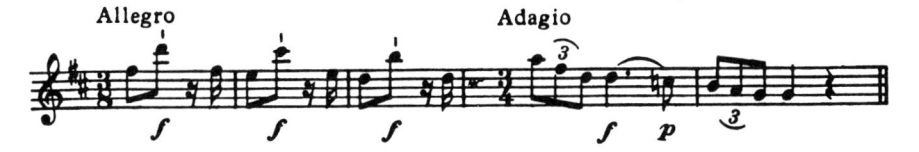

## § 15

It can be seen from the last example that in the first bar the dotted crotchet (D) is slurred on to the quaver (C) following it. Accordingly there must be no after-pressure of the bow on the dot; but here, as well as in all similar cases, the crotchet must be attacked with moderate strength; the length of the dot sustained without after-pressure; and the quaver note following it slurred quite quietly on to it. I have already mentioned this in the third section of the first chapter, § 9.

## § 16

In the same manner, the notes which are divided by the bar-line must never be separated; neither must the division be marked by an accent but must be merely attacked and quietly sustained; not otherwise than if it stood at the beginning of the crotchet. Read § 21, § 22, and § 23, of the fourth chapter, in which there are enough examples. Here belongs also what has been said at the end of § 18 in the third section of the first chapter; and let the footnote on no account be forgotten. This style of performance makes a certain broken tempo which, since either the middle part or the bass appear to separate themselves from the upper part, has a very strange and pleasing effect, and is also the reason that in certain passages the fifths do not collide with each other so greatly but are accented alternately, one after the other. For example, here are three parts:

## § 17

In the same way as in the cases given here, so, wherever a *forte* is written down, the tone is to be used with moderation, without foolish scrapings, especially in the accompaniment of a solo part. Many either omit to do a thing altogether, or if they do it, are certain to exaggerate. The effect must be considered. Often a note demands a strong accent, at other times only a moderate one, and then again one which is hardly audible. The first occurs generally in a forceful expression mark which all the instruments play together, and this is usually indicated by *fp*. For example:

*fp*

The second happens on the specially important notes, of which mention has been made in § 9 of this chapter. The third occurs on all the other notes first indicated in § 10, where a hardly noticeable accent is used. But when in the accompaniment of a solo part many *fortes* are written down, the stress must surely be played in moderation, and not so exaggeratedly that the chief part be overpowered. Such a slight and short accent should rather bring out the principal part, inspire the melody, help the performer, and lighten his task of characterizing the piece rightly.

§ 18

Just as the slurring and detaching, the *forte* and *piano*, according to the demands of expression, must be observed in tl. most exact manner; so must one not play continuously with a lagging, heavy stroke, but must accommodate oneself to the prevailing mood of each passage. Merry and playful passages must be played with light, short, and lifted strokes, happily and rapidly; just as in slow, sad pieces one performs them with long strokes of the bow, simply and tenderly.

§ 19

In the accompaniment of a solo part the notes are mostly not sustained but played quickly, and in $\frac{6}{8}$ and $\frac{12}{8}$ time the crotchets are to be played almost as quaver-notes, so that the performance be not sleepy. But the equality of the time-measure must be considered, and the crotchet must be heard more than the quaver. For example:

**Andante**

So is it written.          *f   p   f   p   f   p   f   p*
                           Thus is it played.

§ 20

Many, who have no idea of taste, never retain the evenness of tempo in the accompanying of a concerto part, but endeavour always to follow the solo-part.

These are accompanists for dilettanti and not for masters. When one is confronted by many an Italian songstress or other such would-be virtuosi, who are not able to execute in correct time even that which they learn by heart, even entire half-bars have indeed to be allowed to drop out in order to rescue them from public disgrace. But when a true virtuoso who is worthy of the title is to be accompanied, then one must not allow oneself to be beguiled by the postponing or anticipating of the notes, which he knows how to shape so adroitly and touchingly, into hesitating or hurrying, but must continue to play throughout in the same manner; else the effect which the performer desired to build up would be demolished by the accompaniment.[1]

§ 21

Moreover, in music-making, if it is to be good in other respects, all the ensemble-players must observe each other carefully, and especially watch the leader; not so that they begin well together, but that they may play steadily in the same tempo and with the same expression. There are certain passages in the playing of which it is easy to be betrayed into hurrying. Remember § 38 of Chapter IV. And in the sixth and seventh chapters the importance of evenness of tempo has been emphasized more than once. Further, care must be taken to play chords smartly and together, but the short notes, following a dot or short rest, late and rapidly. See what I have taught in the second section of Chapter VII, § 2 and § 3; and there seek out the examples. When in the up beat, or after a short rest, several notes are to be played, it is usual to take them in the down stroke and to slur them on to the first note of the following crotchet. There the ensemble-players must specially observe each other and not begin too soon. Here is an example of chords and rests.

[1] A clever accompanist must also be able to sum up a concert performer. To a sound virtuoso he certainly must not yield, for he would then spoil his tempo rubato. What this 'stolen tempo' is, is more easily shown than described. But on the other hand, if the accompanist has to deal with a *soi-disant* virtuoso, then he may often, in an adagio cantabile, have to hold out many a quaver the length of half a bar, until perchance the latter recovers from his paroxysms; and nothing goes according to time, for he plays after the style of a recitative.

# TWELFTH CHAPTER

## § 22

Now everything that I have written down in this last chapter relates, properly speaking, to reading music correctly, and in particular to the right and reasonable performance of a well-written musical piece. And the pains which I have bestowed on the writing of this book have for their aim: to bring beginners on to the right road and to prepare them for the knowledge of, and feeling for, musical good taste.[1] I will therefore close here, although there is still more that I could have said for the benefit of our worthy platform artists. Who knows? Perchance, I may again venture to bestow upon the musical world another book—if I see that this my zeal to serve beginners has not been entirely without avail.

[1] *From this point, the edition of 1787 concludes as follows:* 'I will therefore close here, but will repeat that which I said at the end of the first edition of this "Violinschule", namely, that much remains which might be said for the benefit of our worthy platform artists, and that I shall perhaps venture to bestow upon the musical world another book. I should unfailingly have so ventured, had not my travels hindered me. The Preface to this edition contains my formal apology. I still hope to redeem my word, as I see that my zeal to serve beginners has not been in vain, and that the learned Musicians have judged my modest effort with much kindness.'

# Index

## Of the Most Important Matters

The Roman Numeral indicates the Chapter; whereas the Arabic Figure gives the Paragraph. But where two Roman Numerals occur together, the first indicates the Chapter; the second in italics signifies the Section. E denotes the Introduction.

### A

Abfall, a musical embellishment. *See* Rückfall.
Accent of musical notes and on which it occurs, XII, 9, 10.
Accompanying, some rules thereto, XII, 9, 17, 18, 19, 20.
Adagio, is often played badly, XII, 2.
Affect, is often indicated by the composer, VI, 3. The bow must contribute greatly to the production of affects, VII, *I*, 1. The affect must be sought in a piece, and observed in the performance thereof, XII, 3, 7.
Alphabet on the Violin, I, *I*, 14. When it must be learned, II, 6. Must be learned well, II, 7. One through (♯) and (♭), III, 6.
Amphion, E, *II*, 5.
Anschlag, IX, 12 (footnote).
Apollo, E, *II*, 5.
Applicatur,[1] what it is, VIII, *I*, 1. The reason for it, VIII, *I*, 2. Is threefold, VIII, *I*, 3. The Whole Applicatur, VIII, *I*, 4, 5, 6. How to make oneself adroit therein, VIII, *I*, 8, 9. How to play it up and down, VIII, *I*, 8, 9, 10, 11, 12, and so on. The Half Applicatur, VIII, *II*, 1, 2, 3, and so on. The Mixed Applicatur, VIII, *II*, 1, 2, 3, and so on.
Aristotle, E, *II*, 5.
Arpeggiare, what it is and how it is made, VIII, *III*, 18.
Authors, good musical, E, *II*, 5.

### B

(B) This letter must be especially observed, I, *I*, 14. (b), what it is and how used in music, I, *III*, 13, 14, 15.
Back of the Violin, E, *I*, 3.
Barydon, so-called, E, *I*, 2.
Battement. *See* Zusammenschlag.
Beginners must not begin to fiddle at once, I, *I*, 1. How to teach them to play in time, I, *II*, 8, 9, 10, 11. How to test them in the division of notes and rests, I, *II*, 12. How a beginner is to hold the Violin, and to draw the bow, II, 1, 2, 3, 4, and so on. Beginners are often spoilt, II, 2. How to teach them with profit, II, 8. Why they should mostly at first play the set pieces in C major, II, 9. One should not write the letters on the Violin, II, 10. Beginners should always play strongly and with earnestness, II, 11. How they shall learn to recognize the keys, III, 2, 3, 4. Shall learn to know all intervals, III, 5. Shall use the fourth finger frequently, III, 7. What they shall play after learning the alphabet, III, 8, 9.
Boëthius, E, *II*, 5.
Bow. How the Violin-bow shall be held and drawn, II, 5, 6.
Bowing, Rules of the Up and Down stroke, IV, 1, 2, 3, and so on. Examples thereof, IV, 38. Division in soft and loud, V, 3, 4, and so on. Must be made now near the

---

[1] [*The word 'Applicatur', as used by L. Mozart, may be understood as Position or Fingering. He often uses it when speaking of the third position exclusively.*]

# INDEX

bridge, now far away from it, V, 11. The strokes must be well united, one with the other, V, 14. Change of the stroke in triplets, VI. 3, 4, and so on. With similar notes, VII, *I*, 1, 2, 3, and so on. With unequal notes, VII, *II*, 1, 2, 3, and so on. The bowing distinguishes everything, VII, *I*, 1.
Bratsche (Viola di Braccio), E, *I*, 2.
Bridge, on the Violin, what it is, E, *I*, 3. Can improve the sound of the Violin, E, *I*, 7.

## C

Canonici, who they were, E, *II*, 5.
Character, of a piece must be examined, XII, 4, 5, 7.
Chords. How to play them, XII, 21. Broken, *see* Arpeggiare.
Circle and Half-Circle of musical ornamentation, XI, 19. The Half-circle of the slur, I, *III*, 16. As a sign to sustain, I, *III*, 19.
Clef, the so-called musical, I, *I*, 9. How one transposes it on the wind-instruments, and why on the Violin it can be written otherwise, I, *I*, 10.
Composers must indicate the change of bowing, VI, 3. But must make a reasonable choice in their directions for performance, VII, *I*, 1.
Concerto-Part (Solo-Part), how it must be accompanied, XII, 9, 17, 19, 20.
Control of the bow, V, 10.
Corona, what it is, *III*, 19.
Corpus or body of the Violin, E, *I*, 3.
Cross, so-called, I, *III*, 13, 14. *See* Sharps.
Custos musicus, what it is, I, *III*, 26.

## D

Detaching of the notes, as indicated, I, *III*, 20. How the notes are to be played, IV, 38, and VII, 2. The detaching of notes must be exactly observed according to the directions of the composer; and one must even know how to apply it frequently oneself, XII, 3, 11.
Didymus, E, *II*, 5.
Diodor, E, *II*, 5.

Division of the bow-stroke in soft and loud, V, 3, 4, 5, and so on.
Division of a note, how to learn it, I, *III*, 7.
Divisions, V, 14.
Doppelschlag, a musical embellishment, IX, 26.
Dot, what it means, I, *II*, 8, 9, 10. New teaching of the double-dot, I, *III*, 11. If it stands over or under the note; what it indicates, I, *III*, 17.
Dotted notes. *See* Notes.
Double-Stopping. *See* Stopping.

## E

Embellishments, must be used with moderation, and when they are to be used, XI, 22.
Emphasis. *See* Accent.
Examples. Why I have set them mostly in C major, VI, 19.
Expression. *See* Accent.

## F

(*f, p*) What these letters indicate, XII, 8.
Fiddle. Difference between the word Fiddle and Violin, E, *I*, 1. The different species thereof, E, *I*, 2. *See further under* Violin.
Fiddle-bow, is also already used with some instruments by the Ancients, E, *I*, 8. *See* Bow.
Fifth, is threefold, III, 5.
Figure (Certain notes belonging together) can, by means of the bowing, be many times varied, VI, 3.
Fingers, Method of the same on the Violin, I, *III*, 14, and III, 6.
Flageolet, so-called, must not be mixed with other natural Violin notes, V, 13.
Flats, I, *III*, 13. An alphabet thereof, III, 6. The double-flat, I, *III*, 25.
Forte (forte). *See* Loudness.
Fourth, is threefold, III, 5.
Frequently the fourth finger must be used, III, 7. Why it is often necessary, V, 13, and VI, 5, 17. How the fingers are used in the third position, VIII, *I*, 4, 5, 6, 8, 9, and so on. In the first, VIII, *II*, 1, 2, 3, and so on. In the mixed, VIII, *III*, 2, 3, and so on. The interchange or overlapping of the

## INDEX

fingers, VIII, *III*, 15. One has often to move back with all the fingers, VIII, *III*, 16. Extension of the fourth finger, VIII, *III*, 9. Or even drawing the first backwards, VIII, *III*, 10. But oft-times extending two fingers, VIII, *III*, 11.

### G

Gamba, E, *I*, 2.
Greeks. They sang above their letters, I, *I*, 3. Their time-measure, I, *I*, 4.
Gregory the Great, E, *II*, 5. He changes music, I, 1.
Groppo, a musical embellishment, XI, 18.
Guido d'Arezzo, E, *II*, 5. Made a change in music, I, *I*, 5, 6.
Gut strings. *See* Strings.

### H

Half-Circle. *See* Circle.
Half-Trill, IX, 27.
Hard Key. *See under* Scale.
Harmonica. Who they were, E, *II*, 5.
History of Music, E, *II*, 5.
Homer, E, *II*, 5.

### I

Instruments, musical, of ancient times, E, *II*, 4. The inventor thereof, E, *II*, 4, 6, 8. Stringed-Instruments change in warmth and cold, XII, 6.
Instrumentalists, must direct their performance after the manner of vocal music, V, 14.
Intervals, musical. What they are and how many, III, 5.
Inventor of Music, E, *II*, 3. And of musical instruments, E, *II*, 5.

### J

Jubal, E, *II*, 3.

### K

Key, description, and manifold varieties, III, 2, 3, 4.

### L

Lactantius, E, *II*, 5.
Leader must be well observed by all in concerted music, XII, 21.
Letters, the musical, I, *I*, 12. Where they are, on the Violin, I, *I*, 13, 14. One must not write them on the Violin for beginners, II, 10.
Lines, musical, I, *I*, 8.
Loudness, where it can be obtained with the Violin-bow, V, 3, 4, 5, and so on. Must not be overdone, V, 13. Where to apply it in the slur, VII, *I*, 20. Must be used adroitly, XII, 3, 8. Rules for the control of loudness, X, 17.
Lucian, E, *II*, 5.
Lyre of the Ancients, what it was, and its origin, E, *II*, 6.

### M

Major Tones. *See* Key.
Marcus Meibomius, E, *II*, 5.
Marine Trumpet, E, *I*, 2.
Mathematicians, must come to the aid of Violin-makers for the making of Instruments, E, *I*, 6.
Mercury, E, *II*, 5, 6, 8.
Minor Tones. *See* Key.
Mizler, a learned music-connoisseur, E, *I*, 6.
Mordent. What it is and how many varieties, XI, 8, 9. Is ascending and descending, XI, 10. One must use it with moderation; and where, XI, 11, 12, 13. Must be performed right crisply, XI, 14.
Movement of the hand when sustaining a long note, V, 5.
Murs. Jean de Murs or Johann von der Mauer, E, *II*, 5. He changes music appreciably, I, *I*, 7.
Music. Etymology, E, *II*, 2. The discovery, E, *II*, 3. Vocal music must be the focus of Instrumentalists, V, 14. Change therein, I, *I*, 4, 5, 6, 7.
Musical Authors, many good ones, E, *II*, 5.
Musical History, E, *II*, 5.
Musical Society. *See* Society.
Musical technical words, I, *III*, 27.

## N

Nachschlag, an embellishment, IX, 28.
Naturals, I, *III*, 13.
Notes. Why they were devised, I, *I*, 2. How they were devised, I, *I*, 7. What their appearance now is; and what purpose they serve, I, *I*, 11. How they are used for the Violin, I, *I*, 13, 14. Their duration or value; and how one must apportion them in the bar, I, *III*, 1, 3, 4, 5, and so on, together with the Table, as also IV, 37. How the notes are named before which a (♯), and those before which a (♭) stands, I, *III*, 13. When a note must be sustained, and how, I, *III*, 19. What the Vorschlag-Notes are. *See* Vorschlag-Notes. Examples of rapid and otherwise mixed notes, IV, 38. Notes played in absurd manner, VI, 7. Many slurred in one bow-stroke, VII, *I*, 11, 12, 13. Many detached notes in one bow-stroke, VII, *I*, 15, 16, 17. How to perform the slurred ones tastefully, VII, *I*, 20. The dotted ones; how they are to be played, VII, *II*, 2, 3, 4, and XII, 15, 21. The ruling or strong beats; what these are, XII, 9, 10. Various notes slurred; how they are to be performed, XII, 10, 12, 16, 21. Which are to be apportioned in the bar, XII, 16. After a short rest; how they are to be played on the Violin, XII, 21.

## O

Octave, III, 5.
Olympus, E, *II*, 5.
Orchestral Violinist. A good one is to be valued more highly than one who is purely Soloist, XII, 4.
Ornamentation. *See* Embellishments.
Orpheus, E, *II*, 5.

## P

Pauses. What they are, and their value, I, *III*, 2, 3, 5, 6.
Parts. Difference between the high and low in playing, V, 11.
Passage. One varied thirty-four times by means of bowings, VII, *I*, 19. Special passages, XII, 12, 13, 14.

Performance, often varied by means of the bowing, VI, 3, 4, and so on; VIII, *I*, 1, 2, 3, and so on; VII, *II*, 1, 2, and so on. Particularly by means of loudness and softness, VII, *II*, 4, 5, 7. Good performance is not easy, XII, 2, 3. *See further*: Reading music.
Performance, upon which all depends, XII, 1.
Phrases, V, 14.
Piano. *See* Softness.
Playing, must be performed at all times strongly and with earnestness, II, 11, and V, 2. One must play as one sings, V, 14. Some rules for a good manner of playing, XII, 7, 8, 9, and so on, to 21.
Pliny, E, *II*, 5.
Ptolemy, E, *II*, 5.

## R

Reading music. Good reading is more difficult than studying Concertos, XII, 3. Few Soloists read well, XII, 4. A few rules, XII, 7, 8, 9, and so on, to 22.
Repeat-Marks, I, *III*, 22.
Ribattuta. *See* Zurückschlag.
Ribs of the Violin, what are thus named, E, *I*, 3.
Rückfall or Abfall, an embellishment, IX. When it is good or bad, IX, 25.
Rules of the Up Stroke and Down Stroke, IV, 1, 2, 3, and so on. For the furthering of good tone on the Violin, V, 4, 5, and so on. For good reading of music, XII, 7, 8, 9, and so on, up to 22.

## S

Sappho the Poetess, is supposed to have invented the Fiddle-Bow, E, *II*, 8.
Second is threefold, III, 5.
Seventh is threefold, III, 5.
Sharps, I, *III*, 13. Wherein often other fingers must be used, I, *III*, 13, 14. The fourth finger is here necessary, III, 6. The double-sharp, I, *III*, 25. A scale with (♯), III, 6.
Shot, a musical, XI, 20. *See* Tirata.
Signs. Slurs, Repeat-Marks, I, *III*, 22.
Singingly must one play, V, 14. Signum intentionis, remissionis and restitutionis, I, *III*, 13.
Sixth, is threefold, III, 5.

# INDEX

Slur, the, I, *III*, 16. Dots or little strokes often stand below it, I, *III*, 17. Applied in a different fashion, I, *III*, 18.

Slurring, how it is indicated, I, *III*, 16. How one must slur, VII, *I*, 20; VII, *II*, 2, 3, 4, 5, 6, 7. One must observe the slur with exactitude and also know, oneself, how to apply it, XII, 3, 10, 11, 15.

Society, musical. Account thereof, E, *I*, 6.

Soft Key. *See* Key.

Softness, whereabouts in the bow to produce it, V, 3, 4, 5, and so on. Must not be exaggerated, V, 13. When slurring, VII, *I*, 20. Must be used rightly, XII, 3, 8.

Solo, must be played only when one can accompany well, XII, 5.

Sospire. What are named thus; and their value, I, *III*, 3, 5, 6.

Soundpost. What it is, E, *I*, 3. It can improve the sound of the Violin, E, *I*, 7.

Stopping, on the Violin, I, *III*, 14. Double-stopping, VIII, *II*, 11, and VIII, *III*, 8, 9, 10, 11, 12, 15, 16, and so on. A very useful remark regarding double-stopping, VIII, *III*, 20.

Stringed-Instruments. *See* Instruments.

Strings. The instruments of the Ancients were already then strung with gut string, E, *II*, 7. How the four open strings on the Violin are named, I, *I*, 13. How, by means of the movement of the strings, sound arises, V, 10. One can always attack the thicker and lower, more strongly than the weak, V, 11. One must often avoid the open strings, V, 13.

Stroke. *See* Bowing.

Strokes, small, over or under the notes; what they indicate, I, *III*, 17. At the end of every bar, I, *III*, 5. Are used for the division of a piece, I, *III*, 22.

Sustaining of a note, signs thereof, and the time of the same, I, *III*, 19.

## T

Table (Belly, or 'roof') of the Violin, E, *I*, 3.

Tempered Tuning, what it is, I, *III*, 25.

Tempo, broken, XII, 16.

Termini technici, I, *III*, 27.

Tevo, a musical author, E, *II*, 8.

Third, is threefold, III, 5.

Time, its description and its operation, I, *II*, 1, 2. The times of the Ancients, and the explanation of the time-measure of the present age, I, *II*, 3, 4. On the main beat depend the others, I, *II*, 5. The Allabreve, I, *II*, 6. The explanation of the kind of movement: how one recognizes it, and how it should be taught to the pupil, I, *II*, 7, 8. Faults of the teachers, I, *II*, 9. They must watch the pupil's temperament, I, *II*, 10, and not give him difficulties too soon, I, *II*, 11. One must never omit to attend to the evenness of the time, I, *II*, 12. In similar, rapid notes one is easily betrayed into hurrying, IV, 35. The evenness of time must be perpetually inculcated, VII, *I*, 8, 11, 16, 17, and VII, *II*, 2, 3, 5. Time must not be varied when accompanying, XII, 20.

Time-Measure, the musical. *See* Time.

Tirata, what it is, XI, 20, 21.

Tone, to draw a good one out from the Violin, V, 1, 2, and so on. To maintain purity of tone, V, 10. One must observe the tuning, V, 11. To play with conformity of tone in loud and soft, V, 12. Conformity of tone in singing and playing, V, 13, 14.

Tremolo, its origin, and how it is made, XI, 1, 2, 3. Is three-fold, XI, 4. Further description thereof, X, 5. On two strings, XI, 6. Is mostly used in Cadenzas, XI, 7.

Trill, how it is indicated, I, *III*, 21. Is described, X, 1, 2. Must be made with the major or minor second, and not out of the third, X, 3. This rule appears to have an exception: which, however, does not stand the test, X, 4. How one begins a Trill and finishes, X, 5, 6. It is threefold, X, 7. Goat's trill,[1] X, 8. One must also accustom oneself to a long one, X, 9. And practise all fingers in the Trill-fall, X, 10. How one uses the Trill in the Vorschlag and

---

[¹ *'Goat's Trill.'* In the editions of *1756* and *1787* an error is present. L. Mozart speaks of this Trill making a bleating effect. The German for goat is *'Geiss'* and not *'Geist'* as printed.]

Nachschlag, X, 11, 12, 13, 14. Where one should make a Trill, X, 15, 16, 17, 18, 19, 20. The ascending and descending Trill, X, 21, 22, 23. Through the semitone, X, 24. In leaping notes, X, 25, with the Abfall on an open string, X, 26. The Double-Trill, X, 27, 28. Examples thereof through all tones, X, 29. The ascending and descending Double-Trill, X, 30. The Trill in sixths, X, 31. The accompanied Trill, X, 32. The Half-Trill, IX, 27.

Triplets, what they are, VI, 1. Must be performed evenly, VI, 2. They can often be varied by the bowing, VI, 3, 4, 5, and so on.

Tuning, purity is extremely necessary, XII, 6.

## U

Ueberwurf, an embellishment, IX, 22. When to avoid it, IX, 23.

Unison, III, 5.

Up stroke, I, *III*, 24.

Ut, re, mi, fa, &c., the origin thereof, I, *I*, 5.

## V

Variety of bowing in triplets, VI, 3, 4, 5, and so on. In even notes, VII, *I*, 2, 3, 4, and so on. In uneven notes, VII, *II*, 1, 2, 3, and so on.

Viola. *See* Bratsche.

Viola d'Amor, E, *I*, 2.

Violet, the English, E, *I*, 2.

Violin Clef. *See* Clef.

Violin, difference between the Fiddle and Violin, E, *I*, 1. Description of the Violin, E, *I*, 3. How one must string it purely, E, *I*, 4. Violins are often made badly, E, *I*, 5. How one must hold it, II, 1, 2, 3, and so on. The letters must not be marked on it, II, 10. One must, at the first, string the Violin somewhat more heavily; and how to seek to draw a good tone therefrom, V, 1, 2, 3, and so on.

Violinist, how he can improve his Violin, E, *I*, 7. How he shall hold the Fiddle and draw the Bow, II, 1, 2, 3, and so on. What he has to observe, before he begins to play, III, *I*, 1. He must play intelligently, VII, *I*, 1. Must observe well the directions of the composer, IX, 21. The tuning must be according to that of the leader, XII, 6. Must observe the character of a piece before he begins to play, XII, 7. Must use embellishments in the right place, and not too frequently, IX, 21.

Violino piccolo, E, *I*, 2.

Violon, E, *I*, 2.

Violoncello, E, *I*, 2.

Vorschlag-Notes, what they are, I, *III*, 23, and IX, 1. How many varieties thereof, and how one must perform them, IX, 2, 3, 4. The longer, IX, 4, 5. How they have originated, IX, 6, 7. What one must observe further therein, IX, 8. The short Vorschläge, IX, 9. The descending Vorschläge are better than the ascending, IX, 10. One can make them from the Third, IX, 11; and from the next tone with two notes, IX, 12. When the descending Vortrag sounds best, IX, 13. Is often used maladroitly, IX, 14. The ascending arise also out of distant notes, IX, 15. Passing Vorschläge, IX, 16, 17, 18, 19. One must apply the Vorschläge in the right place, IX, 21. How to use them with the Trill, X, 11, 13, 14.

## W

Wallis, a musical author, E, *II*, 5.

Words, musical technical terms, I, *III*, 27.

## Z

Zurückschlag (Ribattuta), where and how this embellishment is used, XI, 17.

Zusammenschlag (Battement), what kind of embellishment this is. Its origin and use, XI, 15, 16.

Zwischenschlag, uebersteigender; or that which is used in the descending Vorschläge, IX, 19. Untersteigende; or those which are used in the ascending Vorschläge, IX, 20.

# Translator's Appendix

*Pages 104, 114, 215*

There is no English noun of to-day which quite conveys the meaning of 'Affect' as employed by eighteenth-century German writers on music. The corresponding English term of the period was 'the passions'; but this again does not quite mean to the present-day reader what it did to the English poets and aestheticians of that epoch. The notion underlying the doctrine of the 'Affecte' was that each piece of music expressed, and could only express, one 'passion', one 'movement of the soul'—tenderness, grief, rage, despair, contentment, &c.—and Leopold Mozart is at pains to insist that before a player can perform a piece of music in accordance with the composer's intention he must understand the 'Affect' from which the music originated. So rooted in the eighteenth-century mind was this doctrine that a work could delineate only one 'passion' that some aestheticians even contended that the new sonata, with its attempt to run in harness together two 'passions', represented by two utterly contrasted subjects, was an impracticable form.

*Page 173, chapter IX, § 11*

*The 1787 edition reads as follows:*

It is customary, too, to make the ascending appoggiatura with two notes from the third below and to slur them together on to the principal note, even if at first sight the appoggiatura should flow from the neighbouring note. This appoggiatura with two notes is called the slide. For example:

The first and dotted note is attacked more strongly and sustained longer; the second, shortened note however is slurred quietly on to the principal note as quickly as possible. The slide is used also with equal notes, as we see in example 3. But here, too, the stress falls on the first of the two appoggiatura notes.

## TRANSLATOR'S APPENDIX

*Pages 180 to 185*

*The number of paragraphs in chapter IX differs in the First and Third editions, thus:*

| First edition | | Third edition |
|---|---|---|
| § 22 | is divided into | 22 and 23 |
| 23 | becomes | 24 |
| 24 | ,, | 25 |
| 25 | ,, | 26 |
| 26 | ,, | 27 |
| | | Here the Third edition adds a new paragraph: |
| | | 28 |
| 27 | ,, | 29 |
| 28 | ,, | 30 (modified) |

*The new § 28 of the Third (1787) edition reads as follows:*

But the Doppelschlag can also be applied between two principal notes lying near each other, or between two principal notes lying far apart, both notes being thereby united.

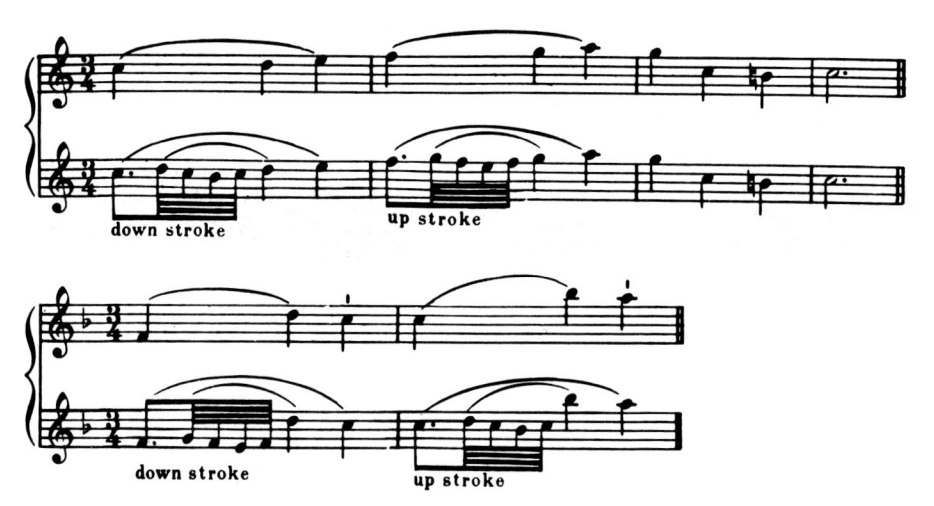

*In the 1787 edition, § 30 reads as follows:*

Now I will add yet another kind of embellishment belonging hereto, which I will call Nachschläge. These same are a couple of rapid little notes which one hangs on to the principal note, in order to enliven the performance. The first of these two notes is taken

# TRANSLATOR'S APPENDIX

by the neighbouring higher or lower note, and the second is a repetition of the principal note. Both little notes must be played very rapidly and be taken only at the end of the principal note before the lead into the following note.

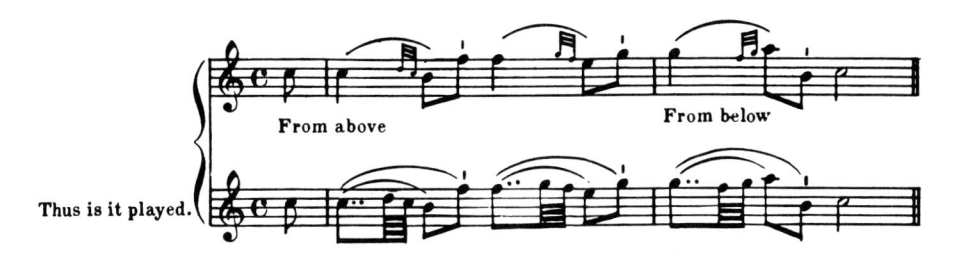

Thus is it played.

*The concluding sentence of chapter IX is as in the First edition.*

### Page 195

*In the 1787 edition the following is added to the end of § 20:*

But these trills are only short and rapid trills without Nachschlag (*trilleti*), or so-called Pralltriller, which are never difficult to learn for those who can in any case already make a good trill. These short trills look thus:

# TABLE
The paragraphs given here refer to the rules on bowing, given in Chapter IV.

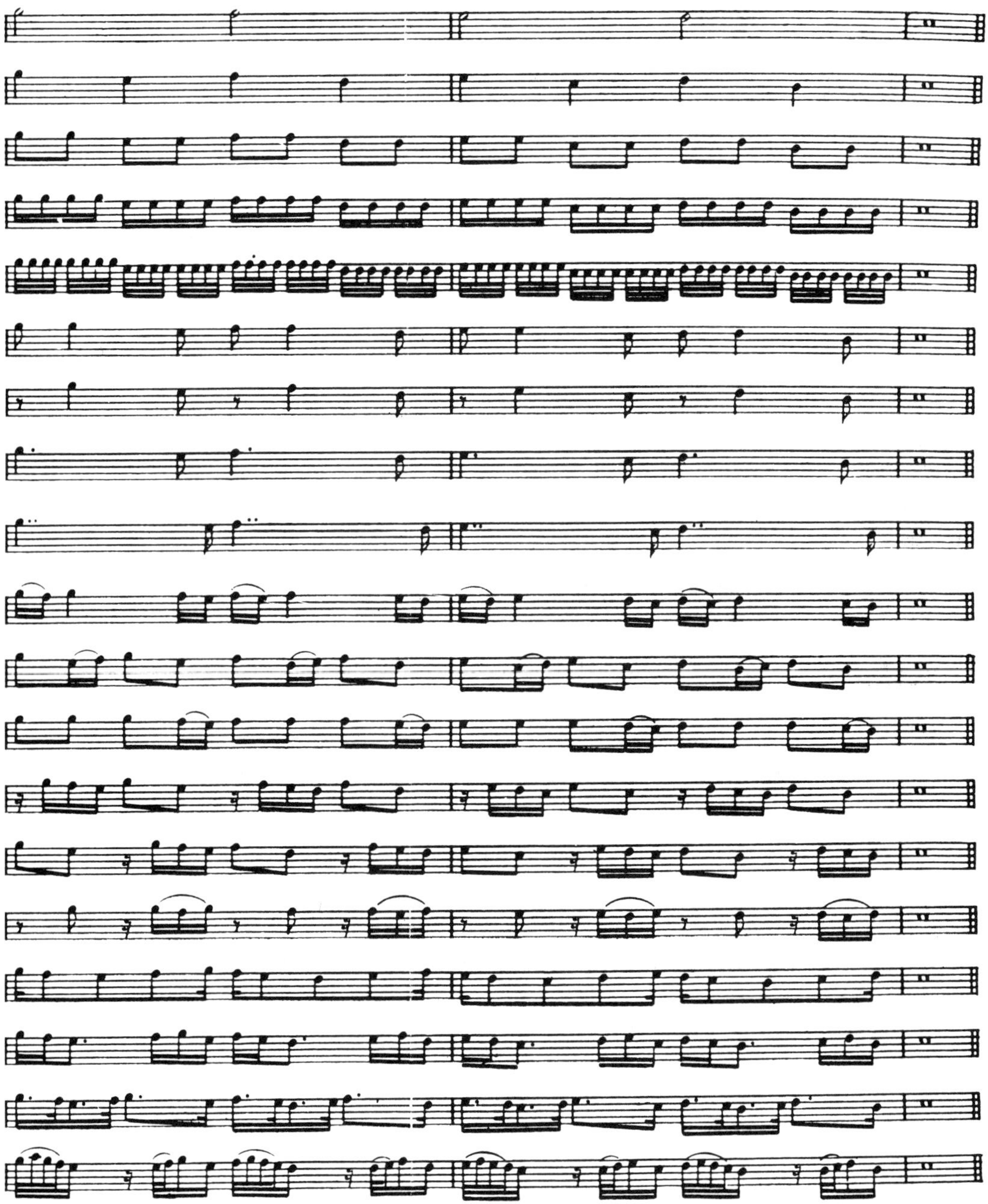